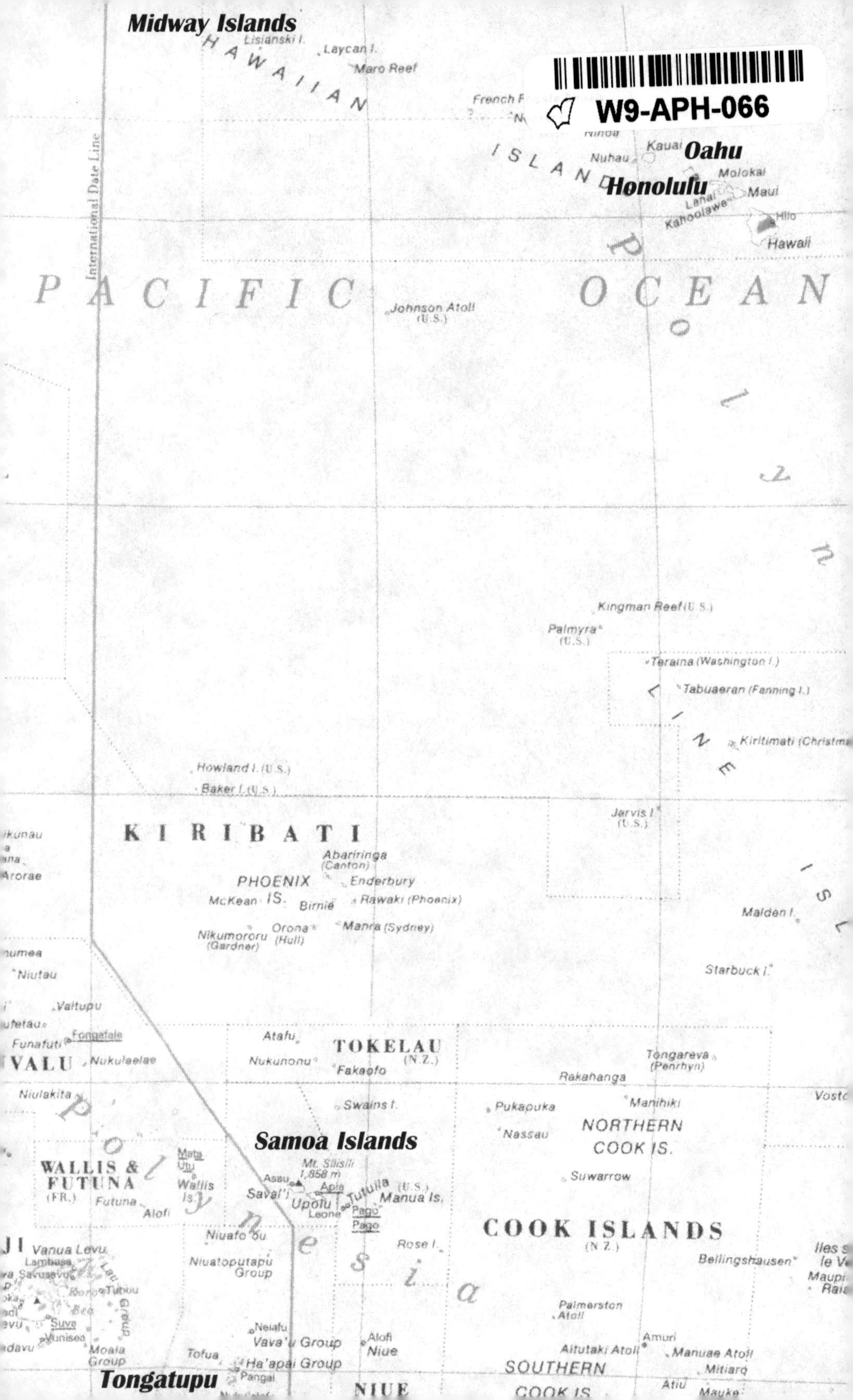
Midway Islands
HAWAIIAN ISLANDS
Lisianski I.
Laycan I.
Maro Reef
French F
Niihau
Nuhau
Kauai
Oahu
Honolulu
Molokai
Maui
Lanai
Kahoolawe
Hilo
Hawaii
W9-APH-066
International Date Line
PACIFIC OCEAN
Johnson Atoll (U.S.)
Polynesia
Kingman Reef (U.S.)
Palmyra (U.S.)
Teraina (Washington I.)
Tabuaeran (Fanning I.)
LINE IS.
Kiritimati (Christma
Howland I. (U.S.)
Baker I. (U.S.)
KIRIBATI
Jarvis I. (U.S.)
Abariringa (Canton)
PHOENIX IS.
Enderbury
McKean
Birnie
Rawaki (Phoenix)
Orona (Hull)
Nikumororu (Gardner)
Manra (Sydney)
Malden I.
Starbuck I.
Niutau
Vaitupu
Funafuti
Fongafale
VALU
Nukulaelae
Niulakita
Atafu
TOKELAU (N.Z.)
Nukunonu
Fakaofo
Swains I.
Tongareva (Penrhyn)
Rakahanga
Manihiki
Pukapuka
Nassau
NORTHERN COOK IS.
Suwarrow
Vosto
Samoa Islands
WALLIS & FUTUNA (FR.)
Futuna
Alofi
Wallis Is.
Mt. Silisili 1,858 m
Asau
Savai'i
Apia
Upolu
Leone
Tutuila
(U.S.)
Manua Is.
Pago Pago
Rose I.
COOK ISLANDS (N.Z.)
Niuafo'ou
Niuatoputapu Group
Vanua Levu
Lambasa
Savusavu
Lau Group
Suva
Vunisea
Moala Group
Neiafu
Vava'u Group
Alofi
Niue
Tofua
Ha'apai Group
Pangai
Tongatupu
NIUE
Bellingshausen
Palmerston Atoll
Aitutaki Atoll
Amuri
Manuae Atoll
Mitiaro
Atiu
Mauke
SOUTHERN COOK IS.

NO HIGHER HONOR

THE U.S.S. *YORKTOWN* AT THE BATTLE OF MIDWAY

NO HIGHER HONOR

JEFF NESMITH

LONGSTREET
Atlanta, Georgia

Published by
LONGSTREET, INC.
A subsidiary of Cox Newspapers
A subsidiary of Cox Enterprises, Inc.
2140 Newmarket Parkway
Suite 122
Marietta, GA 30067
www.lspress.com

Printed in the United States of America

2nd printing 1999

Library of Congress Catalog Card Number: 99-61750

ISBN: 1-56352-552-6

Jacket design by Burtch Hunter
Book design by Megan Wilson

To Achsah

THE U.S.S. *YORKTOWN* AT THE BATTLE OF MIDWAY

NO HIGHER HONOR

1

Pete and Walter had been talking about stickball. Each had just learned the other was from New York. They agreed that the street game of hard rubber balls and broom-handle bats was played best in Manhattan. Pete said he was a three-sewer hitter. He said he had known of games on which bookies had put down as much as $1,000. Walter said he could believe that. They decided that 109th Street between Broadway and Amsterdam Avenue was the Yankee Stadium of stickball.

When the Japanese Nakajima D3A1 "Val" dive-bomber came into view, their attention shifted from boys' pursuits to those of men. Walter Maurice moved to his assigned battle station, helping to load an antiaircraft gun that pumped a stream of exploding shells into the plane. The Val continued to plunge at the ship, strafing as it dived. Its 7.7-millimeter shells clattered against the flight deck. Pete Montalvo gazed up at the plane. In seconds, a 500-pound bomb exploded 50 feet from where he stood.

"I called out to my mother," he would say more than half a century later, his old man's voice breaking up on the memory.

It was June 4, 1942. The United States had been in World War II for less than six months. But for the U.S.S. *Yorktown*, an aircraft carrier, the war was just about over. She would take on waves of assault from Japanese attackers, the first coming only a short time after planes had left her own decks to attack Japanese ships. She would absorb the unleashed energy of tons of explosive and resist it. Eventually, when she could take no more, she would roll over and sink, never to be seen again until a day 56 years later when the remote cameras of undersea explorer Robert Ballard found her, resting upright on the floor of the Pacific Ocean.

Her last fight was part of one of the great naval battles of history, one that would turn the momentum of the war in the Pacific away from Japan in favor of the United States.

Most of the men who fought that battle were young and, by later standards, extremely naive. They would not know at the time what they had done. Although they came from many backgrounds, they were mostly children of the 1930s. The times had taught and enforced a spare and stern life code that had not been assaulted by the forces that would bring ambiguity and skepticism to the hearts of their grandsons several decades later. They brought to the battle an uncluttered and unapologetic love of their country.

The *Yorktown* had gathered them up like a hen clucking in her biddies, some from every direction. One of them came from a small dirt farm in central Florida, a tall, skinny kid with a durable sense of humor and an eye for occasional mischief. A couple of others were quiet descendants of Norwegian settlers on the rolling plains of North Dakota. They had left their fathers' wheat farms, signed papers offered them by a recruiter in Fargo and ridden the "Sioux Line" train down to Minneapolis to be sworn in. An Iowa boy, of soft voice and modest phrase, had lived in an orphanage and, after running away from there, a reform school. Finally, at 18, he had come to a place in life from which there seemed to be no other place to go, so he joined the Navy. A factory worker's son from Asheville, N.C., the son of a German-immigrant butcher in Colorado Springs, a Georgia farm boy who one day decided he was done with "staring at a mule's ass," there were more than 2,500 of them, the men who fought on the U.S.S. *Yorktown.*

When her last battle was over, many would look back from the decks of the ships that had rescued them and cry the salty tears of sailors as they watched her disappear into the gray and indifferent ocean.

They had known the Japanese planes were coming. At 11:59 A.M., the *Yorktown*'s radar picked up the approaching bombers, 18 of them, escorted by six of the dreaded Zero fighters. The planes were 46 miles away. Word that "bogeys" were closing on the ship was relayed to the entire crew through an intercom system.

On the basis of continuing radar contact and wind data, gunnery officers plotted the best point to begin throwing flak into the enemies' paths. Their calculations were used to direct the fire of the ship's largest antiaircraft weapons, guns with barrels five inches in diameter, mounted in pairs on platforms at four corners of the ship. There were two at forward starboard, two at forward port, two at the aft starboard corner and two at the aft port corner.

The guns could send projectiles weighing 54 pounds a distance of several miles. Based on the gunnery officer's calculations, a dial was hand-set on the side of each projectile to determine when it would detonate, making it something of a soaring time bomb. If all went well, it would explode at some hoped-for point of rendezvous with a Japanese bomber, flinging shards of flak into the plane. If the dials were set wrong, the projectiles might explode too soon and the flak rain harmlessly into the ocean. Or they might whiz past their targets and explode among the *Yorktown*'s own fighters as they pursued the bombers. When this happened, angry fighter pilots would radio the ship to "shorten your fuses."

Every four or five seconds, each gun hurled flak into the path of the attacking Japanese bombers. While the guns coughed and roared, the exploding shells filled the air around the ship with black balls of smoke and the sulfurous smell of cordite.

This battle was only the second major carrier battle in history. The first had been fought less than a month earlier. The men of the *Yorktown* had been there, too.

Despite its short history, the art of carrier warfare had matured to a surprising degree. Repeated exercises had developed a simple strategy for trying to evade a dive-bomber: keep moving and keep turning. Yorktowners would remember that Capt. Elliott Buckmaster took the ship into a full-rudder turn to port, followed shortly by a full-rudder to starboard. The wake drew a huge "S" in the ocean.

A few of the men had served under Buckmaster during an earlier tour, when he was executive officer to the captain of another carrier, the U.S.S. *Lexington.* In that job he had seemed nervous and fussy, and when they learned he was to become their captain, they were uneasy.

"When we heard it was to be Buckmaster, people were saying, 'Holy cats, we got Buckmaster as a captain? What kind of captain will he be?'" said Frank Baldino, a saxophonist in the ship's band. He added, "Of course, it was just crew talk. Down below. It's how crews think."

Buckmaster's steady hand under attack earned the admiration of Baldino and others. The eventual loss of the *Yorktown* would change the direction of his Navy career, and he would never command men at sea again. But half a century after this battle, many of the old men who had sailed under him would seem to forget how close they stood to the door that opened onto their eighties (or in some cases, already had passed through it) and would offer to fight just about any man who had a bad word about their skipper.

The sprays of metal chunks from the five-inch guns tore into some of the attacking Japanese bombers and brought them down. Fighter pilots in the ship's combat air patrol got others. But as desperate as the men of the *Yorktown* were to defend their ship, the Japanese attackers were just as desperate to sink her. Seven of the 18 bombers that had originally set out in search of the *Yorktown* made it through the clouds of smoke and flak.

Their target was the ship's flight deck, 805 feet long and slightly over 88 feet wide. The deck was covered with planks of Douglas fir, four inches thick by six inches wide. Most of the bombs that hung beneath the Japanese planes were equipped with fuses that were delayed by a fraction of a second. The delay meant the bombs would explode after they had buried themselves deep inside a ship, where they would create the greatest havoc.

On the starboard side amidships the "island structure" stood more than 30 feet above the flight deck. The island structure was so large that, without offsetting ballast or fuel, it would cause the carrier to list five degrees to starboard. It was the vessel's brain. On it and in it were the bridge, smokestacks, a search light platform, radar antennae, the captain's and admiral's sea cabins, plotting rooms, offices, radio room, the helm and other facilities crucial to the operation of the ship.

The *Yorktown*'s designers had installed four batteries of antiaircraft guns to defend the island, Mounts One and Two before it and Mounts Three and Four abaft.

These guns fired shells 1.1 inches in diameter and roughly seven inches long, designed to explode on contact.

The weapon made a POMH!-POMH!-POMH!-POMH! sound and was sometimes called a pom-pom gun. Some called it a "Chicago piano." But for the most part, guns on the *Yorktown* were referred to according to their size—the five-inch guns, the 20-millimeters and the .50-calibers. So it was customarily called the "one-point-one."

Under the supervision of a junior officer, a crew of around 20 men operated each of the four one-point-one gun batteries. A "trainer" sat in a small metal seat on the right side of the gun and a "pointer" sat in the corresponding seat on the left, the four barrels between them. With a two-handle crank between his knees, the trainer swung the barrels from side to side. The pointer moved them up and down with a similar crank. When this cooperative effort found an enemy plane in the pom-pom's sights, it was the pointer who pressed the trigger. If need-be, the pointer would call over to the trainer and tell him to adjust his aim, to "train right" or "train left."

The pilot of this "Val" was diving toward the *Yorktown* deck at an angle of about 70 degrees, almost straight down. The pointer was firing directly at him. Walter Maurice and others "passed ammunition" from hand to hand to keep the guns loaded. Pete Montalvo was standing by, in case one of them fell.

In his damage report following the battle, Buckmaster would write that none of the seven dive-bombers that finally attacked him survived to return to their own ships. In fact, the plane at which Walter and his comrades were firing apparently was chopped into three pieces. One section crashed into the side of the ship. The other two fell into the ocean, close aboard on the port side.

Maybe the Japanese pilot released the bomb just as his plane was starting to break up, or maybe the antiaircraft guns separated it from the plane. Whatever the cause, the bomb was not dropped in the customary fashion, for instead of plunging toward the ship like a bullet, it tumbled, bright and shiny, from a sky painted with white puffy clouds and floating black balls of smoke.

Some recalled a loud noise, above the roar and clatter and pomh!-pomh!-pomh! of the various antiaircraft guns. Others heard nothing but saw a bright flash over the mid-ocean glare. The bomb hit the flight deck and exploded on contact.

"There was a hole in my helmet you could stick your fist through," said Pete Montalvo. "I had to rip it off to get it off my head. That's when I knew I was wounded. Blood was coming down in my face. The guy I was talking to, Walter, my shipmate, he was laying down with no legs. I tried to help him. I remember I was rubbing him or something, but he was dead. He was gone. One of the two guys that was on the guns, the pointer or the trainer, I don't remember which, from the waist up, he had nothing."

Montalvo had joined the Navy at 17, partly because of a little trouble for playing hooky from school, partly because he felt his life stalling. His mother, an immigrant from Spain, not yet a citizen of this country, had refused at first to sign the papers. He wasn't learning anything in school, he argued, but still she would not listen to him. He nagged her for days and finally she gave in.

Others had been unable to find the work that was both promise and obligation of approaching manhood. Economic hard times and a variety of other factors—a little scrape with the law down in Chattanooga or curiosity about the world outside of northeast Washington state, a lifelong fascination with anything nautical in Norwich, Connecticut, and Mobile, Alabama—had sent hundreds of others into the service and through the mystifying channels by which the Navy bureaucracy would guide them to the decks of this aircraft carrier on this spot of relatively calm ocean, 1,200 miles northwest of Hawaii.

Most of them were just boys—17, 18, 20 or 25 years old—trapped at the friction point between two empires that scraped together like tectonic plates colliding beneath the continents. Of course, wars have always been fought by the young, so it would be easy to overemphasize the youth of the men of the *Yorktown*.

Ens. John D'Arc Lorenz of Portland, Oregon, commanded Mount Three. He was 22.

Lorenz was attending Portland University in 1940, when a recruiter signed him up as an apprentice seaman and potential officer's candidate. From 600 young men recruited around the country, 300 eventually had been selected for commission training at North River, New York, and of these, 258 ultimately became Navy ensigns.

Years later, someone would tally up: the class had accounted for one Medal of Honor, four Navy Crosses (one of which went to John Lorenz for the things he would do that afternoon at Gun Mount Three), one Legion of Merit, six Silver Stars, four Bronze Stars, thirty-two Purple Hearts and many other decorations.

The force of the explosion drove Lorenz into the "splinter shield," a quarter-inch-thick steel shell that surrounded the gun mount to a height of about three feet, and knocked him out. A piece of shrapnel tore into the head of the gun captain, a second-class boatswain's mate, who had been standing next to him. Lorenz was unconscious for only a few seconds.

A grim scene lay before him when he came to. Some of his men were dead, killed instantly by shrapnel. Others were dying. Less than an hour earlier they had been sitting there smoking and chatting with him about whether there would even be an attack that day.

"We'll knock the hell out of them," he had assured them.

Now he had two tasks, to care for his men and to get the weapon back into operation. He helped some men into a battle dressing station and gave them morphine.

A medical corpsman appeared almost immediately, accompanied by musicians from the ship's band, men whose battle station assignments were to carry stretchers. "Okay, fellow, we've got to get you below," the corpsman told Montalvo, who could still walk, despite the head wound and shrapnel wounds in his legs and shoulder. Two volunteers stepped up to help their wounded shipmate down the narrow, steep, ladder-like stairway that led to a temporary battle dressing station, several decks below. The stretchers would be used for others.

In a magazine article he wrote nearly a year later,

Lorenz described the bomb attack and the men who served under him.

"They were just plain, young Americans, out to fight for their country," he wrote. "There was Zimmerele, my battery gunner's mate. He was a quiet fellow, who never talked about anything but guns, and then there was no stopping him. It was only about a week before that he had shown me a picture of his family and of his girl. I know that his folks were proud of this son. . . .

"Johnson, a second-class boatswain's mate, was my gun captain. He was typical of his rate. Tough, hard to get along with and knew all the answers. He was very well built and could have handled any half-dozen of the rest at a single time. He kept the gun on line, all right, because they knew he meant business. . . .

"Donald Smith was a second loader. He was the youngest of them all but put in the best performance on that afternoon, if one could make such a distinction. He was shy and frail. It seemed strange to see his young face in this world of battle. . . .

"Prince, a loader, was very unfortunate. I know the rest of the others must have felt sorry for him. His wife and child had been killed in an automobile accident a few months before. Little wonder that he never had much to say. I have often wondered what was in Prince's heart and mind as he sat waiting for the Japs. . . .

"I was very proud of my crew. I regret now that I never told them so. . . ."

Lorenz also wrote that the night before, in the tiny room he shared with another ensign, he had written a prayer on a piece of paper about the battle he knew was ahead. "May God keep us safe tomorrow."

Ten feet behind Mount Three, at Mount Four, there was far less activity. That's because Mount Four was much closer to the bomb blast and the crew was virtually wiped out: 12 killed and four wounded.

Among those who had passed ammunition at Mount Four was Curtis Owens. When he was not at his battle station, Owens's endless task on the *Yorktown* had been to chip off old paint and spread new paint in its place.

He was from Buffalo, South Carolina, a tiny town built around a textile mill. Nothing about Curtis Owens, not the South Carolina drawl that was thicker than sorghum syrup on a cold day or even a degree of naivete that could endure only in a tiny southern town in a pre-television era, was more distinctive than his nose. It was a bulging, hooking prominence that dominated first impressions of him and led merciless shipmates from places Owens had never even heard of to assume the right to rename him. Pelican.

On another day, six months earlier, Owens and his best friend, James E. "Chick" Liner, also from Buffalo, stood on Pier Seven at the Norfolk Naval Station in Virginia, fresh from boot camp, holding their seabags and gazing at the carrier that was about to become their home.

"Chick, if they take them ropes off of that thing, it's going to sink, sure as hell," Owens declared.

"I don't believe it will," Liner replied thoughtfully.

"What's going to hold it up?"

"I don't know, but I don't believe those lines are holding it."

Years later, Liner would recall that he had "never seen anything as big as that ship in my life. There was more people on that ship than there was in Buffalo."

Liner's battle station had been at the forward five-inch gun on the starboard side of the ship. When the gun fired, it ejected a hot, brass shell onto the deck. Wearing gloves, Liner picked up the used shells and tossed them into the sea. When bullets from one of the Japanese bombers killed the first loader, Liner stepped forward and took his job. At one point during the battle, the officer assigned to the gun had told Liner that the Old Man himself had telephoned down from the bridge and observed, "That gun must be an automatic, judging from how fast you men are firing it." The call may have been a bit of fiction, created on the scene by the officer to keep his crew's morale boosted, but the 17-year-old Liner went for it.

"Just tell him you don't need no automatic," he said, heaving another shell into place, "'cause you got yourself a scared Rebel down here."

Almost abruptly, the battle quieted.

During the lull, Liner stood on the platform that held the large gun, gripping a handrail. He noticed that the hands that had lifted 54-pound projectiles into the gun so rapidly minutes earlier were now trembling and he could not stop them.

"That's when I knew I was really scared," he would recall. "I had done passed scared and had gone to shaking."

A shipmate, someone Liner would remember only as "a boy from West Virginia," reflected the tension in a different way. Staring in the general direction of Japan, he hurled his anger across an empty sea.

"You son-of-a-bitches!" he screamed again and again. "You son-of-a-bitches!"

Soon the word passed about the bomb that had taken out the two gun mounts abaft the island structure. Liner knew that one of the one-point-ones had been Curtis Owens's battle station.

Other planes might come to press against the *Yorktown*'s defenses. Other bombs might hit the ship. Liner could not leave his battle station. He could only wait and worry about his best friend.

Three bombs from the attacking planes had hit the *Yorktown*, in spite of Buckmaster's desperate, S-turn maneuvers. Others, near misses, had fallen into the ocean close aboard, and their explosions had sent geysers towering over the ship. The seawater fell on the flight deck and mixed with men's blood in slick, pink pools.

The crew had seen Japanese dive-bombers crash into the ocean all around the *Yorktown*, often in flames. The sky had been filled with smoke from bursting shells, the air saturated with the noise of guns and airplane engines and the shuddering, groaning sound of the ship as Buckmaster twisted and turned to evade his enemies.

One bomb crashed through the flight deck at an angle that caused it to penetrate the funnel and explode in the air uptakes of the ship's boilers. The explosion blew out the fires in five of the six boilers and sent an enormous cloud of black smoke and soot rolling out of the stack. Steam pressure from the five boilers dropped to zero. Within minutes, the *Yorktown* was dead in the water.

2

Joe Fazio was proud of the fact that he worked after school at Longo's Fruit Store to help support his family, proud enough to have the job listed in his high school yearbook, where it also was noted that he ran track, that he was a member of the How and When Club and that his "highest ambition" was to become a chief petty officer in the U.S. Navy.

When Joe was in the eleventh grade at Norwich Free Academy, in Norwich, Connecticut, his English teacher had her students write papers on what they hoped to be when they "grew up." He had never given that question much thought, but he went to the school library and did some research. Ultimately, he decided he would like to become a chief petty officer in the Navy. The class assignment unearthed the usual assortment of would-be doctors, lawyers, bankers and, that being Connecticut, insurance company executives. Other kids joked about what seemed to them Joe's more modest ambition. But determination runs in the Fazio family and with the kind of singlemindedness that had enabled his Italian immigrant father to buy a house and rear a family on a construction laborer's pay, Joe stuck with his new plans.

The following year, the Free Academy yearbook carried his picture on page 45, smiling and Vaseline Hair Tonic straight, above the following sketch:

"'Foz'

"Cross country 3 and 4

"How and When Club 3

"Track 4

"Foz, a hardworking and good-natured student, is well-liked by his friends. Foz hasn't much time for extra activities because he works in a fruit store, but he was a great asset on the track team. His ambition is to join the Navy, which he is well fitted for, and he will be missed greatly when he goes away. Noted for being a member of 'the Gashouse Gang.' Highest Ambition: to become a chief petty officer in the U.S. Navy."

Before the end of his senior year, he asked the principal if he could graduate early, so that he might enlist in the Navy. Unknown to Fazio, the mother of one of his future shipmates, Anthony Brunetti, had campaigned to get Connecticut school requirements changed to allow early graduation by boys who wanted to join the military. She wrote to Clare Boothe Luce, the journalist-turned-political activist, and the change was instituted. On May 16, 1941, a month before the rest of his class graduated, Fazio took his oath to defend America and departed for Navy boot camp in Newport, Rhode Island. When he left home, his father cried. Joe would finish boot camp and move on to aviation machinist's school at Jacksonville and eventually become a "plane captain" on the *Yorktown*.

With the year 2000 looming, many old Yorktowners would look back on those days and recall what seemed a simpler, more clean-cut America, one that accommodated the straightforward ideals of kids like Joe Fazio. Before AIDS and crack cocaine and Elvis and Watergate and television networks and Vietnam, it was an America that held up cultural signposts like the value of hard work, Gary Cooper in *Sergeant York*, Joe DiMaggio and Joe Louis and Bob Feller, Glenn Miller and "Chattanooga Choo Choo." The past may always look simpler. After all, the 1930s had seen labor riots and veterans' riots, soup kitchens and heated national debates about the country's proper role in the world. The old men of those days must have looked back over the decades to the 1880s and yearned for simpler days past. But the letters the men who fought on the *Yorktown* wrote home and the memories they would describe more than five decades later hold up a not-distant mirror of America at a time when a kid would devote precious yearbook bragging space to the fact that he worked after school at a fruit stand.

That war was coming was clear. Not so clear was where it would start. U.S.-made arms and other desperately needed supplies were being convoyed across the Atlantic to aid in England's war with Nazi Germany, but under the Neutrality Act, the United States was legally barred from entering the conflict. In what would become known as the Battle of the Atlantic, German U-boats converged in "wolfpack" attacks to sink one merchant ship after another in the Atlantic convoys. A Nazi war communique on April 4 boasted of sinking nearly 90,000 tons of shipping, most of it in the North Atlantic.

In an April 10 speech to the House of Commons, Prime Minister Winston Churchill announced that his government had been "loaned" 10 U.S. Coast Guard cutters, which he said were "fast and well-armed," having been equipped to enforce Prohibition. Then, looking directly at U.S. Ambassador John G. Winant seated in the balcony, Churchill reiterated the crucial importance of armed escorts for the Atlantic convoys.

"The defeat of the U-boats and surface raiders has been proved to be entirely a question of adequate escorts for our convoys," Churchill declared. "It will, indeed, be disastrous if the great masses of weapons, munitions and instruments of war of all kinds made with the toil and skill of American hands at the cost of the United States and loaned to us under the Aid to Britain Bill were to sink into the depths of the ocean and never reach the hard-pressed fighting line. That would be lamentable to us and I cannot believe it would be found acceptable to the proud and resolute people of the United States."

The week before Churchill made the speech, President Franklin D. Roosevelt had directed the Navy to bolster its Atlantic fleet in preparation for defending the shipments.

April 1941. It was a strange month, judging from what they put in the papers back then.

It began with protests from Italian and German authorities over U.S. seizure of 89 Axis merchant ships, which were being held in "protective custody." German and Italian ships in Boston and Mobile harbors had been damaged by what the Justice Department called "sabotage," purportedly by members of their own crews. In the name of "protecting" the ships, the Justice Department seized them and had their crews deported. While outraged representatives of the Third Reich condemned the actions as illegal, Mexico, Venezuela, Cuba and Peru began seizing German merchant ships in a show of solidarity with the United States.

War between Germany and Yugoslavia became inevitable when efforts by the Italian government to "mediate" differences between the two failed. There were labor riots at an Allis Chalmers strike in Milwaukee, and John L. Lewis warned that if he decided to lead his mineworkers on a strike against the soft coal industry, he would refuse to accept government mediation.

Spring training was over, and on April 1 in Selma, Alabama, the New York Giants won the first of a floating series of exhibition games against the Cleveland Indians. The Yankees and the Dodgers began to make their way north for their respective season openers, playing exhibitions in minor league towns along the way. DiMaggio homered twice as the Yankees beat up on Oklahoma City. Playing in front of 417 paying fans, the Dodgers beat the Fort Worth Cats, 6-4.

In Manila, representatives of the United States, the Netherlands and Britain met to discuss strategies for defending the Orient against Japanese expansion. Nazi troops marched across Hungary to mass on Yugoslavia's borders. The White House said President Roosevelt would intervene in the Allis Chalmers strike if necessary. A Ford plant in Detroit was shut down by the United Auto Workers. The Indians and Giants continued their exhibition series in Talladega. This time, the Indians won. Brooklyn played the Dallas Rebels at Waco and won, 5-1, and the Yankees defeated the Tulsa Oilers, 14-5.

Lou Nova knocked out Max Baer in the eighth round at Madison Square Garden.

The Nazis moved into Yugoslavia and marched toward Greece. Secretary of State Cordell Hull said the United States would ship arms to Yugoslavia. Mediators negotiated an end to the Allis Chalmers strike. The Yankees "routed" the Memphis Chicks. The Dodgers "subdued" the New Orleans Pelicans. The Giants "blanked" the Atlanta Crackers.

The U.S.S. *North Carolina*, a 35,000-ton battleship that was the largest and most powerful warship ever built in America at that time, was commissioned at the Brooklyn Navy Yard. A Greek War Relief Association was organized and took out full page newspaper ads soliciting donations. German bombers struck London for the first time in 18 months. The Yankees and Dodgers played an exhibition in Atlanta and the Dodgers won. The Indians and Giants resumed their series in Greenville, S.C. Feller struck out seven Giants in seven innings and the Indians won. Joe Louis, in his sixteenth title defense, knocked out somebody named Tony Musta in the ninth round in St. Louis. The Brown Bomber received $17,508 for the night's work and Musta was paid $8,754. In Japan, the foreign minister said his country's policy would continue to rely on the Three-Power Pact with Germany and Italy, even though the treaty had displeased the United States, Britain and the Netherlands. The Royal Air Force bombed Berlin. German troops moved into Thrace, which had been abandoned by beleaguered Greek forces.

And on April 22, the *Yorktown* abruptly cut away from a Pacific Fleet training exercise near Hawaii and, in the company of four destroyers, headed for the Panama Canal. By nightfall, the ship grapevine had successfully winnowed a collection of rumors and virtually every man on board knew that the *Yorktown* was headed for the Atlantic and that the trip had something to do with sealed orders delivered to the skipper at sea.

The sudden move meant an overhaul scheduled for August 4 at Pearl Harbor would have to be postponed. It was only the first of a series of postponed or abbreviated repair and maintenance stops for the *Yorktown*. But as the next nine months would demonstrate, she was tough.

In her engine room, steam turbines converted thick, gummy bunker oil into the pulling strength of 120,000 horses. The turbines spun far too fast for the ship's four screws, each about 16 feet in diameter, so reduction gears were used to lower the RPMs to a maximum of only a little more than 300. With a displacement of 20,000 tons, she was capable of 34 knots and could heel easily through turns tighter than anything a battleship or heavy cruiser would even attempt. America's fifth aircraft carrier, she was designated CV-5 under the Navy's convention for numbering its vessels.

James Liner and Curtis Owens worked the midnight shift at Buffalo Mills, the textile factory around which the town of Buffalo, S.C., was built. They got off at around daylight, usually worn out from the night's work. Then they walked to their homes for breakfast and caught the bus to high school in the nearby town of Union. Both boys lived in homes in which both parents also worked at the mill. They each brought home about $10 a week, and their parents allowed them to keep one dollar.

"I decided there ought to be something better out there somewhere," Liner recalled. "I asked my father if I could join the Navy. He said, 'If that's what you want, go ahead.'" Liner had been talking to his cousin, Willis Kingsmore, and to Owens about joining the Navy together. In addition to the pressure of working full-time and going to school, they wanted to avoid the Army, a common urge which seems to have been rooted partly in the horrors of World War I and its muddy trenches. Most of the *Yorktown*'s crew and officers were too young to remember that war, but they had heard about it.

"I didn't want to be one of those doughboys," one Yorktowner recalled.

Years later, Liner talked of the Army almost as if describing a band of kidnappers that raided homes in the South Carolina night and took away children. He said: "We were over in Union one Saturday and they marched the National Guard down Main Street. I told Willis Kingsmore, my cousin, 'Willis, if we're going in the Navy, we'd better get our butts out of here. The Army'll get us, sure as the devil.' Some of those kids in that National Guard were our age and they marched them right down to the train station and took them to Ft. Jackson."

The following Monday, when they got off work at the mill, Liner, Owens and Kingsmore drove to Spartanburg to talk to a Navy recruiter. He gave them a test, signed them up and told them it would be several weeks before they were called. Four days later, they were at Navy boot camp in Norfolk, Virginia. Others would come from other places.

In Dover, a rural community in central Florida, Joseph Wetherington saw hard times apply a familiar squeeze to a farming economy based on strawberries and spring vegetable crops: strawberries were cheap, but fertilizer was not. The berries were grown in the winter to take advantage of Florida's mild climate, then packed and loaded onto trucks and refrigerated rail cars to be shipped north. Carl and Burter Wetherington had reared two sons and two daughters on the income from strawberries and other small cash crops. Joe was the youngest. In January 1940, Carl Wetherington died of pneumonia he had developed while working in his strawberry field. Joe, 23, had already joined the National Guard and could be called up at any time. He was over six-feet-four and weighed only a little over 130 pounds. His legs were so long that friends joked he must have a forked liver. There was no way the Navy would take anyone that tall, he was told. In 1941 he tried anyhow, and a recruiter in Tampa signed him up. Soon he was at Norfolk.

John Underwood had no reason to fear being drafted into the Army, at least not for a few years. He was only 15 years old, growing up on his grandfather's large farm near Chattanooga. His father had been killed in a car wreck when his mother was pregnant with him, and she had come home to her family's farm in Tennessee. "I was parented to death," Underwood recalled. "My mother, my grandparents, my two bachelor uncles and my two maiden aunts all lived on that farm." The aunts taught him to play gin rummy. The uncles provided advanced courses in poker.

Once, on a lark, Underwood agreed to drive a bootlegger's car loaded with illegal whiskey to the town of Lafayette in Georgia, where liquor sales still were prohibited in the summer of 1941.

Two-by-fours, studded with nails and left in the highway by federal revenue agents, sent the 1941 Ford coupe skidding off the mountain road and into a tree. John Underwood's career in the illegal liquor business came to an end.

"Well, this one's only a baby!" a revenuer exclaimed as he shined his flashlight into the car.

The baby was in serious trouble and the only way out seemed to be for his mother to sign an affidavit, falsely declaring that he was 17 years old, so he could get into the Navy. With that and his grandfather's political influence, he could avoid prosecution on the bootlegging charge.

Matthew Blount, a black kid in Norfolk, finished high school in 1940 and found the only job available to him was bagging coal for a dollar and fifty cents a week.

"You'd put the bag on the scales and open the chute and let the coal pour in," he recalled. "When the scales said 100 pounds, you took it off and put another bag in there."

He signed up for the Navy on May 27, 1941, and, along with about 60 other black men, attended an abbreviated and segregated boot camp a few miles from his home. After several other ships, he wound up on the *Yorktown*. As a mess attendant and "cabin boy" in the officers' quarters, he earned $21 a month, but some things did not change. He still was restricted to water fountains marked "colored."

Not all of the men who would sail into war on the *Yorktown* in 1942 had been recruited the previous year. In fact, most had been in the Navy for a year or more and some for many years.

Working in Minnesota's snow at a Civilian Conservation Corps camp, Lynn Forshee of Britt, Iowa, began to develop an interest in the scenes from South Pacific islands featured on some Navy "see-the-world" recruiting posters. That fascination brought him ultimately to boot camp in Great Lakes, Illinois. One day he would see those islands. Jerry Lemberger's father died when he was a small boy, and during the Depression the family had a tough time. He worked in the CCC camps for a year, then joined the Navy. Carl "Red" Maag, the tall, red-haired son of a German-born butcher in Colorado Springs, joined the Navy in 1935, following his own CCC stint. John Anthony Kasselman, whose father ran a grocery store in Cincinnati, had served a hitch in the Army. When it was up, he changed his mind and joined the Navy.

The Depression was coming to an end but the good

news had yet to reach large areas of the country. Jobs still were scarce in Asheville, North Carolina, and in June 1937, Joseph Lewis, son of a furniture factory worker, chose the Navy.

After slipping through the Panama Canal on the night of May 6, 1941, the *Yorktown* set out on the first of a series of "neutrality patrols" across the Atlantic. The cancelled overhaul in Pearl Harbor was rescheduled for October 6 in Norfolk.

The ship made several Atlantic crossings, sometimes escorting merchant trips to "MOMP," the mid-ocean meeting point where they were turned over to British escort ships. In September 1941, the October overhaul in Norfolk was cancelled and rescheduled for December.

News of war in Europe continued to dominate the front pages. On October 17, a German U-boat torpedoed and badly damaged the U.S. destroyer *Kearny* and 11 men were killed. The secretary of state said the United States would not even bother to send a protest to "international highwaymen" in the Third Reich. On November 1, a U-boat sank the destroyer *Reuben James* with terrible loss of life.

Newspapers gave little space to the growing tension between the United States and Japan. After "negotiations" with Vichy France, Japan had sent troops to southern Indochina in July. The United States, Great Britain and the Netherlands responded by imposing an oil export embargo against Japan.

Navy Secretary Frank Knox, in "extemporaneous" but carefully leaked remarks to a group of naval ordnance manufacturers, warned that a "clash" with Japan appeared likely. "The Orient is like a vast powder keg, potentially ready to explode with a roar that will be heard all the way across the ocean," he said on October 24.

Despite several false alarms, during which its fighters and bombers were scrambled, the log of the *Yorktown* indicates it never had a confirmed encounter with German submarines or surface ships during its Atlantic patrol duty. In fact, the worst stress members of its crew could remember from those days resulted from a north Atlantic storm in early November 1941. The ship groaned as it wallowed through storm-driven seas. Expansion joints, a relatively new design innovation installed to increase flexibility during sea battle maneuvers, opened by as much as a foot. Green water sloshed over the flight deck, some 30 feet above the water line.

William Harkins had grown up in Mobile, Alabama, and the sailors who swaggered about the docks in the Gulf seaport town planted in him a lifelong fascination with the Navy. He joined in January 1941, after graduating from high school. Following boot camp and aviation ordnance school, Harkins went to the *Yorktown*. He spent much of his first year on scullery duty, washing dishes and disposing of garbage. The latter task involved heaving heavy garbage cans filled with plate scrapings into a chute, through which the refuse slid into the ocean. The process required a series of tasks and opening and closing of doors. When Harkins had made certain a door on the outside of the chute—below the waterline—was closed, he opened a similar door on the inside. After he dumped the garbage, he closed the inside door to seal off the chute and pulled a lever to open the outside door and allow ocean water to surge into the chute and rinse it out.

Unknown to Harkins, the storm had torn the exterior door off the garbage chute. Thinking it was closed, he dumped in a can full of kitchen grease and leftovers, all of which immediately came sloshing back out of the chute and all over him and the maze of pipes that lined the overhead. He and another sailor were up all night cleaning up the mess. The experience would prepare Bill Harkins for a gruesome task that lay ahead.

On December 2, the *Yorktown* pulled into Norfolk and that afternoon moored to Pier 7 at the Norfolk Naval

Operating Base. The ship had steamed 17,000 miles in Atlantic patrol duty and was about to get its twice-postponed overhaul. The bridge was to be substantially rebuilt. New radar equipment and new antiaircraft guns had been requisitioned and fire bricks in the crumbling linings of her boilers were to be replaced. Some of the parts would not even arrive until January, and members of her crew looked forward to long liberty. None of them knew that the vast powder keg in the Orient was about to explode.

Forshee, the Iowa-born graduate of the CCC camps, had finished aviation radio school and was a radioman-gunner in the *Yorktown*'s bomber squadron, "Bombing Five." On the night of December 6, he took liberty and rode a trolley filled with other sailors into the zone of bars, tattoo parlors, pawn shops and other establishments catering to the needs of sailors. Also on the trolley, Forshee recalled many years later, was a British sailor from the carrier H.M.S. *Illustrious* in port for its own repairs. The boisterous Englishman, perhaps a bit resentful of America's reluctance to enter the European war, asked a *Yorktown* sailor, "When are you chaps going to get the extra stripe on your uniforms?" After a pause, he added, "The yellow one, down the back."

A fight almost started, but cool heads prevailed. After all, someone said, the British sailor should be treated as a guest. The "hosts" then escorted their obliging guest to a bar and began buying beer for him. When he neared his capacity, they took him for a short stop at a tattoo parlor, then put him on a trolley back to his ship. The unfortunate Brit awoke the next morning to find the American flag permanently flying over his heart, along with the words, "God Bless America."

The evening also saw more formal celebration, when Louise Frances Kennedy, daughter of a Navy doctor, was married in Our Lady of Victory Chapel at the Navy base to Ens. Leslie Lockhart Bruce Knox, an Australian-born *Yorktown* fighter pilot. The next morning, the "News of

Society" pages of the Norfolk *Virginian-Pilot* described the ceremony in the kind of detail such weddings commanded. Chaplain J. N. Moody officiated. The chapel was decorated with palms, white chrysanthemums and candles.

"The wedding music was played by Miss Grace Price and before the ceremony, Richard Robinson sang Shubert's 'Ave Maria.' The bride was given in marriage by her father. She wore a gown of white lace over satin, long sleeves ending in points over the hands, long torso bodice and full skirt. Her fingertip veil of illusion was arranged from a tiara of white flowers and she carried a bouquet of white roses and bouvardia. . . ."

The bride's sister was maid of honor and bridesmaids wore emerald green gowns and carried green muffs covered with orchids. Ensign Knox's brother was his best man, and the ushers were other *Yorktown* fighter pilots, Lt. (jg) Richard C. Crommelin and Ensigns Roy M. Plott, Arthur J. Brassfield, B. T. Macomber, Elbert Scott McCuskey and Edgar Bassett. The reception was at the Officer's Club.

The newspaper account noted that "Ens. and Mrs. Knox will reside in the Glencove apartments." They resided there for 10 days and never saw each other again.

The following afternoon, aboard ship, at stores, in bars, in the Navy base dormitory, at private homes, the crew heard with the rest of America the news that would interrupt yet another scheduled *Yorktown* overhaul and change their lives forever. Japanese planes had bombed Pearl Harbor in Hawaii. Some crewmen were at the Norfolk train station, looking forward to trips home, when they heard the news and orders that all military personnel report to their base or ship.

Before the day was over the city manager of Norfolk ordered a dozen Japanese-American men who lived in the town rounded up and arrested. The *Virginian-Pilot* ran a picture of Norfolk businessman Seyomatso Mitzutani, wearing a three-piece suit and raincoat and staring stoically away from the camera while being "frisked" by Police Captain Ted Miller.

Ens. John Paul Adams did not hear about the attack immediately. The son of a Methodist minister, Adams had lived in several northeast Kansas towns as his father moved from church to church. He had hoped to become a physician, but as he neared graduation from the College of Emporia in 1940, he learned there was no money to send him to medical school. He joined the Navy, qualified for flight school and eventually found his way into the *Yorktown*'s fighter squadron. He would become the last pilot ever to take off from the deck of the ship.

In flight school, he and a North Carolina farm boy named Gus Palmer became friends. On December 7, Palmer fixed up a date between his sister, Dixie, and Ens. Adams. They would "double-date" with Gus and his date. Out of touch most of the day, the two young couples drove down to Virginia Beach that evening and parked. Adams flipped on the car radio. The weekly comedy, "The Great Gildersleeve," was to be on at 6 o'clock, the Jack Benny Show at 7 P.M. and at 8 o'clock ventriloquist-comedian Edgar Bergen and his wisecracking dummy, Charlie McCarthy, were to broadcast live before a "studio audience" of 30,000 soldiers at Ft. Ord, California, along with singer Judy Garland and comedians Bud Abbott and Lou Costello. But instead of the scheduled programs, Adams, Palmer and their dates heard continuing reports from Pearl Harbor.

The following day, the *Yorktown* received new orders. She would return to the Pacific in a few days. New guns would be installed and some changes were made in her radar equipment. The bridge would not be rebuilt, or the tired boilers rebricked.

Joe Fazio had finished boot camp at Newport, Rhode Island, and aviation machinist's mate school in Jacksonville, Florida. He was assigned to VF-42, the *Yorktown* fighter squadron. Since spring, pilots in the squadron had been flying the F4F-3, the new single-wing Grumman fighter the Navy had named "Wildcat." Still parked at the Norfolk air field, the F4F-3s underwent a pair of modifications between December 7 and the day the ship left port. Machinists installed bulletproof windshields and gas tanks were replaced with new tanks that were lined with "self-sealing" rubber. Panels under the fuselage had to be removed to get the old tanks out and the new ones in.

Fazio reported to VF-42 on December 9 and went to work removing fuselage panels. He counted up. Taking off one panel and the tank above it required removing 700 screws.

On the night of December 16, amid secrecy so strict that members of the crew were not even allowed to write home, the *Yorktown* stood out from Norfolk and turned back toward the Panama Canal.

3

Members of the crew hit San Diego's streets to find that during their voyage from Norfolk, the country was gearing up for war and getting itself in the mood. After leaving Norfolk on December 16 and squeezing back through the Panama Canal, the carrier docked for a week at the San Diego Naval Air Station. As they rode the city's "Nickel Snatcher" trolley into town, they heard news vendors hawking stories of atrocities by "Japs."

Jap. The word had found quick welcome on the national tongue. For one thing, headline writers loved it for its economy. "Japanese" would eat up as much space as "Japs Fall," more than "Japs Hit." But the word had more in it than headline convenience. Hawaii was regarded as a part of the country, even though it was not yet a state. Attacking U.S. facilities and personnel in Hawaii was attacking America. Moreover, there was concern that the Japanese might try to take Hawaii outright, then attack the West Coast. To be sure, much of the concern rested in the minds of editorial writers; but it also troubled such thoughtful government officials as Secretary of War Henry L. Stimson. In the business of rapidly summoning national resolve against such threats, a word like "Jap" packed a punch.

The music of national anger was on the air and more was on the way from New York's Tin Pan Alley. Less than a week after the bombing of Pearl Harbor, at least two new songs were in the hands of printers, Sam Lerner's "The Sun Will Soon Be Setting (for the Land of the Rising Sun)" and a forgettable collaboration by James Cavanaugh, John Redmon and Nat Simon, "You're a Sap, Mister Jap," which contained this chorus:

> You're a sap, Mister Jap,
> To make a Yankee cranky.
> You're a sap, Mister Jap,
> Uncle Sam is gonna spanky.
> Wait and see, before we're done
> The A, B, C and D will sink your Rising Sun.
> You're a Sap, Mister Jap.
> You don't know Uncle Sammy.
> When he fights for his rights,
> You'll take it on the lamee,
> For he'll wipe the Axis right off the map.
> You're a sap, sap, sap, Mister Jap.

Other titles included, "Let's Take a Rap at the Japs," "Taps for the Japs," "The Japs Don't Have a Chinaman's Chance" and "Goodbye Mama, We'll See You in Yokohama."

The effect of the war could be found in some news stories while others reflected a country continuing with its business.

Sydicated columnist Drew Pearson got wind of the fact that Republican Rep. John M. Vorys, whom Pearson called a "militant Ohio isolationist and Roosevelt-hater," had the odd hobby of climbing trees. Weather permitting, Vorys would take a Sunday in Washington's Rock Creek Park, pick himself a worthy tree and shinny right up. Pearson declared that recent photographs had shown Vorys "out on a limb."

Babe Ruth, then 47, was in a New Year's Eve wreck somewhere in New York and was hospitalized two days later "in a highly nervous condition," according to an unnamed friend. The friend said the Bambino had swerved "to avoid another car" and his car had plunged from the road. In Boston, the Red Sox front office announced that outfielder Ted Williams had been given a draft classification of 1-A and would take the physical examination immediately. The previous year, Williams had become the first major leaguer to finish the season with a batting average over .400 since George Sisler of the old Boston Browns did it in 1922. As his fans would remember forever, Williams would put down his baseball bat for military service, both during World War II and the Korean War.

Mickey Rooney and Ava Gardner went ahead with their plans to get married and Mrs. Reginald C. Vanderbilt of New York announced that her daughter, society glamor girl Gloria Vanderbilt, would marry actor Pasquale "Pat" Di Cicco. The Commerce Department released retail sales figures for 1941. On a per capita average, Americans spent $93 each in food stores, $64 with automobile dealers, $32 in restaurants and bars, $31 on apparel, $28 on "hardware etc.," $20 in furniture stores and $14 at drugstores during the year.

The Chicago *Herald American* reported that in the aftermath of the declaration of war, prices for corn, soybeans, wheat, rye and lard had jumped on the Board of Trade.

On the first day of 1942, hours after the ship arrived at San Diego, Rear Adm. Frank Jack Fletcher came aboard—"broke his flag," in Navy terminology. Fletcher was to be the commander of a new carrier task force, TF-17, and the *Yorktown* would be his flagship. He was a 1906 graduate of the Naval Academy, where he was known as "Flap Jack" Fletcher and sometimes as "Black Jack" Fletcher. He participated in the U.S. expedition against the city of Vera Cruz, Mexico, in 1914, where he was awarded the Medal of

Honor, along with his uncle, Rear Adm. Frank Friday Fletcher, and 53 other participants in the two-day exercise. When Frank Jack Fletcher's personal gear was taken to his *Yorktown* quarters, it included a stainless steel sword that had belonged to Frank Friday Fletcher. The sword is still on the ship.

With the advantage of hindsight, some naval historians who analyzed the decisions Frank Jack Fletcher made in battles during World War II would conclude he was a hell of a guy and a so-so admiral. One of his contemporaries was allowed to say anonymously that Fletcher was "a big, nice, wonderful guy who didn't know his butt from third base." In fact, the men who served under him said he could be affable or prickly. He loved cigars, slept in his shorts and, according to a Marine guard responsible for waking him, had tattooes on his upper arms. A Marine caught smoking a cigar he had lifted from the admiral's box said Fletcher surprised him with, "How's that cigar, Marine?", then walked away chuckling. A cryptanalyst who irritated the admiral would find his intelligence information ignored, sometimes to the endangerment of the task force.

The *Yorktown*'s first mission under Fletcher's flag would be to escort three converted ocean liners from San Diego to Samoa. The liners would be used to transport the newly formed Second Marine Brigade to the island. The carrier stood out from San Diego on January 6, along with the three liners and its task force consorts of two battle cruisers and four destroyers.

Hundreds of new crewmen taken on at Norfolk were still having the ship's culture—its operations, its procedures, its formalities, its physical features—pounded into their heads by merciless boatswain's mates. Among them was John Underwood, the 15-year-old Chattanooga boy who had lied about his age in order to get into the Navy. Underwood was assigned to VF-42, the fighter squadron, commonly called "Fighting Forty-two." He quickly came under the protection of three men, George Barnes, Carl Maag and Wayne Souter.

Barnes, a fatherly 54-year-old chief petty officer, was up for retirement when the outbreak of war caused these plans to be put on hold. He was the "leading chief" of the ship's fighter squadron, meaning he ran it.

Born in 1892 on a farm near the town of Albion, Maine, he became the principal breadwinner for his mother and six siblings in 1907 when his father was kicked in the head while hitching up a horse. George Barnes joined the Navy in 1916 and became a pilot during the Navy's embryonic venture into aviation. He told members of his family that he became a carrier-based chief because he had not liked flying.

Barnes was quiet, but Maag and Souter were anything but.

Glenn Capps, of the town of Sale Creek in the east Tennessee hills, recalled that the first time he saw Maag, the six-foot-four, 200-pound aviation machinist's mate from Colorado Springs was standing in line in the main mess hall, a white bandage all but covering his red hair.

"Who's that?" Capps asked.

"That's Red Maag," the next sailor in the chow line advised. "Don't fuck with him."

Nearly 60 years later, Maag, in his eighties, took time from fishing in Titusville, Florida, to gleefully recall his hell-raising days in the Navy. Other sailors said seaport police chiefs from Portland, Maine, to Elizabeth City, North Carolina, had learned to dread any Saturday night that Maag and Souter rode into town. The story that it once took seven Norfolk policemen to get the two of them into a paddy wagon was "absolutely true," Maag declared. "Billy clubs" used by the policemen on this occasion appear to have accounted for the white bandage Maag was wearing when Capps first saw him.

It is a reflection of the youthful character of the *Yorktown* crew that Maag was remembered years later as "one of the older guys." In fact, he was 27 in 1942.

"Remember this: Never belay a sheet," he would tell a young sailor, then walk away, chuckling to himself as he imagined the youngster's bewilderment over the meaning of the old Navy admonition. Maag had heard the expression from an old salt he met somewhere. Literally translated it meant, "Never tie down a sail." The rope that holds a sail should not be tied—or "belayed"—to the deck cleat, but simply looped around it, according to this bit of wisdom from the days of the sailing ship Navy. That's because a sail that is tied down cannot be loosened quickly enough to respond to a sudden shift in the wind. But if the line is looped around the cleat several times, it can be quickly loosened.

Within days of his appearance on the ship, the fact that Underwood was only 15 was known to many of the enlisted men, at least those in Fighting Forty-two, and he had picked up the nickname "Chicken." Barnes assigned him to be the squadron's compartment cleaner and kept an eye on him while he performed tasks like sorting laundry and mopping the compartment where the squadron bunked.

Underwood also became the unofficial custodian of a Packard-Bell radio-phonograph that the squadron had pitched in to buy. Radios had to be removed before the sets could be brought onto the ship. Sailors were told this was because of concern that when it is playing, a radio broadcasts a weak signal that might be used to locate the ship. When the phonograph was installed in Fighting Forty-two's compartment, it was played almost constantly, Underwood recalled years later. He and others said the most popular record among the squadron's young sailors, who were thousands of miles in distance and even further in circumstance from the nearest fraternity house, was Bing Crosby's 1941 version of "The Sweetheart of Sigma Chi." One by one, the brittle 78-rpm records were dropped and broken until only two were left. They would sink with the ship: "The Last Time I Saw Paris" and a country classic-to-be recorded at a Ft. Worth radio station in April 1941 by a struggling Texas dance-hall singer named Ernest Tubb, "Walking the Floor Over You."

Meanwhile, don't mess with Red Maag or Wayne Souter was soon known also to mean don't mess with Chicken Underwood, and the youngster slipped easily into the carrier's routine. Some of his shipmates would learn only when it was too late that behind the ever-present grin was a poker brain that knew when to draw to an inside straight or raise on the come-card, and they would pay dearly for being unable to find in the wide blue eyes any reliable indication of whether Chicken Underwood was bluffing or holding.

Maag, Souter, Underwood, Barnes and all other enlisted men assigned to any of the four air squadrons were known as "airedales," as opposed to men who served in the "ship's company." Although air squadrons had to provide a few men for kitchen duty and other chores that had nothing to do with aviation, members of each squadron generally occupied themselves chiefly with the maintenance and arming of their airplanes.

On the other hand, the ship's company was made up of the people who ran the carrier, tended its turbines and boilers, cooked its meals, washed its mess trays, barbered its hair, cobbled its shoes, printed its newspaper, laundered its clothes, pulled its teeth, treated its sick, chipped off its paint and spread on its new, ran its post office, served meals to its officers and cleaned their rooms, ministered to its spiritual needs, checked its weather, played its music, prepared its dead for burial at sea and carried out a nearly endless series of other tasks.

It is unlikely anyone who sailed on the *Yorktown* ever saw the entire ship. Enlisted crewmen were not encouraged to visit "Officers Country," also known as "Green Country," because the bulkheads and overheads were painted pale green, instead of grey. They had little reason or time to venture outside their own routines. However, there were common areas, such as the main mess hall, the ship's post office and the ship soda fountain. Known to crewmen as the "Gedunk," the fountain served soft drinks and sold candy and even freshly made ice cream.

In the heads were toilets built over troughs through which a steady stream of sea water flowed. The toilet seats consisted of two parallel boards about six inches apart on top of the troughs. In heavy seas, the sea water would sometimes reverse course.

Another common area was the "scuttlebutt." Yorktowners sailed at about the halfway point of a century-long evolution in the meaning of this old nautical term. In the 1880s, when fresh water had to be provisioned onto ships, a "scuttled butt" was a small keg in which water was kept available on deck. A hole was bored—"scuttled"—into the side of the keg, then closed with a plug that could be pulled out to release a stream of water. Sixty years later, on the *Yorktown* and other Navy vessels, the two words had been joined in "scuttlebutt," which had nothing to do with kegs but had come to mean any ship drinking fountain. The term also expanded to take in ship gossip, the kind exchanged at a drinking fountain. After the war, sailors brought the word back with them to stateside factories and office buildings. In another 60 years, with the Twenty-first Century heaving into view, the word had wandered further on the uncertain seas of the English language, leaving behind any reference to drinking fountains and meaning simply gossip or inside information.

In addition to Rear Admiral Fletcher, the *Yorktown* took on one of its most unusual crewman in San Diego when Thomas Coleman, a 62-year-old El Cajon chicken farmer, appeared at the aft gangway one day with a duffel bag on his shoulder and walked aboard.

Coleman was a retired chief carpenter's mate with 40 years of know-how, and the war could have made it easy for an experienced hand to talk his way back into the Navy. However, an early note in his service record may provide a clue to why he was able to get on this particular carrier at this particular time. Like Fletcher, CCM Thomas Coleman had been present at the 1914 Vera Cruz action.

Coleman's military record seems to sketch a more or less unresolvable love-hate relationship with the Navy. He first enlisted on August 2, 1902, in St. Louis and was discharged in 1906 in Bremerton, Washington. He signed up again in 1913 and served for a little over a year, during which he went to Vera Cruz. In 1917, he reenlisted at San Francisco and served for two years, part of the time in New York. He was discharged August 21, 1919, having made chief carpenter's mate. Two months later, he reenlisted, served mainly in the Philippines until October 21, 1921, was discharged and, four days later, reenlisted. Discharged on November 7, 1925, he reenlisted two days later.

Coleman transferred to the Fleet Naval Reserve on January 16, 1928.

He ran his chicken farm a dozen years, until 1940, when at age 59 he returned to active duty and was assigned to the *Yorktown*. He served for a little over a year. His retirement papers were signed on December 8, 1941, the day after the attack on Pearl Harbor, while the ship was in Norfolk.

He had made it back to Route 1, Box 857, El Cajon, but on January 2, 1942, got himself recalled to active duty. He was ordered to report on January 9.

But by January 9, Coleman already had been at sea three days on his old ship, the *Yorktown*.

As the 10 ships slashed through the Pacific toward Samoa, a "combat air patrol" of four or six F4F-3 Wildcat fighters circled the task force much of the time. In addition to guarding against attack, this activity allowed Fighting Forty-two's commanding officer, Lt. Cdr. Oscar Pederson, to drill his pilots and squadron "plane pushers" in the handling of the aircraft.

The drilling appeared to be needed. The *Yorktown* had been out of San Diego only two days when Ens. William S. Woolen lost power and crashed his F4F-3 on takeoff.

In speed, climbing strength, range or firepower, the Wildcat was never a match for its chief Japanese adversary, the Zero. But it was a sturdy aircraft and it held its own during the first 18 months of the war, largely because of the skill of American pilots. It was cranked with a "shotgun starter." A gunpowder-packed cartridge about the size of a shotgun shell was placed in a cylinder behind the engine. When the pilot fired the shell with a switch in the cockpit, the force of the exploding gases was transmitted to the engine. Two different shells were used, a small one for routine starts and a larger charge for reluctant engines.

A small crank was mounted inside of the cockpit of the Wildcat, beside the pilot's right knee. It was linked to the landing gear by way of a sprocket and a simple bicycle chain. As soon as the plane was airborne, the pilot began cranking up the wheels—27 turns, in all. Deck crews would watch the pilot's brown helmet bobbing up and down as he cranked up his wheels, his left hand on the stick. Sometimes, cranking up the landing gear caused the pilot to inadvertently shake the stick, making the plane wobble as it left the carrier. If a friction brake on the shaft of the crank was loose and the pilot's right hand slipped, the weight of the wheels caused the handle to whirl forward at a ferocious speed. The only way the pilot could stop it was by jamming his knee into it, sometimes at the cost of a chipped bone.

Woolen was fished out of the Pacific but his plane was lost.

On the 12th, Ens. Walter A. Haas crashed his Wildcat on takeoff and was rescued by a destroyer.

The pushers manually moved planes about the flight deck, positioning them for takeoff and guiding them to parking spots or onto the three deck elevators that were used to move them up or down between the flight deck and the hangar deck immediately beneath it. On carriers built a few years later, this job would be done with smaller models of the mechanical "mules" that tow planes at airports.

Besides the landing gear crank and the occasionally cantankerous starter, Pederson's fighter pilots had to learn to deal with the Wildcat's tendency to lift its right side slightly as it accelerated down the flight deck on takeoff. This was because the 1,200-horsepower Pratt-Whitney engine, which drove the plane's propeller clockwise from the pilot's viewpoint, produced such torque force that the plane reacted opposite the propeller's turn and torqued to the left. The effect caused the right-side landing gear to lighten and the left-side wheel to bear down, a difference that made the plane hard to guide on takeoff. It also caused the Wildcat to virtually insist on banking left as soon as it cleared the flight deck—and in an odd way that may have contributed to saving many lives on *Yorktown*.

January 13 was a Tuesday. Joseph Wetherington of Dover, Florida, was summoned from his job pushing planes and told he must appear at a "captain's mast" before Lieutenant Commander Pederson. A captain's mast is a nonjudicial proceeding for dealing with minor disciplinary infractions, but it can end up sending a sailor to the brig. The worried Wetherington reported to the commander and stood at attention with no idea why he was in trouble.

"Sailor, where have you been for the last seven days?" Pederson demanded.

"I've been up on the flight deck, sir, pushing planes," said a bewildered Seaman 3c. Joe Wetherington.

"No you haven't. You've been AWOL since this ship left San Diego."

Now even more confused, Wetherington thought back to the San Diego stop. It was his first liberty since joining the Navy. Then he realized that he had forgotten to turn in his "liberty pass" when he returned to the ship. Until the liberty pass was returned to squadron yeomen, Wetherington was technically not on the ship.

He quickly pulled his wallet from the pocket of his Navy-issue dungarees and offered the liberty pass to the

C.O., along with exaggerated apologies for his negligence. While the attending boatswain's mate struggled to hold a straight face, Pederson examined the pass gravely, then pronounced sentence.

"Sailor, you are confined to this ship for the next seven days."

When he was dismissed, the chastened Wetherington returned to the flight deck. Not until he saw the endless ocean horizon on all sides did he realize that his lesson in the proper use of a liberty pass had come in the form of a joke: The ship's entire crew was "confined."

Pederson had a sadder duty when he sent for Seaman 2c. William Harkins of Mobile, Alabama. When Harkins reported, Pederson informed him that his mother had died while the *Yorktown* was en route to San Diego but the carrier's departure from Norfolk had been such a guarded secret that the Navy had not been able to route the notification to him before the ship had left the California port. She was in her forties and her death, due to a heart attack, had been unexpected. Because of the war, the Navy would not have permitted him to go home for the funeral, even if the ship's command had known about it, Pederson said.

"Sir, if I had have known about my momma's funeral, I would have gone to it," the stunned sailor replied.

The next day, Ens. Richard L. Wright crashed his Wildcat on takeoff. He was picked up by a destroyer. Meanwhile, other fighter planes were sputtering and going dead on the flight deck. The engine failure problem had to be solved. Three airplanes had been lost. Even more important, a fighter that loses power during aerial combat becomes a coffin very quickly. Pederson ordered mechanics and engineers to tear into the engines and find the cause.

4

Something was wrong, something about the compass.

Aviation Machinist's Mate 1c. Charles Fosha stared at the instrument for a moment, then took the microphone from the hook on his instrument panel, switched to intercom and spoke to his pilot.

It was February 1, 1942. Fosha was bombardier of a single-engine, three-seat torpedo bomber that the war and public opinion had launched on a mistake-ridden mission over a suspected Japanese base on the South Pacific island of Jaluit. As the plane left the flight deck of the *Yorktown* nearly four hours earlier, Fosha had thought that someday he might tell his grandchildren that he participated in America's first strike at Japanese positions in World War II. Now, he wasn't so sure.

Still looking at the compass, Fosha asked Lt. Harlan T. Johnson, "What's your heading?"

The pilot told him where the plane was going, then exclaimed seconds later, "Oh, my God!"

It was a drastic but not uncommon mistake. Johnson was "flying the reciprocal," the opposite compass point of his intended heading. In everyday language, he was flying the wrong way. Instead of returning to the *Yorktown* at the end of a bombing run, the three of them, Johnson, Fosha and their radioman-gunner, Aviation Radioman 1c. James W. "Ace" Dalzell in the rear seat, were flying away from it.

What's more, another plane, piloted by Johnson's wingman, was loyally following their lead.

Johnson turned his plane around, and the second plane followed. Using a small pad pilots sometimes strapped just above their knees, Johnson did a quick reckoning of his probable location and estimated the amount of fuel left in the two Douglas TBD Devastators. More bad news. There was not enough fuel in the planes to get them any closer to the ship than 50 or 100 miles. He told Fosha and Dalzell and the crew of the other plane it was up to them. If they wanted him to, he would try to make it as far back as fuel would carry them. They could hope that a destroyer from the *Yorktown*'s Task Force 17 would pick them up. But in the limited visibility of this weather, he thought it unlikely they ever would be found.

The alternative, he said, was to land the plane in the water in the vicinity of one of the tiny coral atolls that dotted the ocean beneath them. This was Japanese-held territory and they would almost inevitably be captured.

It did not take long for the six men, Johnson, Fosha, Dalzell, and the crew of the second plane, Ens. H. R. Hein, Aviation Ordnanceman 3c. J. D. Strahl and Seaman 1c. M. E. Windham, to discuss their grim options and vote.

At 8:11 A.M. local time on January 31, 1942, the *Yorktown* radio room copied the following message from Lt. Johnson:

"This is 77V44. 77V44 and 76V44 are landing at Jaluit . . . are landing alongside one of the northwestern islands of Jaluit. That is all."

America had been at war less than two months. The *Yorktown* had lost 17 men and 10 aircraft.

The Japanese press was reveling in reports of victory at

sea. Guam had fallen on December 10 and Wake Island on December 23. On January 11, the U.S. aircraft carrier *Saratoga* was torpedoed off Oahu. Although it did not sink, it had to be towed to the shipyard at Bremerton, Washington, for repairs that would keep it out of the war for months.

At the same time, the need grew at Pearl Harbor and Washington for some action to which military and political leaders could point, some aggressive strike against the Japanese, to show that the United States was indeed in the war. The men who were getting a war effort organized had to think not just about an enemy and how to attack him and defend against him but about public and troop morale.

Countless typewriters in countless editorial offices in the country's heartland clacked with fervent, if occasionally intemperate, calls for action. Editor James R. Skewes of the *Meridian (Mississippi) Star* was in many ways typical.

In a column of editorials that followed the "Daily Bible Thought," Skewes took out after "Hitler—brothel born and bred" and the "pagan Jap" day after day.

On the day the Daily Bible Thought was taken from Proverbs 16:18, "Pride goeth before destruction and a haughty spirit before a fall," Skewes offered these thoughts:

> Shoot wherever and whenever the rattler shows its ugly head.
> Shoot to sink! And shoot to kill!
> To H— with diplomatic niceties!
> Blast 'tinder' Tokyo from the Oriental map.
> We know only one efficient way to 'play the game.'
> Kill as many foemen as we can—
> As quickly as we can—
> Pagan Japan has started this hellish slaughter.
> Let us finish it!
> Stop talking! Start fighting!

Adm. Chester W. Nimitz, the new commander in chief of the Pacific Fleet (CINCPAC), found himself between that kind of domestic clamor and military realities in which much of his fleet had been sent to the bottom of Pearl Harbor, and he could not accept "losses on a ship-for-ship basis." Therefore, he decided on a strategy of avoiding all-out confrontations with superior Japanese forces, while striking "the enemy a blow from time to time" because "the morale of the fleet and the nation demands it." From that strategy sprang his orders for the *Yorktown* and the *Enterprise* to attack Japanese positions in the Marshall and Gilbert Islands. Nimitz ordered Vice Adm. William F. "Bull" Halsey to take the *Enterprise* and his Task Force 8 to the South Pacific and rendezvous with Fletcher.

On January 19, the *Yorktown*'s first assignment of the war, escorting Marines to Samoa, had been carried out. Task Force 17, composed of the *Yorktown*, the battle cruisers *St. Louis* and *Louisville*, and four destroyers, *Russell*, *Walke*, *Hughes* and *Sims*, steamed northwest from Guam. Buckmaster announced over the *Yorktown* intercom that ship was about to strike a blow against the enemy. The crew cheered.

The Marshall and Gilbert Islands are contiguous chains of coral atoll north of Samoa. American and British missionaries found their way to the islands in the nineteenth century and a fair amount of English was spoken. The adjacent clumps of islands had followed different paths into the 1940s. The northern group, the Marshalls, was seized in 1914 by Japan, which continued to administer the islands on the basis of a 1919 League of Nations mandate. The Gilberts were part of a British crown colony until the Japanese took them over in 1941.

Halsey would send his bombers and fighters against three islands at the north end of the Marshalls: Kwajalein, Wotje and Maloelap. The *Yorktown* moved to a spot of ocean between the two chains with orders to attack

Japanese positions at the Jaluit and Mili atolls, on the southern end of the Marshalls, and Makin, a 10-mile-wide island at the northern end of the Gilberts.

The group sent to Jaluit included 17 dive-bombers and 11 torpedo bombers, the Douglas TBD Devastators.

The operation was a fiasco. A few miles from the ship, pilots encountered rain squalls and a few miles further, a thunderstorm. Planes got separated and pilots of many of the dive-bombers searched unsuccessfully through clouds for targets.

Approaching Jaluit, Ens. J. T. Crawford, a dive-bomber pilot, was flying at about 500 feet when he caught up with two torpedo planes from the *Yorktown* and joined up with them.

"Lousy luck to come this far to try to crank up the Navy's and the country's morale only to have this kind of weather," Crawford's radioman-gunner, Seaman 1c. Lynn Forshee, wrote years later in his privately published war memoir, *Standby Mark*.

"Now it began raining with a fervor. Fierce lightning and torrential rains hit us as we neared the island. It was find whatever target you could and hope for the best. [We] picked as our objective what was shown on the charts to be an administration building."

The bomber climbed to 8,000 feet and Crawford made his dive. As he did, he hit a layer of warm, moist tropical air that fogged his windshield, a problem that would continue to plague dive-bombers in the tropical Pacific. It was like diving "with a white sheet in front of your face," one would observe later. Another called it "aiming by memory." Crawford blew up the target building. As he pulled out of the dive, he and Forshee strafed whatever boats and ships they could find in Jaluit's small harbor.

By then, Lieutenant Johnson and the torpedo plane flying on his wing were lost.

Someone would observe years later that the only people

ever devastated by the Devastator were its own crews. The plane had a factory-rated top speed of only about 125 miles per hour, although men who flew in it said it seldom reached that velocity. It was awkward and underpowered and it was a fire trap. Flotation devices in the wings, installed to keep it afloat if the pilot had to ditch at sea, had a tendency to inflate without warning during flight. Since this circumstance greatly compromised the plane's already challenged aerodynamics, the Navy issued pilots rapier-like tools, with which they could reach out of the cockpit when necessary and puncture a float that had inflated before its time.

When the Devastator carried a torpedo only two men flew in it, the pilot and radioman-gunner. The mid-seat was unoccupied. The rear seat swiveled in order that the radioman-gunner might use either the .30-caliber machine gun mounted behind him or the radio equipment in front. When near a target, the pilot released the torpedo by pressing a small switch, the "pickle," on the side of the stick. If the electrical switched failed to work—and it often did—the pilot could release the torpedo manually.

When the Devastator was armed with bombs, it carried a third crewman, the bombardier. As the plane approached its target, the mid-seater slipped through an opening in front of his seat and knelt inside the fuselage, almost directly beneath the pilot's seat. As he searched for the target, the bombardier took control of the aircraft, flying it with a device known as the Norden Bomb Sight.

Fosha had brought a civilian pilot's license with him into the Navy, and recruiters told him he would be sent to flight school almost immediately with a commission probably not far behind. In fact, it took him five years to get to flight school at Pensacola. While there, he met Edna Warner and they got married. She had moved to Norfolk with him but returned to Pensacola to live with her parents when the *Yorktown* was sent to war. Just before he shipped out, she told him she thought she was pregnant.

Fosha, Dalzell and pilot Johnson circled around Jaluit for several minutes, while Fosha peered into the bomb sight and through occasional holes in the clouds. Finally, he and Johnson concluded that efforts to locate a target were futile. Johnson decided to abort the mission and turn back before the plane had consumed too much fuel.

Dalzell would speculate years later that Fosha's inability to find a target for their three 500-pound bombs was the result of the plane's having strayed to the opposite side of Jaluit from the harbor.

When James Dalzell was an infant, his father was killed in a construction accident at Americus, Georgia, and he was sent to live with his maternal grandmother, Mrs. Tulula Fuller of Albany, Georgia. Together, the two of them clawed their way through the Depression, Granny and James in the boll-weevil South. She took in laundry to get money for groceries and he worked part-time at an A&P store.

He had joined the Navy in 1937, after being allowed to graduate from high school in Albany a few months early.

The water landings were not difficult. Fosha had returned to his spot in the belly of the plane, removed the Norden Bomb Sight and tossed it overboard. The two Devastators settled into the water a few hundred yards apart and their flotation devices inflated properly. When Ensign Hein and his crew attempted to inflate their life raft, they found it was punctured. They told flyers from the other plane they had inadvertently pushed it against a piece of metal protruding from the side of the fuselage and punched a hole in it. However, it was not uncommon for Devastator crews to find their life rafts had been packed with leaks in them. This sometimes happened because packers, trying to roll the raft down to a size that allowed stowing it in the space allotted for it, banged it against work benches. That caused the bottle of compressed carbon dioxide gas wrapped inside to punch a hole in the raft. The three men sank their plane and began swimming toward the Johnson plane.

Meanwhile, Dalzell and Fosha were having trouble deflating the flotation bags in the wings of their plane. It was imperative that the plane be sunk, lest it fall into the hands of Japanese. Finally, Johnson climbed back into the cockpit and retrieved his rapier-like flotation device puncturing tool. It did its work and the plane promptly sank.

The six men began paddling and swimming, three of them in the life raft and the other three hanging on the sides. They would alternate positions.

They worried about sharks and about the "Emily," a Japanese Kawanishi flying boat, which slowly circled overhead then flew away.

5

Newspapers would report the strike on the Marshalls and Gilberts as if the attack on Pearl Harbor had been avenged. In reality, the operation was a bust.

All planes sent against two islands, Makin and Mili, returned safely to the ship after delivering strikes of questionable consequence.

The Jaluit operation was costly, in equipment and in lives.

Planes from that raid groped through the rain to get back to the ship, the first arriving around 9 A.M., nearly five hours after taking off. Several Devastators were down to as little as two or three gallons of gasoline when they landed. Two others ran out of gas trying to make it back to the ship and ditched in the open sea. Crews of other returning planes saw one of the torpedo bombers still riding its flotation devices. A dive-bomber radioman said he had seen crewmen in a life raft and dropped a smoke bomb to let them know they had been spotted. But in the rain, visibility at sea level often was as low as a few hundred yards and destroyers sent back to search for the two crews never found them. The six crewmen were formally listed as lost at sea.

Two dive-bombers, each with a crew of two men, also

failed to return. One was listed simply as "last seen" en route to Jaluit and the other as not seen since taking off that morning. There were reports of a flash in the sky several miles from the ship, leading to at least one published account that shortly after taking off, the two planes had collided in the miserable weather. However, the same weather had sent lightning flashing through the rainy predawn sky and, in reality, no one knows what happened to the two bombers or the four men in them.

A bomber patrolling around the carrier task force crashed in bad weather at around 9 A.M. The pilot and radioman-gunner were picked up by a destroyer but the plane was lost.

Counting the two planes that ditched near Jaluit, six torpedo bombers and three dive-bombers were lost. Sixteen men were lost at sea.

Six of the missing *Yorktown* were paddling around among the spits of land that dotted the ocean at the south end of the Marshall Islands, taking turns riding in a three-man life raft, somewhere near Jaluit.

Dalzell would recall that after several hours of paddling, swimming and riding currents, the six flyers drifted close to a tiny island and waded ashore. The island appears to have been Gebu, which is just north of Jaluit. It is about two miles long and not even a mile wide. As he stood on the beach, Dalzell had the feeling he could have looked across the island to the opposite shore, except for the vegetation in the center. A house was visible in the trees. Otherwise, there was no sign of life. For about an hour, the six men walked along the beach, periodically calling out in an attempt to find out if anyone else was on the island. There was no response.

Finally, an old Micronesian man appeared and walked uncertainly across the sand. In limited island English, he managed to communicate that the only people left on the island were women, children and a few old men. The young men, he said, had been taken away by Japanese soldiers nine months earlier to work on construction of military bases on other islands. Eventually, the rest of the island's residents emerged from bushes where they had been hiding. The Americans counted 55 women and children, three old men.

The flyers ate coconuts and breadfruit, along with a chicken the islanders gave them, for the next two days. Periodically, the "Emily" circled the island. The natives did not have any boats that looked like they could safely carry six men away from Gebu.

On the third day, two barge-like boats circled the island for about an hour. Then around 70 Japanese troops came ashore.

The six Americans hid and watched, along with the worried natives, whose island was being brushed by a world war in which it had not sought a part. The Japanese troops formed a sort of skirmish line on the beach, Dalzell recalled.

"Well, there's no way out of this," Johnson finally said. "I'm going to walk down there and surrender to them. If they kill me, you guys are on your own."

With that, waving a white handkerchief over his head, the six-foot-four, blond Navy lieutenant walked to the beach and gave himself up. The Japanese surrounded him and pointed their weapons at him as he towered over them. For a few minutes, the other five flyers watched the odd scene on the beach, then walked down and gave up also.

The six were taken to the island's only house and kept for a few minutes. During this time, Dalzell recalled, the officer in charge of the Japanese troops directed a thorough search of the island. When he was satisfied there were no other Americans there, he made a simple but welcomed declaration: "Through the grace of His Majesty, the Emperor of Japan, you are permitted to remain alive."

They then were bound and placed on a float plane that had landed near the island and transferred to an air base at Kwajalein and were taken to a guardhouse, bound and blindfolded.

"We sat there on the floor, still blindfolded for what seemed like hours," Fosha recalled. "While sitting there, we heard a noise that sounded like someone falling."

Dalzell started a roll call but was interrupted by Strahl, the Judsonia, Arkansas-born bombardier from Hein's plane.

"Ah, shucks," he drawled. "I fell asleep and fell over."

During their stay at Kwajalein, the six flyers were interrogated at length, individually.

"The main thing they were interested in was what had happened at Pearl Harbor," Dalzell recalled. "They would lay out picture after picture they had taken during the attack on Pearl Harbor. And they would ask us, 'What ship is this? What ship is that?' We didn't even know. We told them over and over that we were not at Pearl Harbor, we were at Norfolk."

He said the interrogators clearly were concerned about the fact that no carriers had been in port during the attack.

It was a widespread concern in the Imperial Japanese Navy.

Mitsuo Fuchida, the lieutenant commander who had been in overall charge of the 353-plane attack force sent to Pearl Harbor on December 7, 1941—and whose famous message, "Tora! Tora! Tora!," informed his carrier that the attack had begun—wrote after the war that it was only one hour before launching the attack that Japanese forces received intelligence reports that none of the U.S. carriers were in port. Despite this supremely disappointing news, the Pearl Harbor strike had demonstrated the primacy of the aircraft carrier.

Vice Adm. Chuichi Nagumo, proud son of a venerable Samurai family, was given the honor of personally delivering a report on Pearl Harbor to Emperor Hirohito, and Fuchida was one of two men he chose to accompany him. But even while these celebrations were underway, Adm. Isoroku Yamamoto, commander of the Japanese Combined Fleet, and others were thinking through the problem posed by the survival of the American carriers. Fuchida would contend that the oil embargo imposed on Japan in 1941 by the United States, Great Britain and the Netherlands had driven the decision to attack the United States and would guide many of his country's subsequent military decisions. To survive, Japan believed it had to seize the rich petroleum-producing areas of Southeast Asia as soon as possible.

But to hold the oil fields of the Dutch East Indies without fear of an attack on its homeland, Japan required free rein in the Pacific. It would not have it as long as the fleet of four American carriers—the *Lexington*, the *Saratoga*, the *Yorktown* and the *Enterprise*—was intact. In some quarters of the Imperial Japanese Navy, the question became a preoccupation: Where were the American carriers and how could they be destroyed?

While Nagumo and Fuchida were describing the Pearl Harbor operation to the emperor, a brilliant naval air tactician who had planned the Pearl Harbor invasion, Cdr. Minoru Genda, was at work on the beginnings of a plan to draw the U.S. carriers into a trap and sink them. Fuchida wrote that Genda "first thought up the basic idea" of picking a fight and trapping the U.S. carriers in it. Others have suggested the idea originated with Yamamoto personally and that Genda merely analyzed it at his request.

Either way, the fate of *Yorktown* sailors was being carried on currents that were invisible to them. In places most of them had never heard of, brilliant men whose names they could not even pronounce were struggling with enormous problems of national wealth and military might. The solutions those men chose and responses of the sailors' own superiors would ultimately bring the *Yorktown* to a place called Midway and another battle. But this battle would not be a haphazard, amateurish exercise like the attack on the Marshall and Gilbert Islands. It would be one of the great sea battles of history, and America would carry it. Like the outcome of any battle, victory would grow from mixed soil; from fate and luck and tactic; from a new technology called radar; from secret, encoded Japanese radio communications snatched like letters written on the wind and deciphered in Honolulu. But as much as any of that, at the Battle of Midway, America would throw at its enemy the character of the young men whom it had bred in the 1920s and reared in the hard times of the 1930s, and that would be enough. The battle would come down to countless acts of courage, at times acts that would be characterized as "suicidal gallantry."

The last torpedo bomber to return from Jaluit landed on the *Yorktown* at around 10 A.M., but the events of the day America launched its first strike against the Japanese were not over.

Ens. J. T. Crawford, pilot of a Douglas SBD dive-bomber, had blown up what he and radioman-gunner Lynn Forshee supposed was an "administration" building at the Jaluit harbor, then strafed a ship in the harbor, before returning to the carrier.

As soon as they had landed, Forshee climbed out of his rear seat and hurried below to get a cup of coffee. He came back up the *Yorktown*'s steep, ladder-like stairs to the hangar deck, where in a little while he would hear a violation of radio silence that *Yorktown* officers and crew would remember for the rest of their lives.

Radio conversations, either between the *Yorktown* and her aircraft or among the pilots could be "piped" throughout the ship. This meant that from the grease-smeared crews in the engine room only a few feet above the keel to the sailors who arranged planes on the flight deck, crewmen could evesdrop on flight chatter, even during battle.

At 11:05 A.M. the *Russell*, one of the destroyers searching for downed airmen, made radar contact with an unidentified aircraft a little over nine miles out and closing slowly. Minutes later, *Sims* and *Hughes*, the other two destroyers, confirmed the contact. Postwar review of

Japanese records showed the plane was a Kawanishi 97, a lumbering, four-engine flying boat used as a bomber and a scout. It and two others had taken off from Jaluit and were searching for the *Yorktown* task force. The *Russell* opened fire with its five-inch antiaircraft guns and the plane retreated into the ragged gray clouds that continued to blanket the area. Minutes later, one of the Kawanishis dropped several bombs but they fell harmlessly about a mile from the *Sims*. The destroyers, which already were giving up their search for the missing flyers, called for fighter support and several Wildcats were scrambled. For nearly two hours, a sort of cat-and-mouse-and-cat game played out, while the Japanese planes looked for the carrier and the Wildcats looked for the Japanese planes. Task Force 17 continued steaming to the east.

Then, at a little after one o'clock in the afternoon, one of the Kawanishis maneuvered to about three miles from the carrier, within range of the ship's five-inch guns. Gunners at platforms around the flight deck sought permission to open fire.

The response from the bridge was emphatic: "Permission denied!"

The reason for the denial was the fact that two Wildcat fighters were ducking in and out of the same now-thinning rain clouds that hid the Kawanishi and would be at risk from antiaircraft flak. The two fighters were flown by Ens. E. Scott McCuskey, an exuberant young pilot known to Fighting Forty-two mechanics and deck crews as something of a back-slapper, and quiet, smallish Ens. John Paul "Johnny" Adams, the Methodist preacher's son from northeast Kansas.

The two pilots broke through clouds at 1:15 P.M. to find themselves staring directly at the large red ball insignia on the side of the Kawanishi. McCuskey, in the lead plane, was too close and going too fast to get off a shot, but flying on his wing was Adams and the Japanese plane was a target

Adams could not miss. He squeezed the switch on the side of the stick, as he had been conditioned to do in hours of flight school training and drills at sea.

In a couple of seconds, the four Browning .50-caliber M2 machine guns in the the wings of Adams's plane threw about a hundred half-inch-thick slugs into the side and wing of the Kawanishi, and flames burst from it. By this time, McCuskey had circled and returned in time to fire his own round of bullets into the doomed Japanese aircraft.

"We just shot his ass off!" McCuskey whooped into his radio microphone.

The words were heard throughout the *Yorktown*. From the flight deck and hangar deck and the decks of the ship's cruiser and destroyer consorts, sailors cheered as burning fragments of the Japanese bomber fell from the clouds into the sea.

"Burn, you son-of-a-bitch, burn!" shouted the ship's bombastic executive officer, Cdr. Joseph J. "Jocko" Clark.

It was the first plane to be shot down by *Yorktown* flyers.

The two new "aces" brought their Wildcats back to the flight deck and were greeted by sailors' cheers and officers' toasts and congratulations in the ready room. But McCuskey would recall years later that after the partying was over and night had fallen, he heard a knock on the door of Room 403, the tiny compartment he shared with Ens. Leslie Knox, the new husband of Louise Frances Kennedy Knox. Adams was at the door.

"How many men do you think were aboard that Jap aircraft?" Adams asked after McCuskey let him in. Until that moment, McCuskey said, that aspect of the day's events had been invisible to him.

"We had been involved in the killing of human beings, instead of just shooting down an aircraft," he recalled.

For his part, Adams was a little embarrassed by published accounts that he felt overdramatized the conversation and neglected the fact that "by the next day, I was ready to go back and do it again, if I needed to."

Fletcher considered launching a second attack on Jaluit, but Halsey, who was senior to him, ordered him to retire from the area.

While the *Yorktown* and the *Enterprise* were attacking the Marshalls and Gilberts, Vice Admiral Nagumo was only 1,000 miles away at a Japanese port on Truk Island, where he had gone after covering the invasion of Rabaul, an island in the Bismarck Archipelago. When he received word of the U.S. carrier attack on the nearby Marshalls and Gilberts, he immediately sortied from Truk Island, in the hope of engaging one or more U.S. carriers. Aboard his flagship, the Japanese fleet carrier *Akagi*, he charged eastward at top speed until the following day, when he concluded that any American carriers involved in the attack were gone. Reluctantly, he turned back.

"This impulsive action really made little sense," Fuchida wrote. "It would take us two full days to cover the 1,200-mile distance from Truk to the Marshalls and, in that interval, the enemy was sure to retire safely. Nevertheless, I inwardly rejoiced. Futile as it seemed, I thought our mad dash might be just the gesture that was needed to persuade Combined Fleet to redirect the Nagumo Force eastward toward its logical and potentially most dangerous opponent, the American carrier force."

The *Yorktown* headed for Pearl Harbor.

The rising hatred for the Asian enemy was most intense among the men who actually fought the battles. Many, though certainly not all, would never let go of the effects it had on them. During the half century after the war ended, strategic alliance, mutually enriching trade and shared economic dominance would change the attitudes of most Americans and draw new outlines of political correctness. But there aren't enough Sony television sets or Mitsubishi video cassette recorders or Honda Accords in the world to change many of those who served on the *Yorktown* and other ships like it or to eradicate "Jap" from their language or the feelings that were packed into it from their hearts.

Many would look back on the *Yorktown*'s February 1941 return to Pearl Harbor as the event that stirred this resentment most, even more than battles they fought. The Marshall and Gilbert raids had been molded by Navy propagandists into the kind of morale-raising news story they believed the country needed. Ordered to muster on the flight deck, the men of the *Yorktown* heard cheers rising from the docks and the decks of other ships as the big carrier quietly stood up the channel and glided to her dock on Feburary 6. They saw, too, the devastation the Japanese attack had left behind.

Harry Schanbacher of Binghamton, New York, a flight deck plane pusher on VB-5, the bombing squadron, described the scene years later in present tense, as if he were still there.

"So this is Pearl Harbor, bastion of the Pacific. My God! This is a regular graveyard for ships! *Nevada* is sticking in the mud of the channel. *West Virginia*'s cage mast is sticking out at a crazy angle. Only *Arizona*'s main deck is visible. *Utah* is on her side, and other hulls are spread around. Fuel oil from sunken ships is so thick on the water that boats don't even make a wake. Fumes are everywhere. No smoking is allowed on Ford Island except in the club and the coffee shop. Buildings have no roofs. Hangars are a sorry mess. Aircraft hulls are burnt to a crisp and machinery in the shops is so much rubble."

In another written reminiscence shared with the author, radioman-gunner Anthony Brunetti of VS-5, the scouting squadron, recalled the *Yorktown*'s return to Pearl Harbor.

"I can still remember catching the lovely, woodsy scent of the land and flowers, even before we sighted the Hawaiian Islands. Then we entered Pearl Harbor. The crew, mostly up on the flight deck, was deathly silent as we counted the seven sunken battleships and the still-smoking wreckage of installations on the beaches. I can still see the bow of that destroyer that was blown up onto the beach and the broad hull of the capsized old battleship. . . . I had the same awful feeling as when Norway fell to the Germans in 1939; it somehow signalled the end of my life as it had been. My hatred for the Japs has never abated since that day."

6

Between the town of Pensacola, Florida, and the Pensacola Naval Air Station on the Gulf of Mexico, there stood in the late 1930s a roadside store where groceries, soft drinks, ice cream and snacks were sold. Navy flying cadets being trained at the air station often stopped there on their way to or from Pensacola to get a cold drink or an ice cream. They called the place the "Halfway House."

It was about five miles from Pensacola, five miles from the Naval Air Station and 9,000 miles from Lae and Salamaua.

Those two towns were on the banks of the Gulf of Huon on the east end of the island of New Guinea. Reports that Japanese ships were delivering troops to the area stirred both concern and excitement among the staff of the CINC-PAC, Adm. Chester Nimitz, at Pearl Harbor in early March 1942. The concern was that the Japanese move threatened Australia, which was only a few hundred miles across the Coral Sea from the long, pointed Papua peninsula at the east end of New Guinea. At the same time, the Japanese landing offered the Navy an opportunity to deliver a serious blow because two U.S. carriers, the *Lexington* and the *Yorktown*, happened to be in the region.

The carriers rendezvoused in the South Pacific when Vice Adm. Wilson Brown Jr., commander of the *Lexington* task force, decided on a plan to attack the Lae and Salamaua harbor. The most direct attack would be from the north, but this would place the carriers at risk from Japanese aircraft based at Rabaul, in the Bismarck Archipelago, just north of New Guinea. Therefore, Brown decided to take the ships south of the eastern peninsula and have his bombers fly across the 100-mile strip of land and attack Japanese assets from the land side.

The *Yorktown* had spent only 10 days at Pearl Harbor, taking on provisions, a passenger and a new executive officer. Cdr. Joseph "Jocko" Clark was promoted to captain and transferred off the ship. At the Newport News Shipbuilding and Drydock Co. in Virginia, a new carrier, which had been named the *Bon Homme Richard*, was nearing completion and awaited his command. Clark was loved by the *Yorktown*'s sailors, who identified with his exuberance. The "burn-you-son-of-a-bitch-burn" remark he hurled at the four-engine Japanese float plane shot down by fighter pilots McCuskey and Adams near the Marshall and Gilbert Islands was an example, as was his favorite exhortation, "Let's go to Tokyo!" Officers, on the other hand, appeared to be somewhat relieved when Clark was replaced by Cdr. Dixie Kiefer, a 1918 graduate of the Naval Academy.

"After the Gilbert Island raid in early February, he [Keifer] had relieved the equally dynamic, enthusiastic, but often bombastic, 'Jocko' Clark, who set high standards for us and drove us hard during the months he was on board," Rear Adm. John R. Wadleigh recalled in 1972. "Dixie Kiefer maintained these standards and was also able to solidify the morale and spirit of the ship in the months before Midway." Wadleigh was a lieutenant on the *Yorktown* in 1942.

The passenger who boarded at Pearl Harbor was William Hipple, a former *Honolulu Star-Bulletin* reporter en route to an Associated Press assignment in Australia. Hipple's brief censor-delayed dispatches appeared in the *Star-Bulletin* under a standing headline, "At Sea on a Carrier." The *Yorktown* was not identified. In a typical column, he wrote:

"Hiking around the ship, up and down ladders, through small, round hatches which a fat man could never navigate, you come across facts and figures and items such as these:

"Potatoes are now peeled by machine, no longer by hand. But, sad to say, the machine doesn't get the eyes of the spud. A daily detail of men sits just off the galley, disdainfully digging out the eyes with little knives after the spuds have gone through the machine.

"Beans are still the Navy staple, and 300 pounds are served in a meal, twice a week.

"Other food figures:

"About four steers eaten a meal when beef is served, (2,300 pounds), 150 pounds of coffee a day, 14,000 pounds of potatoes a week, 1,100 pounds of butter a week, 1,000 dozen eggs a week, 1,500 loaves of bread baked a day, 435 pies baked at a time, 100 gallons of ice cream made a day.

"The ship has a musical unit, which can function as a military band, concert orchestra or dance band. The sailors claim it is the best dance band in the fleet, and you can believe it after listening to a jam session.

"There's not much chance for practice now, but sometimes, in comparatively safe waters, they get in a few licks on the hangar deck after dinner, to the accompaniment of much stomping by the lookers-on.

"Favorite recreation is listening to phonograph records. There are record players all over the ship. Men buy their favorites ashore and add them to the various collections. In the band room, for example, there are 500 records, from the hottest swing to the symphonic and operatic.

"The laundry washes and irons 220,000 individual pieces a month, and the men say, jestingly, 'Our rust sprinkler is unequalled and our button jerker beyond compare.'"

On May 22, the *Star-Bulletin* abandoned this format to carry Hipple's account of the attack on Lae and Salamaua over two months earlier:

"Our Navy Strikes Again! March 10 Blitz Is Revealed.

"ABOARD AN AIRCRAFT CARRIER WITH THE ALLIED FORCES—The powerful air arm of the United States fleet on March 10 struck a paralyzing blow against Japanese forces attempting to establish bases in New Guinea. Attacking within 48 hours after the announcement of the enemy's movement against the undefended ports of Salamaua and Lae, carrier-based aircraft descended in a lightning strike upon Japanese warships, troopships and auxiliary vessels.

"Taken completely by surprise in the act of consolidating their positions, the Japanese ships attempted frantically to scatter.

"But as one high officer's report said, prosaically, 'All except unimportant units were sought out and visited with sudden and very unpleasant destruction.'"

Hipple reported what he was told. He had not flown on the mission, so he had not seen the dud Mk. 13 U.S. torpedoes bumping harmlessly into Japanese ships.

John Smith Thach had.

When Thach, a native of Fordyce, Arkansas, appeared at the U.S. Naval Academy in Annapolis in 1923, someone thought he looked like his older brother, James Thach, who had preceded him there, and began calling him "Jimmy." The nickname stuck until his retirement as a full admiral in 1967.

Before the war began, when Thach was stationed at the San Diego Naval Air Station, he had been shown a copy of a Navy intelligence report describing a new Japanese fighter. The plane had appeared in the skies of China's Szechwan Province, where much of the fighting in what the Japanese called the "second Sino-Japanese War" was centered.

Chinese pilots who saw it said it was long-winged, fast and heavily armed. It climbed easily and maneuvered nimbly in combat. In little over a year, Japanese pilots flying 30 of these aircraft brought down 266 Chinese planes, without losing a single plane to an enemy fighter. The plane was a carrier-based fighter that the Japanese Navy had designated "Type 00," because 1940 corresponded to the year 2600 in the Japanese calendar. Japanese pilots shortened the "00" designation to simply "Zero."

Thach, whose men were flying the new Grumman F4F-3 Wildcats, immediately grasped the importance of the report. Years later, in an interview conducted as part of the World War II oral history series at the Naval Institute in Annapolis, Thach recalled the first time he heard about the Zero.

"It was in the spring of '41, when we received an intelligence report of great significance. This report had come out of China when the Japanese and Chinese were having aerial combat in connection with the war there. It described a new Japanese aircraft, a fighter, that had performance that was far superior to anything we had. It said it had more than 5,000-feet-per-minute climb, it had very high speed and could turn inside any other aircraft. Well, those are the three advantages that a fighter pilot would like to have, or rather, that he needed to have at least two out of the three: one is high rate of climb, one is a tight turn and the other is speed. So, when I realized that this airplane, if this intelligence report was correct, had us beat in three categories, it was pretty discouraging. . . ."

The 5,000-feet-per-minute climb rate turned out to be an exaggeration. Performance requests Japanese Navy officials gave to the American-trained Mitsubishi engineer who headed the Zero's design team called for a climb rate of slightly less than 3,000 feet per minute. But even that was superior to the Grumman Wildcat.

One night as he mulled over the problem the mystery plane posed, Thach took a box of matches and dumped them onto the kitchen table at his home in Coronado, adjacent to the San Diego Naval Air Station. For the next several hours, he played dogfight games with the matches. At around midnight, his wife, Marilyn, interrupted him.

"Jimmy [even she called him Jimmy], you know you are going to fly tomorrow. Don't you think it's time you got some sleep?"

Night after night, they repeated the exercise, with him playing fighter games on the kitchen table until she came and insisted he come to bed.

Then one night, he came to bed early. He had figured out a maneuver that became known among Navy flyers and in air forces in the United States, Great Britain and Russia as the "Thach weave." The tactic was based on Thach's realization that even in slower and less maneuverable aircraft, U.S. pilots could compete with the faster Zeroes if they worked together. This principle of mutual support was the theme of Thach's constant lectures to the young pilots who served under him during the opening weeks of the war. "Don't be a lone wolf," he would tell them. "Lone wolves die."

Thach would command the *Yorktown*'s fighter pilots in the ship's final battle at Midway, but in March 1942 he was teaching his weave maneuver and mutual support philosophy to young pilots on the *Lexington*, where he was commander of the fighter squadron.

Vice Admiral Brown's strategy for attacking Lae and Salamaua from the land side meant the carriers were less at risk from Japanese planes in Rabaul, but it was not without complications. A jungle-covered spine of mountains runs along the center of the eastern New Guinea peninsula, 13,200 feet high. It is known as the Owen Stanley Range. Devastators carrying heavy torpedoes or bombs could not climb high enough to clear the peaks. Between two of the mountains, Mounts Chapman and Lawson, was a 7,500-foot-high pass, which carrier air officers had said the torpedo bombers should be able to clear. Even this route had complications, however, because the pass began to cloud up each morning and typically was enshrouded with clouds by midmorning. It would be necessary for the Devastators to get through it and return before 10 A.M. or pilots would be unable to see to fly between the two mountains.

Yorktown Devastators were armed with two 500-pound bombs each, but the *Lexington* torpedo bombers would each carry a single Mk. 13 Bliss-Leveat torpedo, which was much heavier than two 500-pounders. Dive-bombers and fighter escorts from both carriers also would be involved in the attack.

With Thach's fighters circling overhead, the *Lexington* torpedo planes climbed into the Owen Stanley mountains, but when they reached the pass, they did not have altitude to clear it. Years later, Thach described the scene:

"So, they started out and climbed and climbed and climbed and got to the mountain range. They were still below, looking up at that ridge, and I was sitting right up on top of them, and it looked like they weren't going to make it. They went right at the ridge and then had to turn away. They milled around and tried to get more altitude, couldn't seem to do it."

The skipper of the *Lexington* torpedo squadron was Lt. Cdr. Jimmy Brett. After several unsuccessful attempts to get through the pass, Brett radioed Thach.

"You'd better go ahead, I don't think we're going to make it. You go ahead."

"No, I'll wait here a bit. I've got enough gas. I can wait a little bit."

A few minutes later, Brett came back.

"All right, hold it. I've got an idea."

With that, he started flying parallel to the ridge. His squadron mates fell in behind him. Brett, who had qualified as a glider pilot before taking Navy flying lessons at Pensacola, had spotted a sunny meadow in a mountain valley and remembered that sunny fields provided thermal updrafts, which glider pilots often used to stay in the air. Sure enough, when he started circling his torpedo bomber over the meadow, he started climbing. Members of his squadron followed, while Thach and his fighter pilots watched from above.

Finally, Brett got just enough air under his Devastator to make it through the pass. One by one, other members of his squadron followed and slipped between the mountains, each pilot singing out the agreed-on signal that he had cleared the pass: "Halfway House!"

But pilot ingenuity would not cause a torpedo to explode. While it was not Pearl Harbor, the American planes found several ships in the Lae and Salamaua port and the attack had offered the first clear opportunity to deliver a significant blow against the Japanese.

"The torpedo attack was beautifully executed," Thach recalled in the Naval Institute interview. "You could see the streaks of torpedoes going right to the side of those cruisers and nothing happened. I saw one or two torpedoes go right on underneath and come out on the other side and bury themselves in the bank on the shore. Some obviously hit the cruisers and didn't explode. So we had bad fuses and very erratic depth control, and I didn't see any torpedo explosions. What a heart-breaking thing, after all that effort and all that training and the use of this wonderful experience Jimmy Brett had to get over there and then drop these torpedoes and they're practically all duds."

He said some of the dive-bombers hit ships in the harbor but apparently did not sink any of them.

Fletcher fed correspondent Hipple a different story:

"The box-score of the Japanese losses at the two points—Salamaua and Lae—showed that at least 10 ships were sunk or crippled and five others severely damaged," Hipple reported. "Two cruisers were destroyed, five transports—one of fifteen thousand tons and two others of ten thousand tons—sunk, beached or left blazing; one destroyer was blown up by a heavy bomb, another sunk and others damaged by smaller bombs and strafed by machine gun fire."

Practically none of that had happened.

In his regular "At Sea on a Carrier" column, Hipple also told the beginning of the strange and ultimately tragic story of a *Yorktown* fighter pilot, Ens. Edgar Bassett of Philadelphia.

Hipple identified Bassett only as "Red." Associates said he sometimes was called "Red Dog" because of some notable experience, successful or otherwise, at the card game with that name. Hipple wrote that the slightly rotund pilot had been told by a fortune teller some years earlier that he would not survive his 28th birthday, which happened to be on March 10, the day of the Salamaua and Lae raid. The mysterious forewarning was included in a package of prophesies, some of which already had come to pass. While other pilots and enlisted crew of Fighting Forty-two looked on with bemusement, Bassett got prepared for flying an escort mission to Lae and Salmamaua. He wangled a butcher knife from the galley and loaded his cockpit with it and other survival supplies. Perhaps influenced by Joseph Conrad's great nineteenth-century novel, *Lord Jim*, Bassett declared that if he crashed into the jungles of New Guinea, he planned to use his weapons, his merchandise and his superior Western intellect to "become a king" among the natives. Hipple said the hexed Bassett even declared he intended to "prey on their [the natives'] superstitions."

The ensign flew his mission on March 10 and returned to the *Yorktown* flight deck unscratched. He celebrated his success, within the limits that life on a crowded aircraft carrier permitted celebration. "I beat the jinx!" Hipple quoted him as saying.

Two months later, Ed Bassett's Wildcat would be the first *Yorktown* fighter shot down by a Zero at the Battle of

Midway. Thach was the last person to see it as it plunged in flames into the ocean with Bassett still in the cockpit.

7

After the raid on Lae and Salamaua, the *Lexington* headed back to Pearl Harbor for modifications. The *Enterprise* already was in port, receiving the routine maintenance the *Yorktown* would never get. The *Saratoga* was in Bremerton, Washington, being repaired for the torpedo damage it suffered in January, and the *Hornet* was making its way to the Pacific.

Only the *Yorktown* was left to patrol the South Pacific and oppose any Japanese move that might threaten the supply and communication lines to Australia. The carrier zigzagged about the ocean in what seemed an endless vigil. For 101 days, beginning February 16 when they left Pearl Harbor, members of the crew would not see a pier. Hanging over the tropical heat and the grinding tedium of the daily routine was the fact that every man on board knew that the carrier was hauling bombs, torpedoes and high octane aviation fuel. If a lurking enemy submarine were to put a torpedo in just the right place, it could blow up the ship.

As the days wore on, Joe Fazio set his sights on becoming a "plane captain."

Dean Straub waited for news of his wife's pregnancy.

Red Maag practiced playing the only song he knew on his ocarina.

Chicken Underwood explored the ship.

Lynn Forshee and Johnny Kasselman worked out the details of a plan to buy a sailboat together after the war and sail it to South America.

Forshee came from the tiny town of Britt, Iowa. He had turned 19 the day the *Yorktown* docked at San Diego. Kasselman was a city boy from Cincinnati, son of the owner of Kasselman's Grocery downtown, and was a few years older. Forshee marveled at his friend's inquiring mind and worldliness.

They were both radiomen-gunners in VB-5, the *Yorktown* dive-bombing squadron.

The rear seats of the Douglas SBD Dauntless dive-bombers swiveled like those in the bombers' older cousins, the Devastator torpedo bombers. This allowed men like Forshee and Kasselman to face the rear and the .30-caliber machine gun with which they defended the plane—or to spin around to an instrument panel full of radio equipment in front of the seat.

In addition to the radio equipment, an altimeter was mounted on the panel in the rear cockpit. During dives, a Dauntless pilot kept his eye trained on his bomb sight and thus could not keep track of his rapidly decreasing altitude. The second seater had to watch the altitude gauge and tell the pilot when to release the bomb.

The altimeter responded to changes in air pressure that accompanied changes in the plane's altitude and inevitably lagged by 50 to 100 feet during the high-speed dives. Radiomen were taught to estimate the lag and subtract it from the altimeter reading to get a more accurate estimate of the plane's true altitude. As a plane dived, the radioman would speak to the pilot through the onboard intercom and at 3,500 feet, tell him, "Standby . . ." A few seconds later, at 2,500 feet, he would add, "Mark!" The second word was the signal for the pilot to release the bomb and begin pulling out of the dive.

The plane was most vulnerable as it pulled out.

The Dauntless had a much better reputation than the Devastator. The men who flew it loved it because it was tough and, for such a heavy plane, relatively maneuverable. Still, some joked that "SBD" stood for "slow but deadly," and some called it "the Barge." The plane was built for use both as a dive-bomber and a scouting plane.

In December, when the *Yorktown* passed through the Panama Canal and stopped briefly at Balboa, Kasselman had used a few hours of shore leave to find a bookstore and buy a book of Spanish lessons. He set out to teach himself the language in preparation for the planned sailboat trip to South America and attempted without much success to get Forshee to learn at least a few words.

Red Maag also took up self-improvement. During shore leave at Honolulu, Maag had purchased an ocarina, an egg-shaped music pipe about the size of a potato and known primarily for its limited range. The pipe came with instructions for playing only one song, "What a Friend We Have in Jesus." Maag learned to play that song and played it constantly, to the steadily declining appreciation of his squadron mates. Since he was Red Maag, they endured it.

Maag was a fighter squadron plane captain, meaning he was chiefly responsible for the maintenance of a specific airplane. Pilots were not attached to specific aircraft. They generally flew whichever plane was next in line. But on the scouting, fighting, torpedo and bombing squadrons, each plane was assigned a permanent plane captain, a mechanic whose job was to meet that plane when it landed and service it before it took off. Many treated the planes like personal property, tending them and caring for them like hot rods, decorating them with cartoons, slogans and names of sweethearts. Nearly 60 years later, Maag could still recite the order in which the Wildcat's 14 cylinders fired: 5-14-9-4-13-8-3-12-7-2-11-6-1-10-5. . . .

Once, as Maag lay on the wing of "his" plane on the hangar deck, playing "What a Friend We Have in Jesus" on his ocarina, Dixie Kiefer, the new *Yorktown* executive officer, happened by and paused to listen to a few bars.

"Red, He may be the only friend you've got left on this ship," he said. Then he walked on, laughing and shaking his head.

What a friend Joe Fazio had in Red Maag. When the single-minded Fazio began "striking" for third-class petty officer and a possible job as plane captain, he went to Maag for help in getting ready for the tests he would have to take. He had been told one test required him to plot the fuel and oil systems of the Wildcat's two-row, radial engine.

"They told us one of the things I've got to do on the test was a block diagram of the oil system and the fuel system of the Wildcat," Fazio recalled. "I pulled out the maintenance manual, and it was too detailed for me. So I went to Red. I said, 'Hey Red, I've got to take the third-class petty officer's test and one of the things I've got to do is draw a block diagram of the fuel system and the oil system.' And he said, 'Well, that's not too bad.' So we went back and sat down at the base of a crane on the flight deck. First, he drew the oil system. Then he did the fuel system."

Ens. Leslie Knox waited for mail from his bride back in Norfolk. "I remember he was always looking forward to getting back to see her," Knox's fellow ensign, John Adams, recalled years later.

Forshee recalled the unusual interest bombing squadron mechanic Dean Straub had in the occasional refueling maneuvers at sea and the mail bags that arrived with them. Straub had a pregnant wife back in Norfolk.

He and John Trott were neighbors and their wives were friends.

Once after a refueling session, Forshee said, a group of radiomen, mechanics and other members of the bombing squadron were in the squadron ready room, reading accumulated letters. Straub was searching for news of his wife and the outcome of her pregnancy. But Trott, reading his own mail, came to his wife's account of the blessed event first.

"By the way, Dean, it's a boy," he said.

It may have been the same refueling session that William Surgi of New Orleans, an aviation ordnanceman in the fighter squadron, found himself in the grips of a sailor's craving for fresh fruit. Of all the men and officers who ever sailed on the *Yorktown*, Bill Surgi's relationship with the vessel would be unique. In later years a tireless organizer of veterans' groups and campaigner for preservation of old aircraft carriers, Surgi was chosen by Robert Ballard, the undersea explorer, to accompany his expedition to Midway in 1998 to search for the ship. As a remote-controlled video camera swept past the sunken carrier, Surgi was aboard Ballard's research vessel, watching on a monitor the images of the precise spot where he had taken cover during the *Yorktown*'s last battle 56 years earlier.

But on an afternoon at sea in 1942, his interest was in an orange.

"When the *Neosho* [the tanker] came alongside of us to bring us fuel and supplies, everybody was lined up on the catwalk, all ready to catch oranges and apples, bananas and everything else they would throw over," Surgi recalled. "I couldn't have gotten on that catwalk if I had tried. But I saw a lot of that stuff was going over their heads so I went back on the flight deck, in between all those parked airplanes. Pretty soon, I saw an orange rolling across the deck. Unfortunately some other guys had the same idea and about three of us all dove for that orange. I got splinters in my knees and my hands, but I got the orange. It was already squished, split open. But I tore into it. I ate the orange and then I ate the peel and then I ate the seeds. I enjoyed that orange."

There was little ventilation in the ship and in the tropical heat, crew sleeping quarters sweltered.

The *Yorktown* flight deck was over seventeen feet above the hangar deck, and the space between the two was normally open at the sides, meaning the sea was visible to men at work on the hangar deck. However, during the *Yorktown*'s extended South Pacific vigil in the spring of 1942, large metal "weather curtains"—which in some ways resembled folding garage doors but were much larger—were pulled down at night so crews could work without light giving away the ship's location.

The closed weather curtains further reduced the air circulation below, and some crewmen took to sleeping on the hangar deck or even under the stars on the flight deck, using wooden wheel chocks for pillows.

The tropical heat was probably noticed least by the men who labored deep below the water line on the *Yorktown*'s fire rooms, generators, boilers and turbines. They lived with heat, day in and day out. They also lived with soot and grease and were known as the "black gang," a holdover term from the days of coal-burning ships.

"One evening up on the flight deck, I met a sailor from the black gang," Forshee wrote. "He was Harold Braun from the engine room and he had come up on deck in the cool of the evening because of his heat rash. I soon discovered that he also came from Iowa. St. Ansgar, to be exact, and we had gone into Great Lakes Training station [for boot camp] at the same time. He had also joined the *Yorktown* at Norfolk in the summer of '41, and, as I had, he had anticipated leave in December."

Both men had had their leaves cancelled, as did hundreds of others, because of the outbreak of war.

Harold Ervin Braun would never go home to St. Ansgar, Iowa, again. Less than a month after he and Forshee became acquainted, Braun would be killed in the ship's first major battle.

Captain Buckmaster almost disappeared from view during this South Pacific patrol. The Old Man divided his time between his quarters and the bridge, where he had his meals brought to him. He avoided lights, believing they might cause his night vision to become less acute. When there were movies on the hangar deck, he almost never attended.

Unable to push his ship to flank speed because of unrepaired wear in the brick lining of its fireboxes, Buckmaster nevertheless sailed as fast as possible at night. If the carrier were to be seen by Japanese spotter planes during the day, Buckmaster and Rear Admiral Fletcher hoped the nocturnal dashes would create the illusion that more than one U.S. carrier was deployed in the South Pacific.

As the ship sailed on, men fought the heat and the monotony. Dozens of "anchor pools" circulated. Sailors would each pay a dollar and try to guess the precise date and time the ship's anchor would drop. The winner of the pot would be decided by the timing of the boatswain's "Now hear this . . ." announcement that the ship was at anchor. Poker, craps, hearts, backgammon and cribbage games became marathons.

John Underwood's card training at the hands of his two bachelor uncles and maiden aunts back in Tennessee began to pay off. He kept a growing cache of poker winnings stashed in his locker in the Fighting Forty-two berthing compartment. He also learned to exploit his special status as a youngster. He learned that he could pretty much go where he pleased on the ship when he was not at work.

Once he even found himself on the bridge, outside the helm. Buckmaster, who happened to be in the conn at the time, sent his Marine guard out to find out what the sailor wanted.

"Captain wants to know what you're doing up here," the Marine said.

"Well, I was just looking around the ship, to see how it worked," Underwood replied apologetically.

Hearing him, Buckmaster told the guard, "Bring him in here."

The captain of the ship then gave the third-class seaman a tour of the conning tower, explaining how he gave orders to the helmsman, who turned the carrier's big steering wheel, how this movement was transmitted to electric motors below and how the motors drove pistons that moved the *Yorktown*'s huge rudder.

The conning tower was heavily armored, with slits on the sides. Buckmaster told Underwood that he would look through those slits to see how to guide the ship in a battle.

When the tour was over, Underwood thanked his captain and took his leave.

"Come back any time, son," Buckmaster said with a grin.

When traditional time-killers lost their edge, men got creative. Someone would get a big wad of paper, soak it in aviation fuel and go into one of the heads on the ship. Sailors hunched side-by-side without partitions or doors in these common-seat toilets, above the stream of sea water that flowed continually though the stainless steel trough beneath them. The sailor with the fuel-soaked paper would wait for a spot to become available at the upstream end of a toilet, light the paper and drop it into the water—then run like hell while the furiously flaming wad floated under the exposed rear ends of his shipmates.

At least fighter pilots and SBD crewmen could get away from the ship occasionally, even if it was for lonely "combat air patrols," in which the Wildcats circled the region around the ship, or the scouting missions when the SBDs flew over extended sectors, 100 miles or more from the ship. Forshee wrote that he began to look forward to the long scouting flights, when he could feel almost alone in the rear seat of an SBD Dauntless, scanning the ocean for an enemy ship or the faint "white feather" wake of a submarine periscope.

Afternoon practice sessions of the ship's band afforded another diversion. The band was made up of professional musicians, some with the kind of talent that would take them to jobs in big-name bands or as college music teachers after the war. It was originally attached to Adm. Ernest J. King, and it accompanied him wherever he took his flag. In 1939, however, King was sent to a desk job in Washington, and the band stayed behind on his last carrier, the *Yorktown*.

When bandleader Edgar L. Oakley, a chief petty officer, got his musicians together for hangar deck rehearsals, sailors with nothing to do would gather and listen. Inevitably, the band would get around to a tune from the music craze of the day, jitterbug, or "jumpin' jive," the rock-and-roll precursor that seemed to be almost a cross between dancing and tumbling. Pete Montalvo, the New York stickball player, and Sid Flum, who had grown up in the Bronx and joined the Navy a few months after his father died in 1939, started jumping and jiving and quickly developed their own fans. But few sailors could get away from their work stations long enough to listen to the band's rehearsals.

Food ran low and meals became increasingly monotonous. Bath water had to be rationed when fresh water evaporators, long in need of maintenance, began to fail.

Forshee wrote that he had eaten powdered eggs for so long that "I was convinced that somewhere back in the states, someone in a lab was working on a method to make a powdered chicken."

The *Yorktown* had become the "waltzing Matilda of the Pacific Fleet," in the words of Navy historian Samuel Eliot Morison, and "[h]er sailors felt that this marathon had lasted long enough."

Crew grumbling soon became apparent to Lt. Cdr. Frank Hamilton, the ship's chaplain.

Hamilton, a Protestant minister, was loved by many Yorktowners, though not all. He and Sid Flum became close friends after the war, when Flum moved to Norfolk and Hamilton pastored a church there. According to a story he told Flum, Hamilton and his wife were riding on a trolley in

San Diego one evening shortly after the war ended when a group of sailors, including some who had served on the *Yorktown*, climbed on. The sailors had spent several hours in a tavern, and it showed.

Recognizing Lieutenant Commander Hamilton, they crowded around him, slapping his shoulder and shaking his hand and introducing themselves to his wife with exaggerated, if slurred, gentility. Then, while the embarrassed Hamilton alternately smiled and cringed in his seat, one of the former Yorktowners turned to the rest of the streetcar and announced loudly, "Ladies and gentlemen! Allow me to int'duce you t'best god-damn chaplain in t'United States Navy! Chaplain Hamilton!"

The chaplain's inquiries about the ship's morale soon led him to the fact that only three steaks were left in the main galley cold storage lockers. Turning scarcity into revelry, Hamilton, Flum and others came up with the idea of putting on a ship "Jamboree," at which the three steaks would be raffled off and the winners would be served steak dinners before the entire company and air crews. The steaks were displayed during a parade on the flight deck and the winners drawn.

Someone decided John Underwood should be dressed as a girl to serve as a "waitress." A "wig" was fashioned from a mop and stainless steel bowls from the galley became "breasts." A piece of parachute became what appears in photographs to have been the first miniskirt ever worn by a male sailor in the U.S. Navy, and knee-length white stockings were borrowed from the uniform of a British Royal Navy officer who had boarded the ship in Honolulu as an official observer. Underwood fought furiously to escape the role and gave in only after Wayne Souter, Maag's sidekick, told him, "Go along with it, John. It won't hurt you, and it'll be a favor to the ship and everybody'll remember you for it from now on."

In his miniskirt with his blond mop-wig, Chicken

Underwood didn't look all that bad to some of his sea-weary shipmates.

"Hey, come over here, honey, and let me have a pinch," one or two shouted.

But Souter was close by. "The first guy that touches that kid, I'll knock him on his ass," he warned.

Oakley's musicians struck up "Tuxedo Junction" and Montalvo and Flum performed their jumpin' jive jitterbug for the entire crew and officers.

Standing at the edge of the crowd in a small group were several black mess attendants. The black sailors were rarely even seen by other members of the ship's crew. They worked in Officers' Country, where other enlisted men seldom ventured. They ate together in a small mess hall near the galley where officers' meals were cooked, had their own sleeping quarters and pretty much kept to themselves. Matthew Blount of Norfolk, Virginia, recalled the "white" and "colored" drinking fountains and heads in Officers' Country and the less obvious but always present reminders of segregation that he and his fellow blacks found on the ship.

"We weren't the only mess attendants," Blount said. "They had Filipinos and men from Guam. But you could see that the Filipinos, they didn't want to be with the blacks. The Guamanians didn't want to be with us. You could tell by the way they acted. If you were in charge of them, they would resent you for being in charge.

"But when the Japanese dropped four bombs and two torpedoes on us, nobody looked to see whose name was on it. They didn't look for what color he was and who he was and where he was."

Spotting the black sailors at the edge of the crowd, a master of ceremonies at the Jamboree called over to them, Blount said, and asked "if any of you boys would like to dance." There's no reason a half-century later to attach any significance to his use of the word "boys." Of the more than 2,500 enlisted men on the *Yorktown*, most were white and most were boys. And the invitation was in all likelihood a genuine effort to include the black men in the fun.

But to them it sounded a little like someone thought all black men could dance, "like he thought we were all Bojangles," said Blount. They politely declined and, after a few minutes, returned to their compartment.

When the "last T-bone in captivity" had disappeared down the throat of a lucky sailor and members of the ship's band had packed their instruments back into their lockers, the *Yorktown* continued its vigil. But that would end soon.

8

The mystery of the loss of power by the Wildcat fighters had been solved.

Rubber used to line the new self-sealing fuel tanks was dissolving in gasoline and clogging up the carburetors. Fletcher sent a message to Nimitz at Pearl Harbor that the fighter squadron would have to have new tanks. Replacements were flown to the island of Tongatabu, where the ship dropped anchor on April 20.

Dozens of anchor pools were paid off and the tanks and new provisions were brought aboard. Fletcher and Buckmaster put on their formal blue uniforms and, accompanied by Marine guards, made a courtesy call on Queen Salote, ruler of the Tonga Islands.

Members of the crew who drew shore leave went looking for what sailors always look for when they come ashore after a long voyage, but they did not find it. Queen Salote had ruled her people for over 23 years and was wise about the ways of sailing men. She had the island's entire young female population rounded up and sequestered at a secret location until the ship left. The Yorktowners settled for a chance to walk on firm ground again, to eat coconuts and fresh island fruit and to explore the strange place far from Mobile, Norwich, Chattanooga and Manhattan. Some rented mules from the islanders and rode them to the center of the island, only to learn that inland Tongatabu was home to the animals, who upon arriving there betrayed no inclination to return to the coast. The sailors had to walk back. Some used their time on the island to overimbibe on *kava*, which in the words of Fighting Forty-two's expert on shore-leave revelry, Red Maag, "was the strangest liquor I ever drank, because it didn't make you happy, it just made you numb."

While the carrier was at anchor in the Tongas, the six Devastator crewmen who had ditched near Jaluit February 1 were being taken to prisoner-of-war camps in Japan.

Chuck Fosha, the bombardier on one of the planes, spent a few days in a new camp at Oofuna, near Yokohama. The camp would later become known for the brutal things that happened there, but Fosha said his stay of a few weeks was easy, possibly because he was the camp's only prisoner.

On April 18, 1942, while at Oofuma, he also became one of the first Americans to witness from the ground an event that would have a profound impact on the fate of his shipmates on the *Yorktown* and, indeed, the outcome of the war. It was an event that would push the *Yorktown* in the direction of its final great battle.

While on an exercise walk through some hills near the camp, Fosha noticed a strange airplane and heard antiaircraft fire. Assuming the plane was being used for antiaircraft practice, he looked up to see if it was towing a target but could not find one among the antiaircraft bursts that trailed it. Meanwhile, his guards suddenly grew inexplicably agitated and raced back to the prison camp, forcing him to run with them.

A week later, Fosha was shifted to a camp at Zentsuji on Shikoku Island where several of the other five *Yorktown* flyers already had been put to work loading and unloading railroad cars. There, on a prison camp bulletin board, he found a clipping from the English language *Japan Times & Advertiser*, which explained the mysterious plane he had seen near Yokohama. The clipping described the bombing raid led by Army Air Corps Lt. Col. James Doolittle over several Japanese cities, including Tokyo.

"I was not that familiar with the planes Doolittle was flying, but I'm sure that was one of his airplanes," Fosha said in later years. "It [the Doolittle raid] was the same day and I think the same time that I saw that airplane."

The raid was practically inconsequential in terms of physical damage. Mitsuo Fuchida would write a decade later in his book, *Midway: The Battle That Doomed Japan*, that the Japanese military scoffed at the exercise and said it should be known not as a Doolittle raid, but as a "do-nothing" raid.

Fuchida added: "In point of physical damage inflicted, it was true enough that the raid did not accomplish a great deal. But the same could not be said of its impact on the minds of Japan's naval leaders and its consequent impact on the course of the war at sea. From that standpoint, neither 'do-nothing' nor 'do-little' were accurate descriptions. On the contrary, it must be regarded as a 'do-much' raid."

Fuchida was commander of the bomber squadron on Vice Admiral Nagumo's flaghip, the carrier *Akagi*. The ship was rounding the southern end of Formosa on its way back to Japan from action in the Indian Ocean on the day a Japanese Navy patrol boat spotted the U.S.S. *Hornet* carrying Doolittle's B-25 Mitchells. (The Japanese patrol boat was promptly sunk by U.S. ships but not before it had radioed its report.) Fuchida said he was in the *Akagi* flight personnel standby room when an orderly rushed in and told him that Genda, the carrier's air operations officer, wanted to see him in the operations room. He responded quickly, wondering what was going on.

Genda was only five foot three and weighed slightly more than 100 pounds. He was one of the most colorful characters in the story of the U.S.–Japanese relationship between 1941 and the end of the millennium.

In the early 1930s he had commanded a squadron of Navy test pilots, known even in the West as "Genda Flying Circus." To drum up public enthusiasm for the creation of the Japanese Naval Air Force, the pilots put on barnstorming flying shows throughout Japan, a sort of biplane-era predecessor of teams like the U.S. Navy's Blue Angels, which would put on similar shows for similar reasons decades later in jets.

Later, he would spend two years in London as a naval attache in the Japanese Embassy.

When Mitsubishi engineer Jiro Horikoshi set out to design the fighter plane that would become Japan's fabled Zero, Genda represented fighter pilots on the Zero planning committee and forcefully argued for a maneuverable fighter.

From the design of an aircraft to the design of a battle, it would be Minoru Genda who, at the request of Yamamoto, drew up detailed plans for the attack on Pearl Harbor three years later. One of the first problems he confronted was the fact that small bombs carried by Japanese dive-bombers would have little effect on U.S. carriers in the Hawaii port. He solved the problem by having stabilizing fins welded to the 16-inch exploding shells, which Japanese battleships fired from their big guns. This converted the shells into bombs.

In 1954, nearly a decade after the war ended, Japan re-established its armed services and Genda joined the new Air Self-Defense Force as a general. Two years later, he was asked at a London press conference if he had regrets about the attack on Pearl Harbor.

"I have no regrets," he replied. Then, after a pause, he added: "Yes, I have regrets. We should not have attacked just once. We should have attacked again and again. The mistake we made was in not occupying Hawaii with the Army. If we had then gone on to make a surprise attack on the West Coast of the United States, we might have won."

Six years later, in 1962, President John F. Kennedy awarded Genda the Legion of Merit, the highest honor America can bestow on a foreigner, for his service in the Air Self-Defense Force and his contributions to the U.S.–Japan Security Treaty. Genda had vigorously advocated the basing of U.S. nuclear weapons in Japanese territory. After retiring from the military, Genda served 24 years in the upper house of the Japan Parliament.

He kept seven dogs, a cat and four hawks as pets and served for many years as chairman of the Japan Animal Welfare Society.

In addition to planning the Pearl Harbor attack, Genda first conceived a plan to force the United States into a carrier battle at the Midway Islands in the belief that a much superior Japanese force could sink the U.S. ships, according to Fuchida.

The Japanese Naval General Staff initially opposed the attack, saying Midway was too small to be worth the effort it would take to capture it. Besides, the General Staff had its attention focused on the South Pacific because of concern about possible Allied use of Australia as a base to impede Japan's exploitation of the priceless oil fields of the Dutch East Indies. On April 5, the General Staff had bowed to Yamamoto's wishes and approved the attack on Midway but haggled endlessly over details and did not abandon its interest in Australia and the South Pacific.

The haggling was ended by the Doolittle raid, and the planning for Genda's proposed carrier trap at Midway moved into high gear. Fuchida suggests Genda instantly realized that would happen.

He said that when he arrived at the *Akagi*'s operations room on the morning of April 18, 1942, Genda handed him a copy of the report from the patrol boat that a few hours earlier had spotted the *Hornet* closing in on the Japanese homeland.

"Well, they've come at last!" Genda said.

Chuck Fosha was at the Zentsuji prison camp only a short time when prison officials asked him if he wanted to make a statement on a Japanese shortwave radio broadcast. He was worried about his wife back in Pensacola. He needed to let her know he was alive. She would be about halfway through her pregnancy, and he knew the Navy would have been unable to tell her anything more than that he was missing in action. Yet, he did not want to do anything to assist a Japanese propaganda effort. He went to Lt. Harlan T. Johnson, his pilot and superior officer, and asked for guidance. Johnson told him the War Department had not issued instructions for captured personnel. However, a statement in which Fosha merely identified himself and said he was in good health should not be a problem, Johnson said.

Fosha decided to make a statement. He gave his name, said he was in good health and was being held as a prisoner of war in Japan. He asked any American hearing the broadcast to contact his wife in Pensacola and let her know he was alive.

Within days, Edna Fosha received between 30 and 40 postcards and letters from Americans who monitored the Japanese shortwave broadcasts as hobbies and relayed Fosha's message to her. These cards and notes were the first indication she received that her husband was still alive. Perhaps the most unusual letter was from a minister, who enclosed a small plastic record of Fosha's voice on the broadcast. The record had been cut to be played on a needle phonograph. On the opposite side, the preacher had recorded his own message of counseling and encouragement to her. Beside the minister's message were the words, "Words of Comfort," and the name, "R. Van Dosbree."

Ham radio operators also monitored a Japanese broadcast on which a list of the names of American prisoners of war was read, and James Dalzell's name appeared in a subsequent wire service story about the broadcast. In Albany, Georgia, his mother was contacted by an *Atlanta Journal* reporter, who provided the first word she and Granny were to receive that he was alive in Japan.

Before the *Yorktown* left the Tonga Islands, Yamamoto had organized a critique of his planned Midway campaign.

But the Imperial Navy's General Staff did not completely abandon its idea of controlling the South Pacific. Japan's newest aircraft carriers, the *Shokaku* and the *Zuikaku*, both commissioned in August 1941, were diverted to the Coral Sea to cover the Japanese invasions of the town of Port Moresby on the eastern Papua peninsula of New Guinea.

At Pearl Harbor, Navy code breakers sifting through bits and pieces of Japanese radio traffic became aware of the plan to occupy Port Moresby. Nimitz sent the *Lexington*, by then refitted with 1.1-inch antiaircraft guns, to rendezvous with the *Yorktown* near the New Hebrides Islands, at the eastern perimeter of the Coral Sea. The *Yorktown* weighed anchor April 27, 1942, and bade goodbye to the people of Tongatabu, their beautiful island, their wise queen, their strange liquor and their contrary mules.

Task forces organized around four fleet carriers, two from the United States and two from Japan, headed for the Coral Sea. What happened next was stated best by historian Morison: "The dancing waters of the broad Coral Sea . . . where no more serious fights had taken place in days gone by than those between trading schooners and Melanesian war canoes, became the scene of the first great naval action between aircraft carriers."

9

A week out of Tongatabu, Fletcher rendezvoused with Fitch and the *Lexington* at a spot Nimitz had code-named "Point Buttercup," and the two carriers began patrolling on the western end of the Coral Sea. Fletcher received an intelligence report that the Japanese had begun moving troops and materiel into Tulagi, a mud drop of land just north of Guadalcanal in the middle of the Solomon Island chain. An Australian garrison had been evacuated from Tulagi and the Japanese were planning to set up a seaplane base at the island. Fletcher immediately turned the *Yorktown* task force north, toward the southern coast of Guadalcanal, and prepared to launch his dive-bombers and torpedo planes.

He would later say that the Japanese move into Tulagi, which had one of the best anchorages in the Solomons, was the kind of news he "had been waiting two months to receive." Communication mix-ups and a case or two of possibly justified caution on his part had sown doubt in the minds of his superiors, especially Admiral King in Washington, over whether Fletcher could fight. Here was a chance for him to "strike a blow against the enemy."

It may have been a chance for the admiral to put the *Yorktown* to use. But fate seemed disinterested in the exercise, as if it were saving the old girl for a bigger fight.

For whatever reason, the Tulagi raid, like those on the Marshall and Gilbert Islands and the ports of Lae and Salamaua, was largely a story of near misses and lost aircraft. When the day—May 4, 1942—was over, the Japanese had lost a few barges and a pair of converted fishing trawlers. The captain and nine crewmen of a Japanese destroyer were killed by strafing fire from Fighting Forty-two's Wildcats, but the ship was not sunk.

For that, the *Yorktown* had lost another TBD Devastator and two brand-new self-sealing fuel tanks—along with the two F4F-3 Wildcat fighters in which they had been installed during the stop at Tongatabu.

After reading the action report, Nimitz sent word from his headquarters at Pearl Harbor that the "operation was certainly disappointing in terms of ammunition expended to results obtained."

The two lost Wildcats were flown by John Adams and Scott McCuskey, the same pair who had shot down the Japanese float plane three months earlier, leading to McCuskey's shout, "We shot his ass off!" The remark had been published somewhere, and McCuskey had promptly received a batch of angry letters from schoolteachers around the country, taking him to task for using language that could corrupt America's youth.

After the Tulagi raid, Adams and McCuskey got lost returning to the *Yorktown* because a homing device, which was supposed to receive a secret radio signal that would enable a pilot to calculate the approximate direction to the ship, had malfunctioned on McCuskey's plane. Adams's plane did not have the equipment, but he was sure he knew how to get back to the ship. Meanwhile, McCuskey could not receive radio signals of any kind but seemed able to send messages. When Adams signed with a circular motion over his head that he knew the way back to the ship, McCuskey refused to turn with him.

"Goddamn it, Adams, come back here," he barked into his radio microphone.

Adams radioed the ship and described his dilemma. He felt he knew the way back but his section leader refused to go with him and clearly intended to crash-land on the beach at Guadalcanal. Adams was told to stay with McCuskey, so he radioed directions that he believed would help rescuers find them and followed McCuskey onto the beach. They kept their landing gears up to avoid being flipped over by a rock and bellied in safely at a point near the town of Cape Henslow on the southeast coast of Guadalcanal. The U.S.S. *Hammann*, a destroyer, was directed to leave the carrier's escort screen and search for the downed flyers.

In addition to the homing device, McCuskey's plane was equipped with an identifying transmitter, which sent out an encoded signal that would inform the ship that his approaching aircraft was friendly. It was important that both this equipment and the ZB homing device be removed and destroyed. McCuskey was unable to unbolt either from its cockpit mountings.

A few weeks later, Navy public relations people would set up a "radio interview" with *Collier's Magazine* for McCuskey. With the assistance of magazine rewrite man Frank D. Morris, McCuskey treated readers of the magazine to a colorful account of the two flyers' adventure.

"Our landing gear was carried away and our props ruined," the article ran. "I was busy destroying all confidential gear and equipment when Adams walked over and tapped me on the shoulder. I looked up and he pointed toward an opening in the jungle that fringed the beach. There stood a couple of dozen of the fiercest-looking blacks I've ever seen outside the movies. They were perfect cannibal-types—bushy hair, skewer-pierced noses and the inevitable loin cloths."

McCuskey said that he and Adams went over and stuck our their hands.

"We shook hands all around, but their deadpan expressions did not change a bit and when I started asking them questions, the only answers I got were grunts.

"'Any Australians here?' I asked. Grunts.

"'Any English? Dutch?' Grunts.

"Then I spoke a magic word: 'Americans?' They all became excited, started chattering among themselves, and the first thing I knew there was another round of handshaking. We were accepted socially. . . ."

In fact, it was not unlikely that the "fiercest-looking blacks" McCuskey had ever seen outside of the movies were Christians. In addition to Roman Catholic priests and Anglican missionaries, a South Seas Evangelical Mission Society was active throughout the Solomon Islands. It had been founded in Queensland, Australia, in the late nineteenth century by an Australian woman who felt a need to evangelize among islanders who were being imported to work on sugarcane plantations. The Protestant movement had spread from the mainland back to the islands.

In addition to giving the American flyers oranges and coconuts, the islanders led them to a "spring of cold clear water," McCuskey reported. At Adams's request, they took his white silk parachute and spread it over the top of a coconut palm, hopefully to be seen by lookouts on the rescue ship. Eventually, the islanders pointed out the *Hammann* as it skirted the island, searching for them. At about the same time, crewmen on the destroyer spotted Adams's parachute, and a motor-launch was sent ashore.

McCuskey's account in *Collier's* said he "did what I could" to destroy the radio equipment before taking the launch to the *Hammann*. As it would turn out, that wasn't much.

The following day McCuskey and Adams transferred back to the *Yorktown*.

The homing device on McCuskey's plane was not the

only one that malfunctioned. A torpedo plane flown by Lt. Leonard E. Ewoldt got separated from its squadron, and it too was lost. For a few minutes, Ewoldt's radioman-gunner, Ray Machalinski of Erie, Pennsylvania, heard the *Yorktown* signal, but then it stopped. Radiomen on the ship said that like McCuskey, Machalinski could send radio signals but was unable to receive. He tried to repair his radio but could not get it working.

In 1927, when Ray Machalinski was seven years old, the death of his father in a work accident at the General Electric plant near Erie, Pennsylvania, disrupted the family. Grief drove Ray's mother to a nervous breakdown from which she never emerged, and she spent the rest of her life in a state hospital. His oldest brother, Al, was forced to drop out of school before finishing the twelfth grade and join the Navy. An Erie lawyer was appointed legal guardian of Ray, his older sister, Rose, and Max, a second brother who was just older than Rose. He placed the kids in a Catholic orphanage. They never heard from him again. Nor did they hear anything about the two-story house their father had owned in Erie.

When Machalinski left the orphanage nine years later, he, his sister and his brother had had only a handful of visits, although they had many relatives in Erie. His mother's sister, "Aunt Sophie," brought their maternal grandmother to see them twice, and his father's brother, also named Al—Brother Al of the Order of the Holy Cross in Chicago—came to visit them two other times.

But the Machalinski kids did not complain. They were tough and the Catholic home was a secure and warm place—a lot more secure and a lot warmer than the Pacific Ocean would be on May 4, 1942.

Unable to find the carrier, Lieutenant Ewoldt had finally run out of gas and glided his TBD Devastator into the sea. It was 4:05 P.M. when the *Yorktown* copied Ewoldt's notification that he would have to ditch. The destroyer *Perkins* was sent to search for the downed flyers, but it could not find them.

Since they had left the carrier armed with a torpedo, rather than bombs, there was no midseater and only Ewoldt and Machalinski were in the plane. By then, the bothersome flotation devices had been removed from Devastator wings, and the plane sank within minutes. Machalinski was able to retrieve the rolled life raft from the middle cockpit but did not have time to find the prepackaged supplies of food and drinking water.

After he inflated the raft, he and Ewoldt discovered it was in the water upside down.

It had been that kind of day. The "pickle" torpedo release switch on his stick had not worked, and Ewoldt had been forced to drop the torpedo manually. They had gotten separated from their squadron in the rain, and their homing equipment had malfunctioned. They had run out of gas and crashed, and now they were sitting on the bottom of an upside-down life raft somewhere in the Pacific Ocean without food or water.

When they had righted the raft, they found two small oars and an air pump had been secured to the inside. Ewoldt decided on the basis of the vaguest sort of ocean surface reckoning that currents were moving them in the direction of Australia. Fortunately, that was not true, for Australia was a thousand miles away, on the opposite side of the Coral Sea.

With no food and no water, the two men drifted on the ocean for four days.

Occasionally there were squalls. They leaned back and held their mouths open, trying to catch rain drops. The rainwater that fell in the raft was promptly ruined by seawater that sloshed over the side. They tried wringing out their undershirts and using them to catch rainwater, then wringing the rainwater into their mouths. By the time they had wrung it from their shirts, the rainwater had mixed with spray and was salty.

The raft was spotted by a ship, which turned toward them. As it approached, they realized it was a Japanese destroyer. The anxious Yorktowners waited to see what would happen. Men on the deck of the Japanese ship looked them over carefully. Then, the destroyer went on its way.

The raft started losing pressure and they reinflated it with the small air pump, something like the devices used to inflate footballs. One end of the pump screwed onto a valve in the raft and the other end was covered with a small wooden disk or grommet. The pump handle moved back and forth through a hole in the grommet. When the wood got wet, it swelled and tightened around the handle, which would no longer budge. Ewoldt worked with a penknife to loosen the waterlogged pump handle. The task was made difficult by the fact that the other end of the pump was stuck on the metal tip of the life raft inflation valve and the two men were afraid that forcibly removing it might break the valve and cause the raft to deflate completely.

The sea was their enemy and the sagging raft their only refuge. They were terrified that something might harm it, for without it they were doomed. They threw their canvas helmets overboard out of fear the plastic earphone supports might puncture the raft. Sharks appeared occasionally in the water near them.

On the third day, Ewoldt looked up from his efforts to widen the opening in the end of the air pump and pointed toward a spot low in the sky.

"Look!" he said. "Land!"

At first Machalinski saw no land. Gradually, however, the tip of a mountain became clear to him in the clouds. They were approaching Guadalcanal. They began rowing toward the island, all day and all night.

The next morning, they were close enough that Machalinski could make out a small river flowing into the sea. He jumped into the shallow water and scrambled toward the beach, where he collapsed and crawled, crab-like, toward the fresh water.

After a few minutes, he was joined by Ewoldt and they managed to shake a coconut out of a tree. They were trying to cut away the thick husk with Ewoldt's penknife when friendly natives came up to them.

The two *Yorktown* airmen later said the natives appeared strange with "pierced noses and filed teeth."

For their part, the permanent residents of Guadalcanal Island may have felt there was something unusual about American flyers, pairs of whom had begun to fall from the sky and wash up from the sea.

10

Fletcher decided against sending planes back to Tulagi for a fourth strike. He turned southwest into the Coral Sea to meet the *Lexington* on the morning of May 5.

Talk aboard the *Yorktown* was driven by pilots' vastly inflated assessments of the damage they had wreaked at Tulagi, and sailors believed they had stopped a major Japanese advance of some sort. Rumor began to feast on fantasy, and there was talk of upcoming liberty in Sydney, Australia. Pity the *Yorktown* sailor: Always dreaming of liberty that he would not get.

In fact, the average sailor knew less than folks back home about just how badly the war was going. By the first week in May the Japanese had run up an impressive list of victories. They had sunk most of the U.S. Pacific Fleet at Pearl Harbor, torpedoed the *Saratoga* and sent it to dry dock. They seized Guam, Wake Island, Hong Kong, Singapore, Manila, Burma and most of the Netherlands East Indies, from Java to Timor. Their ports at Lae and Salamaua, on the north coast of the Papua peninsula, gave them a foothold in New Guinea.

On April 9, 12,000 U.S. Army troops were taken prisoner

on Bataan in the Philippines. And before sunset on May 6, Lt. Gen. Jonathan Wainwright would transmit his famous radio message that "with broken heart and with head bowed in sadness, but not in shame," he was surrendering to Japanese forces on the island of Corregidor in the mouth of Manila Bay.

Those victories had been cheap for Japan. Losses included fewer than 30 naval vessels, the largest a destroyer. Together, lost Japanese military vessels had a total displacement of only 26,441 tons, little more than the *Yorktown* alone. In addition, the Japanese had lost 67 transports and merchant ships, a few hundred planes and a few thousand soldiers and sailors.

And if much of America was aghast at Japan's rapid occupation of a vast area of the globe, the mood in Japan was euphoric. In fact, after the war many Japanese military leaders would look back on the spring of 1942 and recall that a "victory disease" had broken out in the Imperial Forces. This growing notion that Japan was invincible appears not to have been limited to the military.

On March 12, speaking before the Japanese Parliament, Prime Minister Hideki Tojo had directed a specific warning to Australia: "Australia and New Zealand are now threatened directly by the might of the Imperial Forces, and both of them should know that any resistance is futile. If the Australian government does not modify her present attitude, their continent will suffer the same fate as the Dutch East Indies."

The following day, Australian Prime Minister John Curtin called on U.S. leaders not to be fooled by a view of geography based merely on the placement of continents on the globe. Though tucked deep in the Southern Hemisphere, Australia stood between Japan and the U.S. west coast, he declared.

"This is a warning," Curtin said. "Australia is the last Allied bastion between the West Coast of the United States and Japan. If she succumbs, the entire American continent will be wide open to invasion. Some people think the

Japanese will bypass Australia and that they will be intercepted and destroyed in the Indies. But I tell you that saving Australia will be the same as saving the western side of the United States. . . ."

Even Yamamoto, despite his preoccupation with the threat posed by the American carrier forces, suffered from the "victory disease," Japanese historians said.

As he worked on his plan to attack Midway and draw the U.S. carriers into a battle where he believed he could destroy them with superior force, he routinely overruled cautionary advice from his admirals. The Midway plan was gamed in a table-top exercise, and Yamamoto's chief of staff reversed the rulings of umpires whenever they declared that Japanese carriers had been "sunk."

At the same time, some elements of the Imperial Navy's General Staff clung to the earlier strategy of destroying supply and communication links between Australia and the United States and eventually occupying at least the northern coast of Australia.

The town of Port Moresby, on the southern coast of New Guinea's Papua peninsula, became the focus of a compromise within the Japanese command. From its position on the north shore of the Coral Sea, Port Moresby could serve as a base to launch attacks on Australia, as well as New Caledonia, Fiji and Samoa, key points in American–Australian supply and communication lines.

And so, as the *Yorktown* turned southwest from Tulagi, two fleets of Japanese warships were on their way to the Coral Sea with plans to seize Port Moseby.

Papua is sometimes called the "tail of the New Guinea bird" because of the way it reaches into the Pacific Ocean. Port Moresby is on its southern coast, directly south of Lae. Planes from the *Yorktown* and the *Lexington* had flown over the coastal town two months earlier on their way to attack Lae and Salamaua on the north coast of Papua.

Japanese commanders were confident the town soon

would be theirs. An invasion force of eleven troop transports, escorted by destroyers, cruisers and the light aircraft carrier *Shoho*, had sailed from the Japanese base at Rabaul in the Bismarck Archipelago. A "striking force" of two fleet carriers, the *Zuikaku* and the *Shokaku*, and their attending cruisers and destroyers had sortied separately from Truk Island. The carrier flotilla was to close with the invasion force somewhere near the tip of the tail and make for Port Moresby.

Waiting for them were the *Yorktown* and the *Lexington*, along with eight cruisers (two of them from the Royal Australian Navy) and thirteen destroyers. Fletcher was in overall command.

Shortly after breaking his flag on the *Lexington* at Pearl Harbor, Rear Adm. Aubrey Fitch, a friend and Annapolis classmate of Fletcher, beached the carrier's fighter squadron commander, Lt. Cdr. John "Jimmy" Thach.

"We've decided that you better stay here at Pearl Harbor because there's a big training job to be done," Fitch said. "We're getting more airplanes, and more pilots are coming out and there are not very many people who have had any combat experience, and you're going to have stay back and train them."

Recalling the conversation in the U.S. Naval Institute oral history interview years later, Thach said he pleaded with Fitch not to beach him.

"I don't think you ought to go to sea without me, without my squadron," said Thach, who had served on the ship under Vice Adm. Wilson Brown during the March raids on Lae and Salamaua.

"Oh, I'm going to take your squadron," he said Fitch replied. "Your squadron is finally going to be increased to 27 aircraft, but I'm taking all your pilots. You'll get some more people, some more pilots, and 27 airplanes."

The 27 aircraft Thach would get were F4F-4s, new versions of the Wildcat. Most of the pilots would be right out of flight school.

The F4F-4s had three .50-caliber guns on each wing, rather than the two installed on the F4F-3s, and the wings could be folded beside the fuselage, making it possible to crowd more of them onto a carrier. Parked with its wings folded, the plane looked something like a short, stumpy grasshopper with a tail fin. Many pilots, including Thach, would say the changes made the Wildcat a less effective fighter. For one thing, there was no room in the wings for additional belts of ammunition. Six guns, rather than four, and no additional ammunition meant the guns ran out more quickly. The F4F-4 carried the same 135 pounds of pilot armor behind the seat and heavy, bulletproof glass on the windshield. Besides that, the additional guns and the wing-folding mechanism added weight, and pilots complained that with no additional power, the F4F-4 felt sluggish.

Throughout May 5 and May 6, the *Yorktown* and the *Lexington* sailed back and forth in the Coral Sea. From intelligence reports out of Australia and Pearl Harbor, Fletcher knew that the Japanese were bringing two fleet carriers to the fight. He also knew that the attack on Tulagi and occasional encounters with Japanese seaplanes meant his presence was known to the enemy.

On the May 6, Vice Adm. Takeo Takagi brought the *Zuikaku* and the *Shokaku* into the Coral Sea.

At one point, Takagi and Fletcher were within 60 miles of each other, but neither knew it because neither carrier had sent out scouting planes. Had either admiral discovered the other at this point, events would have followed a vastly different course.

The next morning, May 7, the two fleets had pulled away from each other.

By then, the liberty rumor had evaporated on the *Yorktown*. Nearly every sailor on the ship knew that something that had never happened before was about to happen and that he would be in the middle of it—but it was not going to happen in Australia.

A letter from one of John Underwood's aunts in Tennessee had inadvertently exposed his underage status. Alarmed at news reports of the war and afraid he would be killed, she had written to urge him to make known the fact that he was only 15 and to come home and take his chances with the illegal whiskey charge. She had not known that sailors' mail was routinely opened and read and their letters home censored. It didn't matter, though. By then, many people on the ship knew Underwood was only 15 and, at any rate, nothing could be done about it now. The ship was at sea and about to go into battle.

"Sir, you know I'm not supposed to be here," Underwood had said in a flight-deck encounter with pilot Scott McCuskey, a favorite of enlisted men on Fighting Forty-two. "I'm only 15 years old."

"Okay, kid. Wait five and I'll call you a taxi and you can go home," McCuskey joked.

The two carrier task forces began searching for each other around 6 A.M. The scouting squadrons on the U.S. carriers flew the same SDB "Dauntless" dive-bombers as the bombing squadron. In fact, members of the bomber squadron often flew scouting missions and scouts often took part in dive-bombing attacks.

Although aircraft carriers had never squared off at sea before that day, Fletcher and Takagi both knew the outcome of their battle could be largely defined by which of them first learned his adversary's whereabouts. Years of table-top war games and at-sea exercises had shown that scouting would be the dominant tactical problem of carrier warfare. The axiom expressed in Confederate Gen. Nathan Bedford Forrest's simple admonition to "get there fustest with the mostest" would be mostest applicable in a carrier battle.

In this connection, Fletcher had one potentially decisive advantage: radar.

The first observation of the radar effect was in Washington, D.C., in 1922, when scientists at the Naval

Research Laboratory beamed a radio signal across the Potomac River and observed that a sailboat caused a disturbance in the signal as it passed between the transmitter on one shore and a receiver on the other.

Coincidentally, that was the year the first radio receiver was built in Bladen, Nebraska, a tiny town in the southeastern corner of the state. Meredith "Mid" Bennett, the bantamweight, 14-year-old son of a wheat farmer and sometime rural mail carrier, built the set from instructions published by *Popular Mechanics* magazine. It had a single vacuum tube and a coil, which young Bennett made by winding copper wire around an oatmeal box.

Three years later, Bennett joined the Navy. He gravitated toward radio work. After some delay, the Navy developed an interest in using radar to detect and track aircraft. The institutional and personal trends converged and in 1939, 15 years after he joined the Navy, Bennett was one of six chief petty officers selected for special radar training and hands-on instruction at an RCA plant in Camden, New Jersey, where six prototype radars were being assembled under a top-secret Navy contract. One by one, the six radar units were installed on ships, their 16-foot-long "bedspring" antennae mounted at the highest point on the superstructure. Each time a unit was installed, one of the six chiefs remained on the ship to operate it. The last radar and Bennett, the last petty officer, went on the *Yorktown* in the fall of 1940. Additional units were rapidly deployed on other ships in the following year.

Radar would provide a carrier commander a few extra minutes' warning that he is about to be attacked, but it was of no value to him in his most urgent and demanding task—locating enemy carriers. Because of the efficiency of delivering destructive force from dive-bombers and torpedo planes, the range of a fighting ship had increased from no more than 20 miles in the case of a battleship to at least 200 miles for a carrier. That meant a carrier admiral could attack another carrier—or be attacked by it—anywhere in an area of over 125,000 square miles of ocean. When two battleships squared off, each commander had only to worry about a little more than 1,200 square miles.

Flying at 2,000 feet, a scout's horizons are about 55 miles away, as opposed to only about three miles for a man standing on a beach. But the scout can't see a ship on the water 55 miles away. In fact, an aircraft carrier appears as a speck on the surface of the water from 30 miles. Scouting was even harder over the varied colors of the Coral Sea, where clear waters constantly changed their hue, from dark blue to nearly yellow, depending on the depth and coral growth at the bottom. Besides, much of a scout's work was subject to factors like judgment and fatigue and boredom. In other words, while each commander was desperate to find the other, neither had available to him a reliable way of doing that. The pressures that this life-and-death arrangement of circumstance imposed on two men, each bent on destroying the other, can only be imagined by those who have not stood on the flag bridge.

But when one of Takagi's scouts erroneously reported at around 8:15 A.M. that he had found a carrier and a cruiser, the Japanese admiral was elated and an all-out attack of "Val" bombers, "Kate" torpedo planes and Zero escorts roared from his decks.

The scout had spotted a small tanker, the *Neosho*, which had refueled the *Yorktown* the previous day and was on its way back to Pearl Harbor, escorted by a destroyer, the *Sims*. Fearful of encountering combat air patrol fighters, the Japanese scout had not gone close enough to the *Neosho* to properly identify it and mistook its wide deck for that of a carrier. Bomber pilots discovered the error but attacked the two ships anyhow. The *Sims* was promptly sunk and the *Neosho* was ravaged by the disappointed Japanese flyers. The little tanker somehow remained afloat and drifted for four days, when a rescue ship found her and scuttled her. There was a terrible loss of life.

While the Japanese were en route to the *Neosho* and the *Sims*, the *Yorktown* recorded a message from Lt. John L. Nielson in a scouting plane. The message was decoded between 8:30 and 9 A.M. to say that Nielson had seen "two carriers and four cruisers." Now it was Fletcher's turn to be elated. The *Yorktown* immediately launched 43 planes, including dive-bombers, Devastators and F4F-3 Wildcat escorts. The *Lexington* launched 50 more.

However, an encoding device used by Nielson to prepare his message had slipped and he had been one line off. What he had seen—and what he thought he was describing to the *Yorktown*—was not two carriers and four cruisers, but two cruisers and four destroyers. Fletcher's mood swung from elation to fury and the unfortunate Lieutenant Nielson was figuratively "sent to his room" after a public dressing down. Although the captains of the two American carriers had held back fighters to defend the fleet should the Japanese spot them, most of Fletcher's attack planes were nearly 200 miles out by the time Nielson had gotten back to the ship and the error discovered. If another scout were to spot the Japanese carriers at that moment, it would be precious hours before the bombers and torpedo planes could be recalled, refueled, rearmed and relaunched. A recall order was about to go out when radio silence was suddenly broken by this transmission from Lt. (jg) Robert Dixon of the *Lexington*: "Scratch one flattop."

The American bombers and torpedo planes never found the four destroyers and two cruisers that had prompted Nielson's miscoded message. Rather, in searching for those ships, they happened onto the *Shoho*, the smaller escort carrier sent to provide air support for the Japanese troop transports. The transports were nowhere in sight, because Japanese commanders had decided to withdraw them until the American carriers were eliminated. Caught by surprise and attacked by 93 airplanes, the *Shoho* did not have a chance. Within five minutes, she was hit by several torpedoes and perhaps as many as 13 bombs. One bomb missed but exploded in the ocean, so close to the *Shoho* that it blew five planes off her deck. Another bomb or torpedo jammed her steering and she could only plunge straight ahead while the American planes descended on her with pot shots. The battle lasted less than 15 minutes, although the *Shoho* had managed to launch a few fighters, which attempted to engage their enemy. Despite the bedlam that surrounded him, *Shoho*'s captain somehow sounded an order to abandon the ship. Still trying to escape, the carrier plowed under the water. All but 255 of the 800 men on *Shoho* went down with her. The *Yorktown* bombing squadron also sank a destroyer that had been sailing with the *Shoho*.

By noon, all American flyers except the pilot and radioman-gunner of a Dauntless dive-bomber were back on the carriers. The Dauntless crew had run out of gas and ditched near Port Moresby. They rowed ashore in their life raft and were taken in by friendly natives.

The searches resumed. By late afternoon, radio intercepts and radar contacts made it clear to Fletcher that the enemy had discovered his location. Still, he did not know where the Japanese carriers were—even though they were only about 30 miles away.

Late in the afternoon, Takagi launched 12 bombers and 15 torpedo planes, flown by trained night-fighting pilots, with orders to attack the American ships at sundown—which would be at 7:45. But bad weather had enfolded both American carriers in squalls, rainclouds and scud, and the Japanese attackers did not find either ship. On the other hand, the attack planes were picked up on *Lexington* and *Yorktown* radar and immediately intercepted by Wildcats. Nine Japanese planes were lost in the fray.

As the rainy daylight dimmed into dusk and the American carriers began recovering their fighters, one of the most bizarre and heart-wrenching events in the *Yorktown*'s voyage began to unfold.

The landing signal officer, unhappy with a plane's approach, waved the pilot off. The pilot complied with the wave-off, but in pulling out of the unsuccessful landing, he banked his plane to starboard. This was opposite the way a pilot would normally fly in such a circumstance, because all American carriers had their island structures on the starboard side of the flight deck. Pilots were trained to bank left when leaving the flight deck, away from the island structure.

Soon, the explanation was all too obvious. The plane was a Japanese bomber whose pilot had finally found the *Yorktown*—but instead of bombing it, had tried to land on it. Since some Japanese carriers were built with the island structure on the port side, flyers assigned to those ships would bank to starboard after a wave-off.

The reason the Japanese pilot tried to land on an enemy ship will never be known. The best guess is that he was confused and in the bad weather had mistaken it for his own ship and the circling Wildcats for his comrades. This explanation is supported by the fact that two other Japanese planes also were flying among the Wildcats in the *Yorktown* landing circle. With their own ship so close to the American task force, it would have been easy for them to find themselves lost and confused in the foul weather.

American flyers were radioed to clear out of the area, and anti-aircraft gunners opened fire on the shocked intruders.

Standing at his battle station at one of the *Yorktown*'s five-inch antiaircraft gun mounts, James Liner of Buffalo, South Carolina, could see the large "red ball" insignia on the side of one of the bombers as shells exploded and tracers glowed in the foggy twilight.

"I think they thought they were going to land on us," Liner recalled. "And when they got to our gun group, somebody hollered 'Open fire,' and damned if we didn't start shooting everything we had at them. I could see them sitting in the cockpit. I saw the pilot sitting in the plane when they went by. I don't think we ever hit a one of them."

Officially, it was deemed likely that at least one of the Japanese planes was shot down, although that is not certain. Whether any of them ever found their way back to the *Zuikaku* or the *Shokaku* also is not known.

While these strange events were underway, the main group of Japanese planes was being tracked by the *Lexington*'s radar as they returned to their carriers. When they went into their landing circles, the location of the Japanese carriers became clear. Now, each admiral knew the other's whereabouts. For separate reasons, they both decided not to attempt further attacks that night.

After it was clear that the Japanese planes were no longer in the area, Wildcat pilots returned and landed.

However, one pilot, Ens. John D. Baker of Plainfield, New Jersey, had strayed too far from the ship and could not be located on the radar screen and given directions by which to return. Turning on the lights and exposing the carrier and nearly 3,000 men to a possible night attack by an enemy lurking just beyond the horizon was unthinkable.

The drama lasted over an hour. Members of the crew listened in disbelief as the young pilot pleaded for directions back to the ship. He was told again that he could not be found by *Yorktown* radar. Lt. Cdr. Oscar Pederson, who had been commander of the fighter squadron when the *Yorktown* left San Diego in January, had moved up to command the carrier's entire air group. He told a radioman to relay directions to the nearest land, Tagula Island, and wish Ens. Baker good luck. Baker was never heard from again.

Years later, Judson Brodie, a Fighting Forty-two ordnance man who had made the Navy a career and retired as a lieutenant commander, placed a model of a Wildcat in a Navy museum at Charleston in his native South Carolina, dedicated to the memory of Ens. Baker.

Brodie said he also talked about the incident with Pederson, by then a retired rear admiral, who had attended a *Yorktown* reunion. Brodie said he asked the former air group commander if the scuttlebutt that the radioman was "crying like a baby" when he relayed the messages to Baker was true.

"I was crying like a baby," Pederson replied.

Baker was not the only pilot from Fighting Forty-two who failed to make it back to the ship on May 7, 1942. Ens. Leslie Lockhart Bruce Knox had married Louise Frances Kennedy in Our Lady of Victory Chapel at Norfolk on the night before the bombing of Pearl Harbor. He spent 10 days with his bride in the Glencove Apartments and for the next four months had plagued his fellow pilots with his longing for her. He had been among pilots sent to intercept the Japanese attackers. He did not return and, like Baker, was never heard from again.

11

When Sid Flum's father died in 1939, Sid became the sole provider for his mother and sisters. Later, when the sisters found jobs, he joined the Navy and had an allotment from his pay sent to his mother. From his home in the Bronx, Flum had gone to boot camp at Newport, Rhode Island, where he and several other boots from New York became close friends. There was Charlie Steiniger of Staten Island, Paddy Raciopi of Yonkers and Bob Hunt of Olean, over in the western end of the state. They were a multiethnic group, an Italian, a German, a WASP and Flum, who was Jewish. They went to the *Yorktown* together, partied together, took liberty together, traded family visits during leave, even served on the same repair party when the ship was at general quarters.

May 8, 1942, would be different, and for the rest of his life Flum would think about that difference.

When dawn swept across the Coral Sea, members of the *Yorktown* crew already were at their battle stations. Fitch and Fletcher wasted no time getting the search planes into the air. In addition to searching for the two Japanese carriers, the scouting planes would scour the ocean around the *Yorktown* and the *Lexington* for submarine periscopes. The sun rose at 6:55 A.M. The sea was calm and visibility was 30 miles. The rain and clouds that had concealed the U.S. carriers from Japanese attackers the previous afternoon were gone.

At 8:33 A.M., the *Yorktown* intercepted the following message from a *Lexington* scout: "Contact 2 carriers 4 cruisers many destroyers bearing 006 dist 125 speed 15 at 0820." For some reason, *Lexington* radiomen did not copy this message and it was relayed from the *Yorktown* at 8:34.

The message meant the Japanese carrier task force was 125 miles nearly due north of an agreed-on reference point known as "Point Zed." Since the U.S. carriers were constantly moving, the scout would not know exactly where they were, so he located the Japanese carriers in relation to Point Zed. In their separate plotting rooms, Fletcher and Fitch each placed the *Zuikaku* and the *Shokaku* 175 miles away, slightly east of due north.

However, three minutes after intercepting the *Lexington* scout's message that he had spotted the Japanese ships, Fletcher sent Fitch another message: "Believe we have been sighted by enemy carrier plane." This message was followed almost immediately by a transmission to the *Lexington* that "enemy received contact report on us at 8:28."

Now Fletcher knew where Takagi was, but he also knew that Takagi knew where he was. Somewhere between them, their attack planes would pass each other.

An all-out attack roared from the decks of the two U.S. carriers. In 15 minutes, beginning at 9 o'clock, the *Yorktown* launched 24 Dauntless dive-bombers, each carrying a 1,000-pound bomb, and nine torpedo-armed Devastators. They were escorted by six Wildcats. The *Lexington* attack group followed a few minutes later.

Each U.S. carrier already had sent up four Wildcats to circle the ships in defensive combat air patrols.

Before reporting to his battle station as a member of a fire control party, Sid Flum sought out Chaplain Hamilton and asked to talk to him. They went to Hamilton's office. Flum explained that before the trouble started, he wanted to say some prayers in memory of his father. Hamilton provided Flum a prayer shawl and a yarmulke and left the room. Flum's prayer sanctuary would be the chaplain's small, somewhat cluttered office. Standing before the metal, Navy-issue desk, Sid Flum repeated ancient prayers in his father's memory.

Then he reported to Compartment C-301-L, adjacent to a crew's mess compartment on the third deck below the hangar deck. Sixty other men, members of Repair Party No. 5, were at the ready if they were needed. At the forward end of the compartment was the "Gedunk," where Yorktowners bought ice cream, cigarettes and other treats. Aft, a hatch led to a passageway, past the bakery and the scullery and, somewhere beyond that, into the main sickbay. Flum's friends, Steiniger of Staten Island, Raciopi of Yonkers and Hunt of Olean, were in Compartment C-301-L when he arrived. Normally, he would have joined them, but he wanted to be alone for a while. They understood.

Elsewhere, several of Fighting Forty-two's enlisted men with no battle station assignment found a steel net hanging beneath a forward area of the deck and climbed into it. It seemed a safe place. Suspended above the sea and tucked against the side of the ship, it was shielded above by the overhang of the deck. They included Bill Surgi of New Orleans, Stan Catha of Glenmora, Louisiana, Paul Meyers of Cleveland and John Underwood of Chattanooga.

Wayne Souter, who along with Red Maag had become Underwood's *de facto* protectors on the ship, went looking for him and found him in the net with the others.

"Chicken, you get the hell out of there," Souter called down to the net. "I want you to take cover up here." He had in mind a small storage area under the flight deck.

Underwood protested, "I want to stay down here. I have a great view down here." Souter's next utterance carried the kind of emphasis that even Chicken Underwood knew not to defy, so the boy climbed out of the netting and into the storage bin as Souter directed.

At around 9 o'clock, time itself seemed to gather speed.

9:30—The *Yorktown* changed course to 125 (east of southeast).

9:48—Radar picked up a "shadower," a Japanese scout, 25 miles due north of the carriers.

10:04—Speed 15.

10:07—Changed course.

10:15—Shadower shot down by *Yorktown* fighter.

10:30—Changed course.

10:30—The *Yorktown* attack planes first sighted the Japanese carriers.

10:40—Buckmaster, anticipating a Japanese attack out of the sun, maneuvered to correct the relative position of the two carriers, so that he would not be firing in the direction of the *Lexington* when he fired on the attacking planes.

10:55—"Mid" Bennett told Buckmaster that a large group of enemy planes had been detected on the radar screen. The planes were 68 miles away.

10:57—The voice of Lt. Cdr. Joe Taylor, commander of the *Yorktown* torpedo squadron could be heard, addressing Lt. Cdr. William O. Burch Jr., commander of the bombing squadron: "Okay, Bill, I'm starting in." Taylor was beginning the torpedo bomber run on the *Shokaku*.

10:57—Bombers approaching the carrier at 200 miles per hour would cover the 68-mile distance in approximately 20 minutes. For three minutes, Buckmaster eased the carrier's battle status to allow the use of ventilation blowers to air the ship "as air below was becoming very foul. Men standing by any openings."

10:58—Enemy planes, 40 miles away. At first glance, this would appear to be an error in the log entries. For planes that were 68 miles away at 10:55 to be only 40 miles out three minutes later, they would have to have been flying over 550 miles per hour. Even the superior Japanese aircraft were not capable of those speeds.

However, closer examination indicates this was not an error at all. Instead, the radar had picked up two different groups of attacking aircraft. Low-flying torpedo planes were beneath the *Yorktown*'s radar beam as it swept above the horizon so that they were detected after the higher-flying dive-bombers, which were actually trailing them.

11:00—The *Lexington* signaled all fighters circling the carriers to draw in and prepare to defend the fleet from attack. The signal was "Hey, Rube!", the traditional battle cry of circus people when fights broke out with locals.

As the Japanese attack planes drew closer, eight *Yorktown* Dauntless bombers that had been deployed on antisubmarine patrol around the fleet tried to intercept them. Four of the heavy dive-bombers were lost almost at once when Zeroes escorting the Japanese planes jumped them.

The Japanese "Kate" torpedo bombers were between 8,000 and 12,000 yards away when they fanned out and headed toward the *Yorktown* in a converging pattern, just above the water. They were out of range of anything but the five-inch antiaircraft guns, which roared on the *Yorktown* and on the three cruisers and four destroyers that accompanied her.

Rather than direct the battle from inside the armored conning tower, Buckmaster stood outside on the bridge, where he had a clearer view of what was going on. He called orders to his helmsman through the slits he had pointed out to sailor Underwood several weeks earlier.

When he saw the first three torpedoes hit the water on his port quarter, Buckmaster ordered a full right rudder and requested emergency flank speed. One of his telephone talkers related the power request to the engine room.

The big ship was heeling through the water like a speedboat. Red Maag and several others had taken cover in a head that was tucked just below the flight deck on the starboard side. Maag later recalled that although the head was normally a good 40 feet above the water, it felt almost like he could have reached out and touched the surface when Buckmaster took the *Yorktown* into the first turn.

The maneuver had presented the carrier's stern to the oncoming torpedoes. Before they caught up with him, Buckmaster had maneuvered between them. One passed within 20 feet on the starboard. Another passed on the port.

More torpedoes fell. Buckmaster began full-rudder turns in an irregular zigzag course and dodged all of them.

"When the ship would make some wild turns it would heel way over and then pretty soon we were going the other way again," said Donald Blessum of Harvey, North Dakota, a little town in the wheat country, just this side of the Canadian border. "Back and forth we went. Well, come to find out the skipper was an old destroyer sailor and I guess they practiced that a little bit and so he made a destroyer out of the *Yorktown*."

As they maneuvered independently to evade their attackers, the two carriers drew apart, largely because the *Yorktown* was quicker and more nimble than the *Lexington*, which was a converted heavy cruiser. The cruisers *Astoria*, *Portland* and *Chester* remained with the *Yorktown*, along with four destroyers, *Hammann*, *Russell*, *Dewey* and *Aylwin*. These ships conformed to Buckmaster's zigging and zagging as well as they could and maintained constant antiaircraft fire on the topedo bombers.

Ten minutes after the torpedo attack began, the enemy dive-bombers screamed down on the ship, out of the sun. Antiaircraft guns on the flight deck and around the catwalk roared desperately. The bomber pilots appeared to be aiming for the island structure, Buckmaster said later.

Again, Buckmaster applied hard rudder turns. In this case, he turned in the direction of the dive, attempting to go under it. That way, the bomber pilots had to steepen their dives to stay with him, a more difficult maneuver than if he had turned away from them. In that case, they could have adjusted their aim by pulling up slightly.

Bombs exploded all around the ship, sending up geysers of sea water.

Three near misses on the starboard quarter lifted the ship and raised all four screws out of the water. Two more bombs exploded off the port quarter. Six exploded in the water between the bow and the bridge on the starboard side. One clipped the flight deck catwalk near a spot where Marine Cpl. Peter Kikos of Minneapolis was manning a .50-caliber machine gun. Fragments from another ripped into the hull and pierced it in many places above the waterline. This bomb also sent shrapnel tearing into the wire mesh where the group from Fighting Forty-two had attempted to ride out the battle. Several pieces hit Paul Meyers. The others scrambled out, yelling for medical corpsmen, who went down to get Meyers.

Jud Brodie watched as Meyers's pale form was carried across the flight deck on a stretcher. The night before, after the confusion with the Japanese planes that tried to land on the ship and the hour-long ordeal that failed to bring home Ens. John Baker, Brodie and Meyers had sat in the darkness on the flight deck and talked about the future, immediate and distant. They agreed the ship was only hours away from a fight. Meyers also said that when his enlistment was up, he intended to leave the Navy and become a civilian again.

The morning following the battle, Brodie asked a medical corpsmen how Meyers was doing. He was told the sailor died in the night and was buried at sea.

One bomb was not a near miss.

It penetrated the flight deck about 15 feet from the island, went through a ready room just below the deck, then went through the hangar deck and the second deck at an angle from port to starboard, leaving holes about 15 inches in diameter as it penetrated successive decks. Then it hit a beam and angled back toward the center of the ship, piercing the third deck at one end of the compartment where engineering party No. 5 waited. Between the third deck and the fourth deck, it exploded. Analysis of fragments would convince *Yorktown* ordnance officers that the bomb was a "high order explosive," probably a 12-inch projectile, the exploding shell fired by guns on a battleship. Vanes had been welded to it, converting it into a bomb, and a delayed-action fuse allowed it bury itself deep in the ship before exploding.

Maintaining the ship's water-tight integrity meant every compartment was sealed off from those around it. Hatches were closed and "dogged," meaning heavy, deadbolt-like rods were cranked into the bulkheads. That way, if the hull were breached, the water would be confined to one or a few compartments and the ship would remain afloat.

But this also meant the only direction the force of the explosion could go was back up through the holes it made in decks on its way down. Bulkheads were torn away, decks warped. Even the Fourth Deck, which was steel armor, two and one-half inches thick, was warped down, away from the blast that occurred a few feet above it.

Directly above the explosion was Compartment C-301-L, where the repair party waited. The instant the bomb exploded, a terrible concussion ripped a hole about 15 feet wide in the third deck. Fragments of the bomb and hunks of metal from the ship itself ricocheted among the men, killing some. The flash of the blast burned others to death and the concussion from the blast killed still more.

Lights went out and electric wires were torn from the overhead. They started sparking and frying on the metal deck. Fires began immediately.

The officer in charge of engineering repair party No. 5 was Lt. Milton Ernest Ricketts, a native of Baltimore and a 1935 graduate of the Naval Academy. The citation for his Medal of Honor, awarded posthumously, stated in part:

"During the severe bombarding of the *Yorktown* by enemy Japanese forces, an aerial bomb passed through and exploded directly beneath the compartment in which Lt. Ricketts's battle station was located, killing, wounding or stunning all of his men and mortally wounding him. Despite his ebbing strength, Lt. Ricketts promptly opened the valve of a near-by fireplug, partially led out the fire hose and directed a heavy stream of water into the fire before dropping dead beside the hose. His courageous action, which undoubtedly prevented the rapid spread of fire to serious proportions, and his unflinching devotion to duty were in keeping with the highest traditions of the U.S. Naval Service. He gallantly gave his life for his country."

Prior to the explosion, Ricketts had separated brothers William and Victor Kowalczewski of Milwaukee, both of whom were assigned to Repair Party No. 5. Without explanation, he directed Bill Kowalczewski to a passage just abaft the compartment and ordered him to remain there. Waiting in the darkness, Bill Kowalczewski knew when he heard the bomb explode that Victor was somewhere near the blast. He was the first man into the compartment when the door into the passageway was opened. The compartment was still filled with smoke and fumes from the explosion. Kowalczewski borrowed a gasmask and a large flashlight from someone standing nearby, but the light would not penetrate the smoke. Finally, he found his brother's body.

"There wasn't a mark on him," he recalled later. "He must have been killed by the concussion."

The fate of the ship and her entire crew was on the line. There was no time to deal with an individual sailor's grief, even when his brother had been killed. Bill Kowalzcewski was placed on the repair and cleanup party in Compartment C-301-L. The first body he removed was his brother's. He hooked his hands under Victor's shoulders and dragged him to the mess hall, laid him down and went back for another.

The list of the names of men killed on the *Yorktown* at

the Battle of the Coral Sea contains an overwhelming preponderance of firemen, an indication of the devastation that flashed through Compartment C-301-L.

Steiniger of Staten Island and Hunt of Olean died at once. Raciopi of Yonkers was wounded. Chances are F2c. Sid Flum would have been on the list had he been with his friends. As it was, he felt the heat and the dust of the blast "like somebody had hit me in the face with a big potato scraper or something. It was the feeling of something rough hitting you.

"I didn't see any fire. I didn't realize it, but I was on fire," he added. Somebody ran up and beat out the flames that covered his clothes. That was the last thing Flum would know for three days.

When Flum was taken off the ship for transfer back to Pearl Harbor, his old jitterbugging partner, Pete Montalvo, saw him on the stretcher. It did not seem possible to Montalvo that Flum could survive. Flum did survive and learned later that Montalvo had been on the crew of Gun Mount Three at the Battle of Midway. Based on an incomplete account, he believed Montalvo had died there.

Many years later, Bill Surgi of Fighting Forty-two organized the Battle of the Coral Sea Association for men who had served on ships that had participated in the battle. Both Flum and Montalvo joined. When Surgi circulated a membership roster, each learned that the other was alive, after all. One telephoned the other (neither would remember which of them actually placed the call) to renew the friendship. But as soon as they had said hello, the two old sailors started crying and neither could talk. Mrs. Flum and Mrs. Montalvo had to take the telephones, introduce themselves and carry on the conversation.

Not all of those who died were in Compartment C-301-L. The force of the blast made itself felt as far up as the hangar deck. There were rumors—and at least one published account—that a sailor on the flight deck ran over to look down into the hole the bomb left in the deck and was killed instantly when the blast of the explosion came back up. This could not be true, because the delay between the bomb's first contact with the ship and moment it exploded was less than one twenty-fifth of a second.

Several compartments abaft Compartment C-301-L, Lt. Edward Kearney, the ship's junior medical officer, waited in the main sickbay with Frank Baldino, a saxophonist on the ship's band. Baldino had grown up in Providence, Rhode Island, tried out for the band in Boston and was sent to Washington, D.C., for further testing. He qualified and spent a year in music school at the Washington Navy Yard.

When the *Yorktown* was at general quarters, members of the band went to one of the toughest jobs on the ship, as stretcher bearers and assistants for doctors and medical corpsmen.

"All right, let's go," Kearney said sharply after the bomb exploded.

Baldino could not move.

"I looked at him and I was scared," Baldino recalled, "I'm telling you. I was shaking like a leaf. I wanted to go but I didn't want to go. I couldn't move."

The doctor stared into Baldino's eyes as if searching for something and immediately realized the saxophonist was paralyzed with fear. He walked around to a cabinet and took out a bottle and poured something in a glass.

"Drink this." Again, sharply. Baldino did not know what he was being given, but in other places on the ship, corpsmen and doctors were using a tried-and-true prescription for men who were too frightened to move: Ten-High bourbon.

The musician drank whatever it was and followed the doctor out of the sickbay and forward through the passageway by the scullery and by the bakery and to the dogged hatch that opened into C-301-L.

It had been jammed by the force of the explosion, so that Kearney and Baldino had trouble opening it. On the other side were the wounded Sid Flum and one or two unhurt sailors, also pulling against the wheel that cranked the "dogs" into and out of bulkhead door frames. Finally, the door came open, revealing to Kearney and Baldino the scene of devastation.

In his report on the battle, Captain Buckmaster noted that some wounded men had been screaming hysterically. He praised the conduct of the medical personnel for the calming effect they had on these men.

"Those poor guys," Baldino said years later. "Some of them were charred so bad they couldn't move or talk. They just moaned. I had to hold them when the doctor cut them on the ankle to put in the IVs. I couldn't look at it. I looked away. I'm telling you, they didn't teach you about that in music school."

For eye injuries, Kearney's medical bag carried a mixture of cocaine and castor oil. A solution of tannic acid and distilled water was sprayed on burns. Baldino carried a bundle of plywood splints for use in setting broken bones.

As Dr. Kearney and Baldino moved from one man to the next in the shattered compartment, they came upon Victor Fazzi of Cranston, Rhode Island. Fazzi and Baldino were friends. They got to know each other on the ship after their mothers had met in Providence and each wrote her son about the other. The two had been at the Norfolk train station, expecting to go home to Rhode Island for leave on December 7, when all sailors were called back to the ship.

"He was lying on his back, looking right at me," Baldino said. "His eyes were still bright and kind of glistening. I said, 'Hey, Doc, can we do something for my buddy, here?'" Again, Kearney looked directly into Baldino's eyes but didn't say anything, just shook his head.

Pete Montalvo at boot camp.

A service photograph of Thomas E. Allen.

Lt. Cdr. John S. "Jimmy" Thach, commander of the *Yorktown* fighter squadron during the Battle of Midway. (Photograph was taken two months earlier in Hawaii.)

Torpedo Squadron Three pilots photographed in Hawaii about a week prior to the Battle of Midway. All but three of the men in this picture died within minutes of each other, attempting to attack the Japanese carrier *Hiryu*. The two pilots who survived the battle were Machinist Harry L. Corl, far left, back row, and Chief Aviation Pilot Wilhelm G. Esders, far right, back row. Also pictured is Ens. Wesley F. Osmus in shadows, second from left, back row. Osmus crawled out of his downed "Devastator" and was captured by Japanese, then murdered while a prisoner-of-war.

Sailor John Underwood, 15, dressed as a “waitress” to serve steak to raffle winners at the *Yorktown*’s April 10, 1942, “Jamboree.”

Pete Montalvo and Sid Flum jitterbugging at the “Jamboree” aboard the *Yorktown*.

Machinist Tom R. Cheek's F4F-4 Wildcat, which flipped onto its back as he was landing on the *Yorktown* on June 4, 1942, and was placed on a dolly before being taken below to the hangar deck, seen here.

The *Yorktown* launching its attack planes at the beginning of the Battle of Midway.

A view aft after the *Yorktown* was bombed on June 4, 1942. The smoke pouring from the stack is from the bomb that exploded inside the funnel and blew out the fires. The flag was run up just before this photograph was taken.

The *Yorktown* gun crew at a pair of five-inch guns. Smoke from the ship is billowing back and settling onto the water. The ship in the background is probably the *Portland*, a heavy cruiser.

Repair work to the flight deck after a bomb exploded on June 4, 1942. This was the bomb that killed so many men on Mount Four and below on the hangar deck.

The scene around Mount Four, the battery hardest hit by the flight deck explosion. The man walking across the middle of the photograph is a chief petty officer. His trousers are stuffed in his socks in the hopes of reducing the risk of skin burns by flash heat from bomb bursts. The men kneeling at right tend to a wounded crewman.

Firefighting crews deploying hoses on the hangar deck following a dive bomber attack in which three bombs exploded on the *Yorktown*.

An *Enterprise* dive bomber that was too badly damaged to reach its own ship and instead landed on the *Yorktown*. There is visible antiaircraft damage to the stabilizer and bullet holes in the fuselage. The plane pusher in the foreground is looking aft, awaiting the next plane.

As members of the crew prepare to abandon ship, Seaman 2c. James E. Liner, whose face is barely visible in the upper left, asks at one of the bombed gunmounts about the fate of his best friend, Curtis Owens, who had been on one of the gun crews.

The torpedo explosion that led to the *Yorktown*'s being abandoned. The white plume is the "geyser" caused by the explosion, which ripped off the catwalk side of the ship, trapping crewman David Pattison and others. The black smoke balls are bursts of antiaircraft fire from the *Yorktown* and the *Pensacola*, from which this shot was taken. The small geyser at right was probably caused by a crashing Japanese plane.

The *Yorktown* goes dead in the water after a bomb exploded in its air uptake funnel and blew out its boiler fires.

Stern view of the *Yorktown*, abandoned and listing heavily to port while a destroyer, possibly the *Hughes*, stands by.

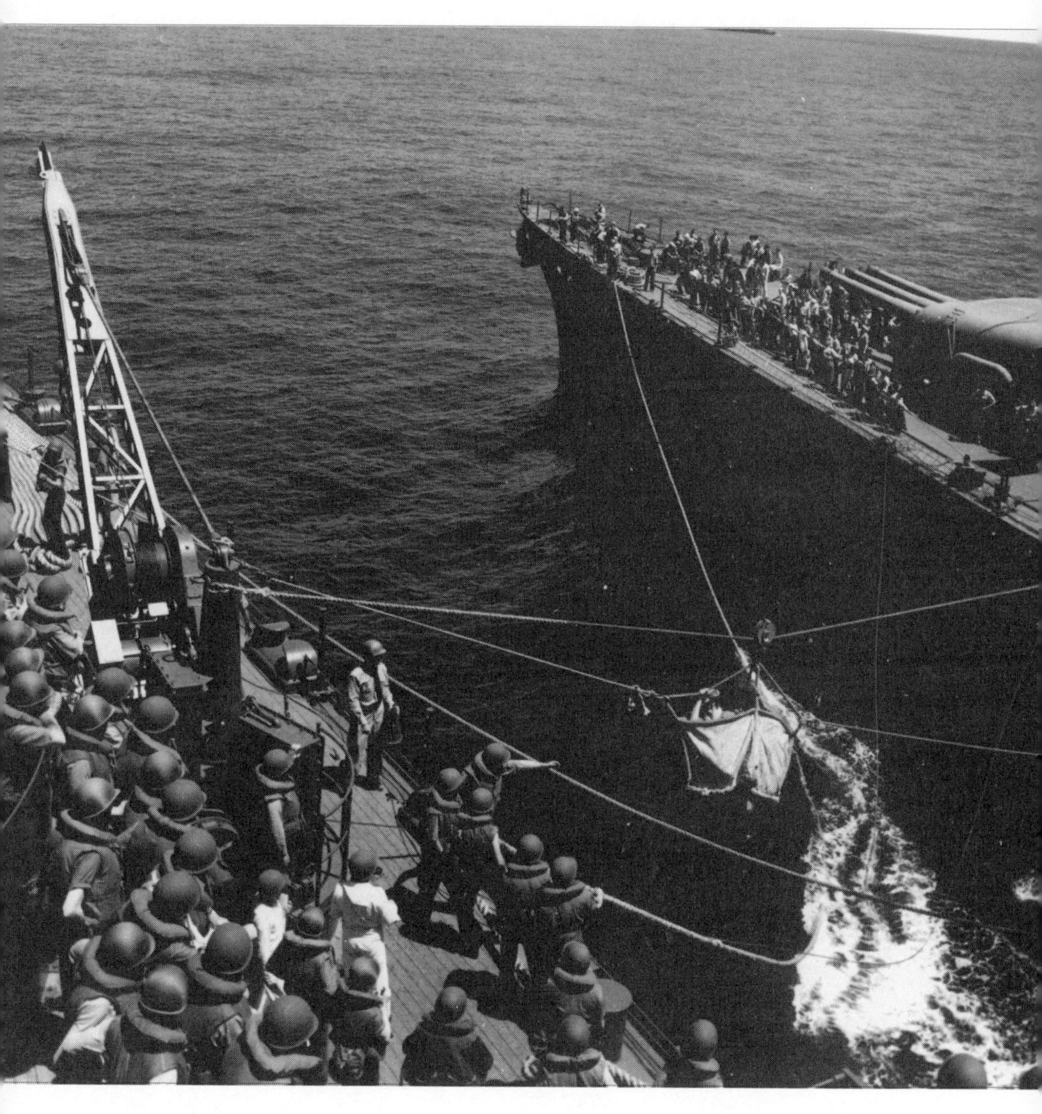

Yorktown survivors ride "coal bags" from the cruiser *Portland*, right, to the *Fulton*, a ship sent to Midway to bring them back to Pearl Harbor.

James Liner, left, and Curtis "Pelican" Owens pose at Liner's grandmother's house after the Battle of Midway. Owens's hand was mangled in the first bomb attack.

12

After finding the Japanese carriers at 10:30 A.M., the Dauntless dive-bombers had to circle for seven minutes, waiting for the slower torpedo planes to arrive. While the American planes killed time, one carrier, the *Zuikaku*, dashed into a rain squall and hid. The *Shokaku* began launching Zeroes.

Forshee was in the rear seat of a dive-bomber piloted by Lt. (jg) W. F. Christie. His best friend, Johnny Kasselman, was flying with Ensign D. E. Chaffee, who was on Christie's wing. Although the two radiomen could communicate visually by making Morse Code signals against the sides of their helmets—a fist was a dot, an open palm, a dash—there would be no chatting now about their plan to buy a sailboat and go to South America when the war was over. Wearing the dashing white silk scarves stitched for them by the boys in the *Yorktown* parachute loft, the two radiomen had other work to do as the bombers circled at around 18,000 feet.

"IAS," Kasselman signed.

Forshee checked with his pilot and signed back their indicated air speed.

"MOPA." Kasselman wanted to check the settings on his radio with Forshee's.

Forshee checked the master oscillator and power amplifier settings and signed them back. "Johnny and Chaffee would be in a position just aft of us in the dive," Forshee wrote in *Standby Mark*. "At about the instant we pushed over for our dive, the Zeroes were on us and my concern was that I would be kept so busy with them on our tail that I would miss giving Christie the standby and mark for a pull-out and with his eye glued to the bomb sight, we would go right in.

"Boy, they were like a swarm of hornets. I got the first one. I believe I got the pilot, as he pulled right up abruptly, did a sort of wing over and nosed down in a spiral. The next one was staying back. I got some hits, but I didn't see what happened to him, other than he broke off the attack.

"One thing about facing aft is that you see all the antiaircraft and tracers (from the ship) converging behind your plane. Facing forward all you see are muzzle flashes and you don't know if they are aimed at you or someone else. . . ."

Spinning around in his seat, Forshee checked the altimeter and prepared to give his pilot the "standby" and the "mark" to release their bomb and pull out of the dive.

"We released and pulled out with what appeared to be a hit on the flight deck," Forshee wrote. "We now headed south at full throttle, trying to get into some of that cloud cover. No other planes joined us. I maintained a sharp lookout for any planes, enemy or ours. . . ."

Minutes after Forshee and Christie dived on the *Shokaku*, a Dauntless flown by Ens. John Jorgenson "turned over" on the carrier, plunging through antiaircraft fire at 250 miles per hour. After Jorgenson had released the bomb and started to pull out of the dive, radioman-gunner Anthony Brunetti of Hartford, Connecticut, felt the plane shudder violently. He looked around for fighters and saw none. Instead, there was a large hole in the right wing with about half of the aileron missing.

"Yogi [Jorgenson] was struggling to right the aircraft

and called for my help on the controls," Brunetti recalled in a written account. "Of course, I didn't have my control stick in, else my swivel seat would've been impeded. About the time I considered turning around and putting the stick in, I saw two Zeroes coming on fast. They were closing from below and dead aft, so I couldn't bring my gun to bear on them without hitting our own horizontal stabilizers. The lead Zero started hitting us with his 7.7-millimeter machine-guns, for some reason not using his cannons."

Brunetti could hear the machine-gun bullets ripping through the plane.

"Brunetti, are you dead?" Jorgenson shouted. "Why aren't you firing?"

At that moment, the Japanese plane pulled up, giving Brunetti a clear shot. He poured a stream of bullets into the canopy of the Zero, which immediately dropped below the Dauntless and plunged toward the sea. Brunetti could not see the cockpit of the Japanese plane as it fell away, but Jorgenson could.

"You shot his head off!" the pilot shouted.

The second Zero dropped below the Dauntless's tail and began firing on them from about 100 yards back.

Brunetti yelled for the pilot to climb and give him a clear shot at their attacker. Jorgenson raised the nose of the battered bomber and firewalled his throttle. The Zero was in Brunetti's sights.

He pressed his trigger, but after firing only a few rounds, the .30 caliber stopped. He could see he had more belt, but the cartridges weren't moving through.

The Zero closed quickly and started firing on them with his 20-millimeter cannons.

Brunetti frantically worked on the gun, charging it again and again, but it was jammed. One end of his white scarf came out of his flight jacket, streamed behind and got in Brunetti's way as he attempted to work on the gun. He snatched it off and released it into the plane slipstream.

Whether it was the sight of the large white object hurling through the air toward him or something else, Brunetti would never know, but at that instant the Japanese pilot broke away and disappeared.

Moments later, Jorgenson spotted two other *Yorktown* Dauntlesses returning to the ship and joined up with them. One pilot looked over at them and shook his head. He dropped below them, then returned to his position and radioed that their landing gear had been shot away and they would have to ditch. Jorgenson informed Brunetti that he had been shot through the leg, was losing strength and needed help controlling the aircraft. Probably because of the hole in its wing, the plane was trying to flip to the left. Brunetti put his stick in the hole between his feet and attempted to help Jorgenson fly the plane.

When they spotted their carrier, they got ready to land in the water.

"Yogi made a beautiful approach, touching down between two swells, and the airplane nosed down, starting to sink. I just barely got the rubber life raft out of its compartment when we had to get clear as the airplane disappeared. With all those holes in it the plane didn't stay afloat long."

Jorgenson, now weak from loss of blood, needed help getting into the raft and Brunetti got under him and pushed him over the side.

"All the time we were in the water, I was thinking about his leg bleeding and wondering when the first shark would hit," Brunetti said. "I remembered that sharks were drawn to blood like moths to bright lights. When I finally got him into the raft, I was damned near too tired to get in myself. But, thank the Lord, we saw no sharks."

They were picked up by the *Aylwin* and transferred back to the *Yorktown*.

The night before the carrier face-off, Lt. John J. "Jo-Jo" Powers of New York City, a bomber pilot, had gathered several pilots and radiomen-gunners from Bombing Five in a ready room to lecture them about the importance of their work the following day.

The process of dropping a bomb on a carrier was something of an art. If the pilot waited too long, he might be unable to pull out of his dive or he might fly into the blast from his own bomb. If he released too early, he might miss. The pilot and the radioman were mutually and totally dependent. The pilot had to rely on the radioman to give him the "standby" signal, indicating they were approaching the 2,500-foot point where the bomb should be released, and the "mark," when they reached the release point. The radioman, of course, was forced to depend on the pilot to pull the plane out of the dive. If the pilot chose to press the attack into the very deck of the enemy ship, the radioman would helplessly ride to his death also.

In the case of Brunetti and Jorgenson, for example, Brunetti gave the "mark" signal, then turned around to his .30-caliber machine gun and attempted to defend the plane, depending on Jorgenson to get out of the dive and head home.

No one knows exactly what happened on May 8, 1942, in the plane flown by Lieutenant Powers and his rear seater, Aviation Radioman 2c. Everett Clyde Hill. The citation on Powers's posthumously awarded Medal of Honor reads as follows:

"For distinguished and conspicuous gallantry and intrepidity at the risk of his life above and beyond the call of duty, while pilot of an airplane of Bombing Squadron 5, Lt. Powers participated, with his squadron, in five engagements with Japanese forces in the Coral Sea area and adjacent waters during the period 4–8 May 1942. Three attacks were made on enemy objectives at or near Tulagi on 4 May. In these attacks he scored a direct hit which instantly demolished a large enemy gunboat or destroyer and is credited with two close misses, one of which severely damaged a large aircraft tender, the other damaging a 20,000-ton transport. He fearlessly strafed a gunboat, firing all his ammunition into it amid intense antiaircraft fire. This gunboat was then observed to be leaving a heavy oil slick in its wake and later was seen beached on a nearby island. On 7 May, an attack was launched against an enemy airplane carrier and other units of the enemy's invasion force. He fearlessly led his attack section of three Douglas Dauntless dive-bombers, to attack the carrier. On this occasion he dived in the face of heavy antiaircraft fire, to an altitude well below the safety altitude, at the risk of his life and almost certain damage to his own plane, in order that he might positively obtain a hit in a vital part of the ship, which would insure her complete destruction. This bomb hit was noted by many pilots and observers to cause a tremendous explosion engulfing the ship in a mass of flame, smoke, and debris. The ship sank soon after. That evening, in his capacity as Squadron Gunnery Officer, Lt. Powers gave a lecture to the squadron on point-of-aim and diving technique. During this discourse he advocated low release point in order to insure greater accuracy; yet he stressed the danger not only from enemy fire and the resultant low pull-out, but from its own bomb blast and bomb fragments. Thus his low-dive bombing attacks were deliberate and premeditated, since he well knew and realized the dangers of such tactics, but went far beyond the call of duty in order to further the cause which he knew to be right. The next morning, 8 May, as the pilots of the attack group left the ready room to man planes, his indomitable spirit and leadership were well expressed in his own words, 'Remember the folks back home are counting on us. I am going to get a hit if I have to lay it on their flight deck.' He led his section of dive-bombers down to the target from an altitude of 18,000 feet, through a wall of bursting antiaircraft shells and into the face of enemy fighter planes. Again, completely disregarding the safety altitude and without fear or concern for his safety, Lt. Powers courageously pressed home his attack, almost to the very deck of an enemy carrier and did not release his bomb until he was sure of a direct hit. He was last seen attempting recovery from his dive at the extremely low altitude of 200 feet and amid a terrific barrage of shell and bomb fragments, smoke, flame and debris from the stricken vessel."

Lieutenant Powers had been a Naval Academy classmate of Lt. Milton Ernest Ricketts, who at almost the exact moment was dying beside his firehose on the *Yorktown*'s fourth deck.

The death of Powers's radioman, Aviation Radioman 2c. Hill, was not mentioned in the Medal of Honor citation. He was the son of Mr. and Mrs. James T. Hill of 3099 Suter Street, Oakland, California. He left his mother $10,000 from a GI insurance policy.

Forshee and Christie were headed back to the *Yorktown* when Forshee noticed strange circles scattered on his dungarees and then realized that sunlight was shining through bullet holes in the fuselage and falling in bright spots on his trousers.

"We joined some others in the landing circle and came aboard," Forshee wrote. "Many of the faces we would normally have welcoming us aboard were strangely white and taut," Forshee wrote. "As we released from the arresting gear and taxied up to the forward elevator for the trip to the hangar deck, a strange feeling came over me. Something was wrong. As I crawled from the plane on the hangar deck, I came upon a pile of bodies, stacked like cordwood.

"I went back topside and discovered that the *Lex* had been hit worse and her aviation gas was burning. I was watching for late returning planes, as Johnny must be short on fuel by this time."

The first carrier battle in history was over before noon, May 8. But before the day was over, another ship would sink. The *Lexington* had been torpedoed and bombed, and aviation fuel had caught fire below. The fire appears to have been started when leaking fumes were ignited by an auxiliary generator. A series of explosions, each worse than those before it, rocked the ship. Finally, the fire reached a forward magazine and the largest explosion occurred. A huge black column of smoke poured out of the horizon, within sight of the *Yorktown*. Finally, Capt. Frederick C. Sherman ordered the *Lex* abandoned. On his final inspection to make sure all wounded had been removed, Sherman had to take cover from the flying debris of yet another explosion. Fletcher later ordered the *Lexington* scuttled, and about 8 P.M. the destroyer *Phelps* did the job with torpedoes.

"Lady Lex," CV-2, had been known as a "happy ship." She took the bodies of 216 members of her crew to the bottom of the Coral Sea with her. Another 2,735 were rescued.

Forshee waited into the afternoon for his friend, Kasselman, eventually admitting to himself that the Dauntless had not had enough fuel to be flying any more. Finally, another rear-seat man who knew that he and Kasselman were close friends, saw Forshee waiting alone on the *Yorktown* flight deck and came over to him.

"Johnny got two Zeroes in his dive," the friend said, "but he and Chaffee went down burning."

In an aircraft carrier, crowded with nearly 3,000 men, there's virtually nowhere to be alone. The 19-year-old Forshee went to the only place that provided even a little privacy, his bunk, and cried quietly for his friend.

Later, he volunteered for a patrol flight, just to get away.

"I ended up flying patrol over the burning *Lex* all afternoon," he said. "It was like watching a person die, I think."

Both sides would claim victory at the Battle of the Coral Sea.

The *Shokaku* was out of commission for several months. The *Zuikaku* was never found by the American ships and sustained no damage, even though it lost most of its aircraft to American planes and antiaircraft guns. Analysis of Japanese records suggested that the *Shokaku* may have been hit by only one bomb, which most likely was the bomb delivered by Lt. Powers and Radioman Hill.

The Japanese had sunk the tanker *Neosho* and the destroyer *Sims*. They would announce that they sank the *Lexington*. The U.S. Navy would flatly deny it for months.

In addition to the men who died on the *Lexington*, flyers from both U.S. ships were shot down or lost at sea.

The final communication of one pilot, Cdr. William B. Ault, a dive-bomber pilot who commanded the *Lexington* air group, was recorded in the *Yorktown* radio room. Mixed into the exchanges between the pilot and the *Yorktown* were desperate dispatches from the *Lexington*.

2:43—CLAG [Commander, *Lexington* Air Group] to *Lexington*: I am steady on course 110. Acknowledge. (No answer from *Lexington*).

2:45—*Yorktown* to *Lexington*: Your 5V33 is asking for instructions.

2:45—*Lexington* to *Yorktown*: *Lexington* has had a serious explosion.

2:48—*Yorktown* to *Lexington*: We do not have 5V33 on screen. Acknowledge.

2:49—CLAG to *Lexington*: Can you hear me and do you have me on the screen? I have gas left for about 20 minutes.

2:49—*Yorktown* to CLAG: I can hear you. You are not on screen.

2:51—CLAG to *Yorktown*: Shall I circle? Do you want me to gain or lose altitude? I have gas left for about 20 minutes.

2:52—*Yorktown* to CLAG: You are not on the screen. Try to make the nearest land.

2:52—*Lexington* to *Yorktown*: Fire is not under control.

2:53—CLAG to *Yorktown*: Nearest land is over 200 miles away. We would never make it.

2:54—*Yorktown* to CLAG: You are on your own. Good luck.

2:54—CLAG to *Yorktown*: Please relay to *Lexington*. We got one 1,000-pound bomb hit on a flat top. Am changing course to north. Let me know if you pick me up.

2:54—*Yorktown* to CLAG: Roger. You are on your own. I will relay your message. Good luck.

2:54—CLAG to *Yorktown*: OK. So long, people. We got a 1,000-pound bomb on a flat top.

2:55—*Lexington* to *Yorktown* [by signal flags]: This ship needs help.

Commander Ault was never heard from again. At 3:06, the *Yorktown* tried to contact him to tell him he had appeared on the radar screen. There was no answer.

13

Bodies and body parts of men killed by the bomb were gathered in piles and covered with canvas sheets. One pile was at one end of the main mess hall on the third deck, and when men went to chow, they often turned back, unable to eat.

Concerned about the crew's morale, Buckmaster ordered burial-at-sea ceremonies that night.

Ship's carpenters rigged a wooden slide, somewhat like a see-saw, on the fantail. After Chaplain Hamilton had said prayers over each body, the forward end of the chute was raised and the body allowed to slide into the sea.

The job of preparing the dead for burial fell to medical corpsmen.

As night fell and work continued, the task took on an eerie quality. Buckmaster had a crippled ship on his hands and was taking extra precautions to avoid being found. The only lights he would allow were flashlights. Bodies were taken to the parachute locker on the hangar deck and in the dim light, corpsmen and volunteers carefully removed dog tags and any other identification, wrapped the bodies in bed sheets and weighted them with spare firebricks.

Howard Stein, a drummer/violinist who earlier in the

day had accompanied a pharmacist's mate in his rounds among the wounded men, volunteered for the burial detail. Stein was in the Navy for much the same reason as hundreds of other members of the ship's crew: the Depression. His father, also a musician, normally played theater orchestra pits in upstate New York, but was often out of work. Howard Stein qualified for Navy Music School and studied in Washington.

Stein recalled years later the tense night when he helped prepare his shipmates' bodies for burial at sea: "I was 20. A couple of years earlier, I had tasted some booze, but I couldn't take it. One sip and that was it. I didn't like the taste. The corpsman came by with this bottle of Ten-High whisky and poured a shot for each of us before we went up to the parachute locker. It went down like water."

It was Stein who prepared the body of Lt. Milton Ricketts. A large piece of shrapnel was stuck through one leg. The heroic Ricketts appeared to have carried the metal during his dying effort to fight fires on the Third Deck.

"What do I do about this?" Stein asked.

The corpsman glanced at the leg under the flashlights' dim glow.

"Just wrap him up," he said.

As they were identified, corpses were taken to the flight deck and stashed near the fantail.

Corpsman Tivis Newberry from the mountains of southwest Virginia worked with the chaplain on the hangar deck as Hamilton began conducting burial services at 2 A.M. on May 9. Volunteers sent from various air group squadrons and divisions of the ship's company placed each wrapped body on the slide and Hamilton committed the sailor's soul to God and his remains to the sea. Then the body slid off and another was placed on the makeshift altar.

Newberry had joined the Navy to get out of the coal mines. He found himself scrubbing decks on the battleship *New Mexico*. To get out of that job, he put in for medical corpsman, qualified and eventually found his way to the *Yorktown*. He had been standing on the hangar deck the previous day when the bomb crashed through and exploded below the Third Deck. Shrapnel had blown all the way back up to the hangar deck with sufficient force to kill two men standing near him. He was wounded slightly.

"We had a time, trying to keep people up there on the fantail to help us," Newberry recalled. "We had a working party that was supposed to be helping us. We were all working in the dark, and you'd have to reach down in that pile of bone and flesh, getting something to take out for the chaplain to say his little piece over and drop it down the slide. It wasn't pleasant, so it wound up that the corpsmen did a whole bunch of that without the help that we thought we would have. They (members of the detail) just evaporated in the darkness. You didn't know where they were."

It seemed that almost everywhere on the ship sailors could see evidence of death, reminders that they were all in danger. As enlisted men from the fighting squadron were cleaning up their compartment and preparing to turn in, mechanic Truxton K. Ford was sent to get some rags. He passed a 10-quart bucket with rags in it and decided to take them, but when he picked up the bundle he found a man's head under it, in the bucket.

Bill Harkins of Mobile, Alabama, was among those chosen to clean blood and flesh out of the elevator pit beneath the hangar deck. It had been only a few months earlier that Harkins had to stay up all night cleaning mess-hall refuse from the overhead when the ship's garbage chute had malfunctioned because of the storm in the north Atlantic.

"It was like a slaughterhouse under there," he recalled of the elevator pit. "And you never get that smell out of your system."

It was still dark when the burials were finished and members of the detail went to their bunks.

"After it was over, I wondered, 'Why did I do this?'"

Stein recalled. "Something to keep busy, I guess. I didn't want to sit around in the compartment. You couldn't read because it was so dark."

Bill Kowalczewski's commanding officer and leading chief both were killed in the bombing attack, and in the confusion his personal tragedy escaped notice. After he had worked on the cleaning party responsible for removing the bodies of his brother, Victor, and around 50 other men from Compartment C-301-L, he was ordered to stand watch. The grieving sailor stood his watch below-decks through the night, unaware that his brother's burial-at-sea funeral was being conducted on the fantail.

The next day, Bill Kowalczewski encountered Lieutenant Commander Hamilton, the chaplain, and asked him what was to be done with the remains of those killed the day before.

"Oh, we buried them at sea last night," the weary chaplain replied and went on his way.

Later, after learning that a member of the crew had lost his brother, Hamilton sent for Bill Kowalczewski and during a brief counseling session told him he should not grieve for Victor, who he said had "gone to his reward."

But the earlier, off-hand treatment of Bill Kowalczewski's inquiry caused pain that would never go away.

After scuttling the *Lexington*, Fletcher was ordered by Nimitz to leave the Coral Sea. He turned his remaining ships east, effectively in retreat. However, Vice Admiral Takagi also retreated, heading north. Besides that, the Japanese called off their plans to take Port Moresby and their troop transport ships were moved back to Rabaul. The dancing waters of the Coral Sea were at peace again.

As the *Yorktown* made its crippled way across the sea, it became apparent that one effect of the near-miss bomb near the bow had been to sever pipes leading from an airplane gasoline storage tank, which was leaking and leaving a slick behind the carrier. Fletcher ordered destroyers to constantly crisscross the carrier's wake in an effort to stir up and disperse the gasoline.

Unaware that the Japanese also were in retreat and knowing their ship was badly crippled, members of the crew were as tense as anyone on the *Yorktown* would ever remember.

"We had gone in there thinking that as soon as we met those Japs, we were going to clean them up," Newberry recalled. "And after seeing what happened to the *Lexington* out there, burning up, watching it, and with what had happened to our ship, we realized we were in a heap of trouble. We all figured if we didn't get the heck out of there, we could be in more trouble.

"And we didn't know if that ship was going to get us out of there or not."

The bomb that exploded above the fourth deck had knocked Mid Bennett across the room in which he monitored the *Yorktown*'s radar. When he got up and returned to his station, he found the screen dark. He and Radioman Alvis "Speedy" Attaway climbed up the mast and found that a coaxial cable had been severed and the radar screen dislodged slightly from its mounts.

While the task force steamed toward the Tonga Islands, Bennett came up with a repair plan. Buckmaster briefly turned the *Yorktown* with the wind and matched its velocity exactly to that surface windspeed. This created an effectively breezeless condition on the mast long enough for Bennett and a crew to remount the radar screen and splice the severed cable.

For years, historians would weigh and compare the evidence in search of a conclusion over which side won the Battle of the Coral Sea. In terms of lost equipment, the Japanese clearly won. Loss of the *Lexington* was a major blow to the U.S. Navy. The addition of the *Hornet* to the Pacific fleet was effectively negated. Besides, the *Neosho* and its escort, the *Sims*, were sunk, and the *Yorktown* was severely damaged.

Japan had lost the small carrier *Shoho* and a destroyer. The *Shokaku* was damaged badly at the bow and could not launch aircraft, although it could land them. It would be out of action for months, but it could be repaired. American planes never found the *Zuikaku*, and it was not scratched. However, it lost many of its planes.

A small carrier and a destroyer sunk and a large carrier damaged, versus a large carrier sunk, a large carrier damaged and a tanker and destroyer lost: The tally would appear to favor the Japanese. On the other hand, America had met the advance toward Australia and turned it back. One view was that the battle amounted to a tactical victory for Japan but a strategical victory for the United States.

Whatever the assessment in terms of one navy versus another or one country versus another, the impact on the men of the *Yorktown* was profound. They were now blooded sailors. They had scrubbed up blood and scraped up flesh and they would never get that smell out of their system. They had seen a head in a bucket and piles of men they once knew covered with canvas. They had heard the explosions of bombs sent for them, had felt their ship tremble from those explosions, had seen the corpses of their buddies slide down the fantail and disappear into the dark and the sea.

David Pattison was placed in an orphanage in Iowa when he was six or seven years old. Later, when he and some other boys tried to run away, he was shifted to a state reform school. When he turned 17 he was "farmed out" to an Independence, Iowa, businessman who had a farm. Pattison lived on the farm and took care of the livestock.

At 18, he joined the Navy. Boot camp at Great Lakes, Illinois, was a snap for him and life on the carrier was pleasant.

"It was fun, living on the ship, until we had that battle in the Coral Sea," he recalled. "After that, it was just war."

At Tongatabu, hasty patch-up repairs were made and fuel was taken from a British ship.

However, at Pearl Harbor, Nimitz had another problem on his hands and he messaged Fletcher to return to Hawaii at "best sustained speed" and the tired, battered vessel again stood out to sea.

On the way from Tongatabu to Pearl Harbor, a change most members of the crew would not even know about was quietly made. There was no announcement and no reason was offered, but the *Yorktown*'s black mess attendants could not fail to observe that "White" and "Colored" signs disappeared from the scuttlebutts and the enlisted heads in Officer's Country.

When it finally seemed safe to believe the carrier was not being pursued by Japanese ships, a movie was shown on the hangar deck. This one would be different in many respects. One difference was Buckmaster's decision to attend. Having apparently decided his night vision could take one movie, the captain appeared on the deck just before the projector started and walked to the chair waiting for him at the front. The master-at-arms roared the obligatory "Attention on deck!" command, and the men snapped to.

Then somewhere somebody started to clap. Yorktowners would recall years later that the applause was picked up and grew into a spontaneous, and even raucous, demonstration. They whistled, stamped and cheered. For a moment, the blooded sailors of the *Yorktown* were kids again and he was the Old Man and he had brought them through it.

The ship was nearing Hawaii when, on May 25, Buckmaster put the finishing touches on his after-action report to Nimitz. It was a lengthy document that described the battle he had fought, sometimes in minute-by-minute detail. He described the kinds of wounds his men had sustained and praised the medical corps. He said that in their first battle his gunners had been steady at their batteries and had never exhibited "buck fever," a term that describes a greenhorn hunter's nervousness at the first sight of game. He called for some way of preventing the fogging of windshields on dive-bombers as they plunge through damp air and said it was imperative that the Devastator be replaced by a faster plane with longer range and that the reliability of torpedo fuses be improved. He noted that there were not enough scuttlebutts on his ship so that some men were unable to get to drinking water during a full day at their battle stations. Portable drinking fountains should be provided to all ships, he said.

And finally, at the end of the report, Buckmaster wrote:

"The conduct in battle of the entire ship's company of the *Yorktown* and her Air Group was worthy of the highest traditions of the Naval Service. With full realization that we were but beginning a long and arduous task, every Officer and Enlisted Man, with tireless energy, unquenchable enthusiasm, grim determination and high courage, gave of himself in full measure to the successful accomplishment of our mission.

"I can have no higher honor than to have commanded them in battle."

14

Once again, the talk was of liberty and shore time.

The bomb had ripped away entire bulkheads, twisted stanchions and pillars and blown loose hatches. Below the point of the blast, the steel armored deck was depressed downward. Decks above were lifted. A steel hatch weighing 200 pounds or more had been torn from its hinges and flipped like a dime 40 feet through a mercifully empty compartment. Fuel lines were ruptured and the ship could make little more than 15 knots.

There was serious damage from the engine room to the flight deck, and members of the crew were sure it would take weeks, perhaps months, to get the vessel in shape for battle again. They were aware that sailors on the *Saratoga* had spent most of the war in Bremerton, Washington, where their ship was in a Navy shipyard being repaired after taking a torpedo in January. It seemed reasonable that they were about to get the same kind of leave.

"We thought every time the *Saratoga* got its paint scratched, they took it to dry dock, so we figured we were on our way to the West Coast," said cook-striker Salvator Monteleone of Duluth, Minnesota.

Rear Adm. Aubrey Fitch, who had been in command of the *Lexington* and her attendant cruisers and destroyers at Battle of the Coral Sea, was now on the *Yorktown*, along with hundreds of members of his crew. He had estimated it would take at least two months to repair the *Yorktown.*

Of course, the scuttlebutt was wrong again.

Isoruku Yamamoto was putting the finishing touches on his plans for a decisive battle, and Chester Nimitz was bent on giving one.

But Nimitz needed another aircraft carrier.

The *Yorktown*'s near-twin, the *Enterprise*, and the newer *Hornet* had completed their mission of launching Doolittle's bombers over Japan and had returned to Pearl Harbor. Under Halsey's command, they had been sent briefly south under the assumption that the Japanese would continue their campaign in the Coral Sea. They were called back because accumulating intelligence convinced Nimitz and King, the COMINCH in Washington, that the next Japanese move would be in the North Pacific, not the South.

The intelligence came from a cluttered suite of basement rooms in a Navy office building at Pearl Harbor where cryptanalysts, language translators and radio operators were collecting scraps of information from Japanese Navy radio communications. The rooms were the headquarters of station "Hypo," one of three Navy listening posts where Japanese radio traffic was monitored. The other two were "Cash" in Melbourne and "Negat" in Washington. "Hypo" stood for "H," which stood for Hawaii. "Cash" was for "C," because the Melbourne station originally was set up in Cavite in the Philippines, later to be evacuated to Australia.

Since early 1940, all three listening stations had been studying a Japanese military code that analysts called JN-25. The designation meant simply that it was the 25th in a series of Japanese codes with which U.S. Navy analysts had grappled since the 1920s.

At the outset of the war, there was only one known form

of unbreakable code, and it was so cumbersome and subject to discovery that it was not used. Sometimes known as the "one-time pad system," it was based on a series of random numbers possessed only by the sender and receiver of a message. Each number corresponded to a word or phrase. The sender directed the receiver to a particular page or line of the jointly held list of the numbers and corresponding words. Then, the sender listed a selection of numbers representing the words and phrases he wished to communicate, as they appeared on that page.

In a simplified example, corresponding pages would have a list of numbers, each representing a word or a phrase such as:

"Troops: 4576"
"Company: 6532"
"Fuel: 6538"
"Supplies: 8901"
"Enemy: 0760"
"Critical: 8965"
"Satisfactory: 5684"
"Division: 3209"
"Withdrawing: 9878"

To send a message, such as "Enemy division withdrawing," the sender would write, "0760 3209 9878." Then both sender and receiver would tear off the page and destroy it. A different list of numbers would be used in the next message, or even within a single message. By creating a new "cipher" with each message, the system denied code breakers the recurrences and patterns that were their stock in trade. But running a modern military organization on the basis of thousands of code books, any one of which could fall into enemy hands at any moment, was unthinkable. Therefore, militaries turned to mechanical encoding systems that attempted to hide messages in proliferations of digits. The German military relied on its famous "ENIGMA" device, which the Polish Secret Service had stolen in the hours immediately preceding the fall of Warsaw and turned over to its British counterpart. While ENIGMA relied on a series of turning wheels, somewhat like the rolling numbers on an automobile mileage indicator, the Japanese used technology based more on electric switches, such as those that routed telephone calls, to hide their messages.

Headed by Cdr. Joseph Rochefort, Station Hypo never actually "broke" the JN-25 code and could read no more than 10 to 15 percent of any message. But that would be enough. A word here, a name there, a ship, an island, even the recognizable telegraph "accent" that betrayed a particular operator as the source of a transmission, were collected and analyzed. Old intercepts were retained and filed, although persons who visited Rochefort's operation said "files" was not really the word to describe the scattered stacks of paper. By mid-April, Rochefort was convinced that a rapidly growing volume of radio traffic emanating from Japan's Inland Sea signaled a plan by Yamamoto to attack the Midway Islands, 1,200 miles northwest of Honolulu. Analysts in Washington thought it more likely the targets would be Dutch Harbor in the Aleutian Islands or Hawaii. Some worried that the U.S. West Coast would be attacked in retaliation for the Doolittle exercise.

Eventually, Rochefort convinced key members of Nimitz's intelligence staff, especially intelligence specialist Cdr. Edwin Layton, that the battle would be at Midway, and Layton convinced the admiral.

Nimitz had been forced to beach Halsey, who had developed a debilitating skin ailment, probably shingles, and had to be hospitalized. Halsey recommended the commander of his cruiser group, Rear Adm. Raymond Spruance, as his replacement and Nimitz had gone along with the suggestion.

"Best sustained speed," Nimitz had said in his message to Fletcher, meaning return to Pearl Harbor at whatever speed the *Yorktown* had left in her.

On May 20, Hypo analyzed a lengthy Japanese transmission, which turned out to be Yamamoto's final operations order to attack and invade the Midway Islands. On May 25, key commanders met on the Yamamoto's flagship, the huge battleship *Yamato*, and with sake provided by the emperor, toasted the anticipated "decisive victory."

Yamamoto and his staff reasoned that Japanese occupation of Midway would pose such a danger to Hawaii that the U.S. fleet would be compelled to react with all available strength. In addition, the two tiny islands that made up the Midway atoll—Sand Island and Eastern Island—were seen as links in a "ribbon defense" line that the Japanese Imperial Headquarters anticipated establishing from the Aleutian Islands to the Coral Sea: the Aleutians, Midway, Wake Island, the Marshall Islands, the Gilbert Islands, Guadalcanal Island and Port Moresby. The failure to take Port Moresby at the Battle of the Coral Sea was seen as nothing more than a postponement. The plan also called for seizing New Caledonia, east of Australia and north of New Zealand, after the ribbon was established.

Elsewhere in Japan, the six *Yorktown* flyers who ditched their Devastator planes near Jaluit in January had settled into the dreary lives of prisoners of war. For the next four years, they unloaded boxcars and ships, repaired railroads, subsisted on diets of mostly rice, slept in stacked "bays" with a dozen or more men crowded side by side on each level and learned, often the hard way, how to get along with and stay out of the way of their guards. Through the Red Cross, they were allowed to receive occasional mail from home, and a jubilant Chuck Fosha learned that his wife had delivered their first son in Pensacola. The baby had weighed over nine pounds and had rolls of fat around his chin.

One night, lying in his bay with other prisoners, James Dalzell experienced the strange realization that he would never again see the grandmother who had raised him in Albany, Georgia. It came to him suddenly, "Granny's dead." He would learn after the war ended that her death had come somewhere during that time, possibly that very night.

On Guadalcanal, radioman-gunner Ray Machalinski and Lt. Leonard Ewoldt were escorted from the beach where they had crawled ashore after four days in a raft. They were taken to a native village and fed. They were shown to a thatched hut with two pallets on the floor. They collapsed and slept for several hours. When they awoke, they were asked if they wanted to take a bath and they said they did. Someone brought them what appeared to be the village's only bar of Lifebuoy soap, and they bathed in a creek. After several hours a stranger walked into the village. He was also an islander but he wore khaki shorts and an undershirt, not a loincloth.

"I am Timothy, of the South Seas Evangelical Mission," he said.

He told Machalinzki and Ewoldt that missionaries in his group had fled to Australia when Japanese troops landed on the island and had left him with a supply of canned food. He suggested they accompany him to the mission. Ewoldt said they were too weak and would need a day or two of rest before they could go. Timothy returned a few days later.

However, as they were about to leave with him, another man, also wearing khaki shorts and an undershirt, arrived with a letter addressed "To the two American airmen." Machalinski and Ewoldt took uneasy note of the fact that word of their presence was obviously spreading.

"We have heard of your plight," the letter stated. "We understand that the Japanese have landed on the island. I have provided horses for you with a runner. God be with you."

The letter was signed by a Father Boudard, a Catholic priest from France. He recommended the flyers come to his mission, and Timothy agreed that would be the best course for them. Before they could leave, the entire village lined up to shake their hands.

They did not teach horsemanship at the Catholic orphanage in Erie, Pennsylvania, and Machalinski's horse bolted. As he struggled to bring the animal under control, he left Ewoldt and the runner behind, and galloped helplessly through several villages while astonished islanders watched. As Ewoldt and the runner followed, islanders brought gifts—fruit, chickens, eggs, whatever they had. The runner struggled to hang onto the donations. Eventually, Machalinski and his horse came to terms. They all linked up again and found their way to Father Boudard's compound.

"Is it true that France has fallen?" he asked after they had introduced themselves. Soon Machalinski came to understand how the French priest, isolated on an island thousands of miles from his home, could be uncertain about events in the outside world. Learning Machalinski was a radioman, Father Boudard asked him to take a look at the mission's radio equipment, which was not working. Machalinski found antiquated equipment and a pair of aged wires with ragged insulation snaking off into another room. He followed the wires to a collection of dry-cell batteries, all dead. There was no way to restore the priest's connection to the rest of the planet without a new power supply.

While the flyers were with Father Boudard, another priest from a still-larger mission arrived in a small schooner and suggested they come with him. They moved on. At times they hid under trees or close to shore while a Japanese "Emily" passed overhead on a patrol flight.

The third mission was an outpost of Marist brothers who ran a school at the village of Avu Avu. When the brothers asked them if they were the two flyers who had landed their planes on the beach a few days earlier, Machalinski and Ewoldt began to learn of the earlier visit to Guadalcanal by their fellow *Yorktown* airmen, Adams and McCuskey. Machalinski's first thoughts were of the radio equipment in the planes. With the help of islanders and priests, he found the two Wildcats, still parked on the beach. Adams's parachute was still draped over a coconut palm. Machalinski removed the radio gear and batteries, planning to assemble a radio station. However, as he worked at this, he realized that in their desperate concern for not puncturing their life raft, he and Ewoldt had thrown over their helmets and ear phones. Once again, he could send messages but could not receive.

The two flyers eventually found their way to the village of Aola on the northern coast and the home of British Resident Commissioner Martin Clemens. Four days after they crawled onto the beach and lay in the sand, trying to suck juice out of a coconut, the two flyers were served martinis—with ice—by the British commissioner. As they sipped, they told him they needed a boat. He said there were no available boats on Guadalcanal, but many had been abandoned by copra traders on the nearby island of San Cristobol. The reason for this, he explained, was that San Cristobol represented the southernmost point in the Solomon Islands and the copra traders were unwilling to take their tiny boats into the open waters beyond. Therefore, they had abandoned the boats there and found other passage in their flight to Australia.

He arranged for them to be taken to San Cristobol on his personal boat. They slipped out of Guadalcanal at night.

At San Cristobol, they met Heinrich Cooper, a man who said he had jumped ship from the Kaiser's German Navy at the end of World War I and married an island princess, Ka Faga Marona, whose name meant "the gift of red money that comes after the feast."

Cooper helped them find a boat, the *Hing Lee*, a small, two-masted schooner with an auxiliary diesel engine. It had been abandoned by a Chinese copra trader. As Machalinski and Ewoldt made preparations to take it, however, two Chinese youths walked up and said the boat was their property, although they did not know how to sail it. They said it had belonged to their father, who had fled to Australia, leaving it—and them—on San Cristobol. Ewoldt told them he was commandeering their vessel in the name of the United States Navy and would give them a letter that they could use in filing a monetary claim against the U.S. government. They took the letter, then asked if they could accompany the Americans as they left the island, and it was agreed. They asked if four of their friends also could come. Ewoldt agreed to that also.

A Church of England missionary donated an ancient sextant. Heinrich Cooper supervised preparation of the *Hing Lee* for what would be a voyage across open seas to the island of Vanikoro in the Santa Cruz Islands, the next stop on their evolving odyssey. And the two Americans waited for good weather and an overcast day when they would be less likely to be spotted by Japanese patrol planes from Tulagi.

Heinrich and Ka Faga Marona Cooper gave them a feast of lobsters and crayfish gathered from the reef during low tide, and the British resident commissioner of San Cristobol gave them a red-and-blue flag to fly on their hopeful little vessel. Machalinski recalls not recognizing the flag but assuming it was some version of the British Union Jack, perhaps something designed for island colonies.

Finally, they sailed. Cooper sketched crude charts of the east end of the Coral Sea for them and told them that Vanikoro was surrounded by fearsome reefs.

"You must approach the island from the south," he said. "As you do, you will see a house with a red roof, up on the hill." He told them that if they kept the bow of the boat pointed toward the house they could make it through the reefs. They kept to a southeastern course, attempting to use the sextant to take sightings of the sun whenever it peeked through the clouds. Machalinski and Ewoldt would brace each other, back to back, while Ewoldt took the latitude readings. On the fourth day, the *Hing Lee* and its eight passengers found the island and the house with the red roof. Following Cooper's instructions, they slipped effortlessly past the reefs and into the calm harbor. It was about May 20.

On May 27 at 1:52 P.M., the *Yorktown* steamed slowly into Pearl Harbor. Fletcher and Buckmaster stood on the bridge and members of the crew mustered in whites on the flight deck, just as they had in February. The men formed a thin white ridge along the edge of the deck. Most of them had not been off the ship since it left Pearl Harbor on February 16—101 days earlier.

Early the next morning, the vessel was tugged into dry dock. Nimitz was told that estimates of the necessary repair time varied from two weeks to several months. He made a personal inspection of the damage and gave repair crews his famous directive: "We must have this ship back in three days."

Then he met with Fletcher and Spruance and told them of the Japanese plans to attack Midway. He said he thought that if the three American carriers could get to the area in time, they might ambush the very Japanese fleet that was being sent to destroy them.

While shipfitters swarmed over the *Yorktown*, welding torches popping and sputtering and hammers banging, new provisions came aboard.

There was no hope of completely restoring the ship's watertight integrity, the design concept in which every compartment could be sealed off from every other. Some bulkheads were beaten back into general alignment and braced with timbers. All "essential watertight boundaries on the second deck and below" were restored. The hull damage from the two near misses on the starboard bow was patched and caulked. Much of the engine room damage was left unrepaired. The boilers could not be fully rehabilitated, just patched up, and the *Yorktown* would never again make the 31 knots its engine crew had given Buckmaster as he waltzed the huge vessel among Japanese torpedoes in the Coral Sea.

Lt. John R. Wadleigh, who as the ship's service officer was responsible for the shattered "Gedunk" soda fountain so loved by the *Yorktown* crew, was ordered by Buckmaster to "get the store operational pronto."

"When we left the Navy Yard three days later, we had a fully stocked, if inadequately shelved store, and over $10,000 worth of ice cream-making equipment," Wadleigh would recall exactly three decades later in a magazine article he wrote as a retired rear admiral, reminiscing about the *Yorktown*. "By the end of our first day at sea, shipfitters and ship's service operators had the ice cream flowing."

Wadleigh also noted that when the loss of the *Lexington* was announced, there was a great deal of publicity, but almost nothing was said or written about the *Yorktown* and her role in the Battle of the Coral Sea. It was not the first time members of the *Yorktown* crew had felt their ship was being given the short end of news coverage. While the vessel patrolled the Pacific through its extended March and April vigil, Halsey was becoming a folk hero. The press picked up on an informal motto *Enterprise* sailors had invented, "Haul off with Halsey," invoking the euphemism for jumping into a fight. Resentful *Yorktown* crew members had their own version: "Haul ass with Halsey, but fight with Fletcher."

Now, in the midst of "Lady Lex" sentimentality, "resentment bubbled through our crew and our air group as there had been no mention of other ships in the Coral Sea battle, and it seemed that *Lexington* had beaten the Japanese single-handed," Wadleigh wrote. "It was a tempest in a teapot, but it seemed important at the time. If it hadn't, we would not have been the ship's company that our veteran carrier deserved."

Wadleigh described the *Yorktown*'s young sailors as "eager and buoyant youngsters who joined the Navy to be 'Navymen.'"

As had happened on previous occasions, plans for leave or even a few hours of shore liberty evaporated for most Yorktowners, who had to help with repairs and provisioning. Liberty was later restored to allow as many men as possible a few hours ashore.

Ship's cook Thomas L. J. Saxon of Columbus, Mississippi, went into Honolulu and, for some reason that has never come to light, bought a white petstore rabbit that he smuggled back onto the ship and into a hiding place in the galley.

And Joel Sledge, an 18-year-old farm boy from Colquitt County, Georgia, wangled some shore time.

Sledge recalled years later that he had joined the Navy "because I was tired of staring at a mule's ass. I decided I was using that mule for a surveyor's instrument and I could do better somewhere else."

He was referring to the process of "laying off rows." The plowman sighted to a distant object, such as a cloud or a tree, and attempted to keep it lined up with the animal's rump. If he succeeded, he would plow a straight row. With his father's consent, Sledge had left his straight rows behind in Colquitt County and joined the Navy.

After a few hours in Honolulu on May 28, he returned to the *Yorktown* and told his envious shipmates, "I have been screwed and I have been tattooed. Now, I am ready for anything."

On one arm, he had had a tattoo artist apply a tribute to his mother, and on the other, "U.S.S. *Yorktown*."

15

Nimitz's orders for the Battle of Midway were issued in a document entitled simply, "Operation Plan No. 29-42." Thanks to the intelligence gleaned from Japanese radio traffic intercepted by Station Hypo, the plan contained a remarkably accurate projection of the Japanese forces: two to four fast battleships, four or five fleet carriers, eight or nine heavy cruisers, up to two dozen destroyers and assorted submarines and sea planes.

In addition to Op Plan 29-42, Nimitz had given Spruance and Fletcher a Letter of Instruction, in which he described the way he wanted them to think as they took their ships to meet what all knew would be a vastly superior Japanese force: "In carrying out the task assigned in Op Plan 29-42, you will be governed by the principle of calculated risk, which you will interpret to mean the avoidance of exposure of your force to attack by superior enemy forces without good prospect of inflicting, as a result of such exposure, greater damage to the enemy."

The *Yorktown* was still high and dry on its blocks in Dry Dock Number One in the Pearl Harbor Navy Yard on May 28 when these documents were delivered. That same day,

Task Force 16, assembled around the *Enterprise* and the *Hornet*, cleared Pearl Harbor and headed for Midway.

The previous day Vice Admiral Nagumo's carrier striking force had sortied from its anchorage in Japan's Inland Sea and headed for Bungo Strait and the Pacific Ocean. It had been hot and muggy in the Inland Sea for the past several days. Mitsuo Fuchida wrote that as Nagumo's flagship, *Akagi*, cruised at 16 knots through Bungo, a sweet and welcome breeze swept across the flight deck. Ahead were cruisers, a 12-ship destroyer squadron and two battleships. Behind was the fleet carrier *Kaga*. Behind it was a second carrier division, assembled around the carriers *Hiryu* and *Soryu* and commanded by Rear Adm. Tamon Yamaguchi. Many members of the *Yorktown* crew who forgot about Yamamoto and Nagumo and never heard of Genda or Fuchida would remember forever the name of Rear Adm. Tamon Yamaguchi.

Fishermen waved and cheered from their boats as the huge flotilla passed.

After clearing the strait, the Nagumo force fell into four columns and headed for Midway. Fuchida and Genda had been Japanese naval academy classmates. They sat in folding chairs on the *Akagi* flight deck, smoking and talking about the upcoming action. Fuchida wrote later that he expressed his concern about intelligence leaks and the fact that every barber in Japan seemed to know what was afoot. He said Genda confided that some parts of the plan didn't "add up" to him but said it probably wouldn't matter because the Nagumo force could handle the operation alone, if need be.

As it happened, neither Genda nor Fuchida would be an active participant in the Battle of Midway. Genda came down with a fever and was sent to sick bay, and Nagumo's four carriers were just out of sight of their homeland when Fuchida learned that a condition doctors had diagnosed as ulcers was actually chronic appendicitis, which suddenly became acute. He was operated on in the carrier sick bay.

On May 29, the Japanese "Main Force" followed Nagumo's carriers out of the Inland Sea, led by Yamamoto's flag ship, the huge battleship *Yamato*. With its sixteen-inch-thick side armor, the *Yamato* displaced nearly 70,000 tons, more than three times the displacement of the *Yorktown*. It was the largest warship on earth, a distinction that would endure until the 1960s, when the United States began launching nuclear-powered aircraft carriers. The Main Force also included the smaller battleships, *Nagato* and *Mutsu*, a light aircraft carrier, cruisers, destroyers and two seaplane carriers, a type of ship that did not even exist in the U.S. Navy. These vessels launched float planes from catapults and then recovered them with cranes when they landed alongside in the water.

The Main Force was followed by a Midway invasion force with cruisers, small carriers and troop transports that carried an invasion force of 5,000 troops.

From other ports in Japan, an Aleutian invasion force set out for Alaska, partly as a diversion but with the intention of capturing specific islands in the Aleutians.

Finally, Yamamoto established three "cordons" of submarines between Hawaii and Midway to wait for the American carriers. The cordons were to be in place by June 2. Because of some confusion in their orders, the submarine pickets were not at their posts until June 3, but the delay of one day would not matter because the cordons would have been too late, even if they had been on time. By June 2, all three U.S. carriers had slipped past the cordon lines and were making ready to rendezvous.

The *Yorktown* had headed back to sea on May 30. As she cleared Pearl Harbor, the ship's band was playing, "California, Here I Come."

Cdr. Ernie Davis, a 1925 graduate of the Naval Academy, was the *Yorktown*'s gunnery officer and almost as soon as the ship had sortied from Pearl Harbor, he started drilling and hounding his gun crews. Some said that Davis, who was from North Carolina, had been raised on North Carolina corn whiskey and it had toughened him from his guts out. After practice produced scores that displeased him, Davis ordered another round and nagged his gun crews that "we needed more hits per minute and we might need them very soon," Wadleigh recalled.

"Almost while we were hearing from our department head, Capt. Buckmaster gave *Yorktown* the word over the public address system," Wadleigh wrote. "The ship was headed for the defense of Midway Island, towards which a strong Japanese force was believed to be steaming."

Buckmaster also relayed to his crew Nimitz's words that he was sorry to have to send them back to sea without the leave they had earned. He said that when the job was finished, they would go stateside for liberty. Then Buckmaster added his own promise, "And not for just two weeks, either!" Once again, the crew of the *Yorktown* cheered.

Three days earlier, as the carrier approached Hawaii, all of its planes that could still fly had taken off and landed at Kaneohe Naval Air Station. Now that it was back at sea, the planes began to return. However, the planes that returned to the ship were in most cases not those that had left it. Over the furious objections of the carrier's air group commander, Lt. Cdr. Oscar Pederson, the air group was drastically reorganized.

Pederson rushed around Pearl Harbor in the day or two available to him, arguing against the decision to replace pilots and support personnel who had seen battle and were familiar with the ship with new commanders, new pilots, new radiomen-gunners, new ordnancemen and new mechanics on the eve of another major battle. But his objections were ignored and the *Yorktown* would take two completely new air squadrons, one old squadron and one mixture of new and old pilots to Midway.

First, the torpedo squadron, VT-5, was beached and an entirely new squadron, VT-3, brought aboard with its own

Devastators. The new squadron was being trained for the *Saratoga*, which had completed its repair visit to the West Coast and was expected in Pearl Harbor within days. Torpedo Three had been together only a few months when its men were ordered onto the *Yorktown*, recalled radioman-gunner Lloyd Childers of Oklahoma. Most of its pilots had never landed on a carrier or dropped a torpedo in combat. The gunners had been given only a handful of practice sessions at firing their .30-caliber machine guns at moving targets, which were towed behind other planes, "and I don't think any of us ever hit one," Childers said. Such a group would have to take on the Zeroes.

A .30-caliber weapon fires a slug that is 30 one-hundredths, or a little less than one-third, of an inch in diameter. A single .30-caliber machine gun seemed a pitiful weapon for use against Zero fighters. In fact, after the Battle of Midway, the Navy would install twin .30-caliber guns in the rear seats of Devastators as well as SBD Dauntless dive-bombers. However, the Zero's most effective defensive tool—somewhat like that of the *Yorktown*—was not how much firepower it could absorb, but how much it could avoid. One way the Zero's designers had reconciled Japanese bombing aviators' insistence on a fast, long-range escort fighter with fighter pilots' demand for a light, maneuverable plane, was to eliminate much of the plane's armor. It was far less rugged than its American adversary, Grumman's Wildcat, which as events over the next few days would show, could continue to fly and fight despite numerous bullet holes. When the carrier was under attack and the need for defensive cover was desperate, *Yorktown* air group officers would not hesitate to send Wildcats back into the air, even though the planes had been "holed" dozens of times.

Zeroes were armed with 7.7-millimeter machine guns, about the same size as a .30-caliber, and a pair of 20-millimeter cannons that fired exploding shells nearly an inch in diameter.

Childers had maneuvered his way into the squadron because his brother, Wayne, an aviation machinist's mate, was already assigned to it. Lloyd Childers's efforts would mean he was one of 20 rear-seaters who would attempt to defend with inadequate weapons a squadron of slow, obsolete torpedo bombers sent on a mission that has been described as "suicidal gallantry."

The commander of the squadron was Lt. Cdr. Lance E. "Lem" Massey, who had been the executive officer—second in command—of the torpedo squadron on the *Enterprise* before being selected to head this new *Saratoga* squadron. Massey was aloof and had little to do with members of his squadron, other than his pilots. He left his executive officer, Lt. Patrick H. Hart, to deal with the needs of radiomen-gunners and the enlisted support crew of torpedo specialists, ordnancemen and mechanics.

A few days before they flew their Devastators onto the *Yorktown*, the pilots of Torpedo Squadron Three posed for the traditional group photograph. But this picture was different in a sad and haunting way.

Mostly ensigns and junior grade lieutenants, along with a smattering of enlisted pilots, known as "NAPs," or Naval Aviation Pilots, the group was arranged in three rows. A first row of men sat on the ground, their arms draped over their knees. Behind them was a middle row of men who seem to have been sitting on chairs or stools. There was an apparent empty place at one end of this row. Then there was a back row of men who stood, shoulder to shoulder, with their hands behind their backs. All in all, it was an ordinary "group shot," the kind Navy photographers snapped by the hundreds—except in this photograph there is another man. He is standing alone, behind the back row. Only his head is visible between two of his fellow pilots as they stand in front of him and he looks over their shoulders. The arrangement was in all likelihood an accident. Perhaps he arrived late and rather than disrupt the arrangement, took a place in the rear. Yet the coincidence of his isolated position and the fact that the lighting caused his face to be in dark shadows seemed to say that there was something different about this pilot in Torpedo Three, and indeed there would be. He was Ens. Wesley F. Osmus of Chicago, and his experiences over the next few days make up one of the most disturbing stories of the Battle of Midway.

VS-5, the *Yorktown* scouting squadron, was also beached at Kaneohe and replaced with VB-5, the carrier's former bombing squadron. Since bombing crews and scouting crews both flew in Dauntless SBDs and had identical missions, the change would make no difference to Lynn Forshee and other pilots and radiomen-gunners in the old bombing squadron.

A new bombing squadron, also being organized for eventual service on the *Saratoga*, VB-3, flew onto the ship as the *Yorktown* bombing squadron.

And finally, VF-42—or "Fighting Forty-two"—more or less ceased to exist, at least on paper. The squadron in which kids like Joe Fazio, Joe Wetherington, Red Maag, John "Chicken" Underwood, Bill Surgi, Stan Catha and Jud Brodie had come to take a lot of pride would become VF-3, even though most of the new squadron's pilots and all of its enlisted support crew were from Fighting Forty-two.

The new designation came with the new commander of the *Yorktown* fighter squadron, Lt. Cdr. John S. "Jimmy" Thach, recently the recipient of the Navy's highest decoration for creating the "Thach weave."

Thach was known as one of the Navy's top fighter pilots and tacticians. He was tall, and photographs from the time indicate that although he was only 37, his face was deeply lined and his eyes, which drooped at the corners, had bags under them. He was variously described as "amiable" and "tough." One writer said he was "tall and soft-spoken, with a pleasant Southern drawl (hailing from Fordyce, Arkansas)."

One of the many legends that surrounded him had that new pilots sent to his squadrons were challenged to mock combat with the skipper. He would easily win these air duels, even though he would fly while eating an apple or even reading a newspaper.

After he was beached as commander of the *Lexington* fighter squadron by Rear Admiral Fitch, Thach had been at Kaneohe getting a new squadron into shape with the new F4F-4 Wildcats from Grumman Aviation.

Most of Thach's new pilots had never landed a Wildcat on an aircraft carrier.

He recalled years later that as he trained them, many were concerned about whether they could handle Wildcats during carrier landings, since their only experience with the planes had been on ground runways. To qualify as carrier pilots, they had practiced landing and taking off from carrier decks—but in training planes, not in the ornery Wildcats.

"I got them together and I said, 'Look, you have landed aboard a carrier, right?'" Thach recalled.

"And they said, 'Yes, sir.'

"I said, 'You have landed this plane, right?'

"And they said, 'Yes, sir.'

"'All right. You are hereby qualified to land this airplane aboard an aircraft carrier. All you've got to do is go out and prove it. Then, that'll be that. I don't want to hear any more about it.'"

Thach said a new pilot once confided in him that he hoped eventually to become a section leader, the pilot who flies at the front of a formation of planes, with other pilots flying on his wings.

"Don't worry. If you live, you will," Thach said he told his student, "and if you're good enough, maybe you'll live."

When rumors began to circulate around Pearl Harbor that "something big" was about to happen and that Thach and his new squadron of fighters were going aboard the *Yorktown*, an old friend, Lt. Cdr. Donald A. Lovelace, offered to accompany him as his executive officer. At that point, Thach did not know what was up, although a friend on the staff of the ailing Halsey had tipped him that it would have something to do with the Midway Islands. Lovelace already had orders to go to San Diego and take over as commander of a new fighter squadron.

"I know that you need fighter pilots and since my squadron is not going to be ready for a while, I'll be glad to come back and help," Thach recalled Lovelace told him.

"You've got orders. You can be on your way back to San Diego," Thach said.

"No, I want to do something," Lovelace replied. "I'd like to come back if you'll have me."

"I'd rather have you than anybody I can think of," Thach said.

And so Thach and Lovelace, their ten new pilots and the sixteen veterans from Fighting Forty-two began flying the new F4F-4 Wildcats onto the *Yorktown*'s deck as it steamed toward Midway. After each plane's tailhook caught the arresting cable and the plane came to a halt, the hook was freed and the plane taxied forward. As an extra precaution, a five-foot-high cable fence was raised with each landing, forward of the arresting cable. If a pilot failed to hook the cable, the fence was there to catch him and protect the planes waiting at the forward end of the flight deck.

Ens. John Paul Adams, one of the veterans of Fighting Forty-two, landed and taxied forward, followed by another plane. Then Lovelace landed and taxied up behind those two. Next to land was one of the new VF-3 rookies. He came in "hot" and missed the arresting cable. His plane then lifted off the deck for a few feet, enough to clear the secondary restraining fence, came back down and rushed forward, climbing upon Lovelace's plane from behind. The propellor of the errant plane killed the new squadron executive officer instantly.

"Had he carried out his orders strictly according to the letter, he would not have been there," Thach said of Lovelace. "But he was a dedicated, loyal individual and he knew he was needed. He knew he was badly needed."

Thach's first concern, however, was the effect the tragedy would have on his young pilots.

"I got them into the ready room immediately and told them that they had to just wash it out of their heads, that if I could do it, they could do it, because he was one of the best friends I ever had and the loss was far greater to me than they may imagine and I was going to forget about it right now," he recalled in his oral history interview with the Naval Institute at Annapolis.

"We have work to do and we're going to do it," he told his pilots. "We're going into a big battle, and we can't let something like this affect our performance in any way. So that's the end of it, and I don't want to hear any more talk about it."

Lt. (jg) William Leonard, one of the VF-42 pilots, was named executive officer of the squadron.

As the *Yorktown* made its way to "Point Luck," the spot of ocean where Fletcher was to rendezvous with Spruance and the *Enterprise* and the *Hornet*, Joe Fazio became a plane captain and was assigned F4F-4 Wildcat fighter Number 23. Different pilots would fly it but only one plane captain would care for it. Number 23 was Joe Fazio's plane now.

"I was real happy that I was getting an airplane, and I was finally not pushing planes anymore," he recalled. "Now, I was a plane captain."

Thousands of miles to the south, the *Hing Lee* had stopped for several days in Vanikoro. Still flying the red-and-blue flag, Machalinski, Ewoldt and their six young Chinese passengers then headed south. The owner of the red-roofed house, a logger named Williams, provided them with simple sailing charts and several ropes of tobacco to use in trading with islanders in the event of an emergency.

Then they headed toward the New Hebrides islands, which years later would become the nation of Vanuatu. The voyage from San Cristobol had covered 250 miles. The next leg of their journey would be about 700 miles.

After eleven days, Machalinski recalled, the *Hing Lee* neared the end of her strange voyage and headed into the harbor of Port Villa on the southern island of Efate. The *Yorktown* airmen found themselves staring at an American flag on a U.S. Navy PT boat—whose small crew stared back at them with a strange ambivalence and waved them away when they attempted to approach. Finally, the crew of the PT boat hung a sign on the back of their craft, "Follow Me." The *Hing Lee* complied and was led into the harbor—where two U.S. destroyers of World War I vintage were docked.

Machalinski and Ewoldt were overjoyed that, thanks to a sagging rubber raft, a runaway horse, the kindness of a succession of strangers and one commandeered schooner, they had survived against unbelievable odds. Even in their exhilaration, however, they were aware they were still being regarded with apparent suspicion—which they came to understand only after they learned that the red-and-blue flag given them by the savvy British resident commissioner in San Cristobol was not a British flag at all, but an international signal flag that told anyone close to the *Hing Lee*, "This vessel has disease."

16

Buckmaster's announcement that the *Yorktown* would go to the West Coast, "and not for just two weeks, either," sent them back to the scuttlebutts.

"We could visualize loved ones coming back to meet the ship, and old-timers could regale newer members of the crew with stories of the *Yorktown*'s 1939 overhaul in Bremerton," wrote Wadleigh. "My roommate and [Naval Academy] classmate, Bill Crenshaw, and I swapped a few yarns about West Coast duty and wondered what Bremerton would be like as a wartime boom town. I don't believe either one of us ever found out. . . ."

On June 2, with the two U.S. task forces observing strict radio silence, Fletcher sent a Dauntless to drop a "bean bag" message onto the *Enterprise* flight deck, informing Spruance that he was approaching with the *Yorktown*'s Task Force 17. The two admirals established visual contact at "Point Luck" at approximately 4 P.M. When the two task forces rendezvoused about 325 miles northwest of Midway, it was the largest naval force assembled by the United States since the bombing of Pearl Harbor. As the senior officer, Fletcher assumed overall command.

A much larger naval force—Nagumo's four-carrier striking force—was 1,000 miles west of the two islands, headed northeast. The following day, when he reached a point 700 miles northwest of Midway, Nagumo turned directly toward the islands and prepared to attack. Everything seemed to be going according to plan for the Japanese forces—but disaster lurked just across the sea.

As Nagumo started his dash toward Midway, the invasion force under Vice Admiral Kondo was 700 miles south of him. This placed the invasion troops almost due west of Midway, waiting to begin landing on the island after Nagumo's carrier planes had successfully eliminated most island-based resistance.

The third element, Yamamoto's "main force," was divided. Part of the main force, including Yamamoto himself, remained 600 miles behind Nagumo, ready to sweep in with battleships and assist when the expected carrier battle began. The plan assumed that the U.S. carriers would appear after the actual landing of troops on Midway began.

The other half of Yamamoto's battleship force moved northward to back up the fourth element of the offensive, which was the attack on the Aleutian Islands.

The precise reason that the commander of the Combined Fleet chose to send three heavy cruisers, four light cruisers, one seaplane carrier and assorted destroyers, minesweepers, transports, tankers and other vessels against the remote, barely populated Aleutian Islands off Alaska never will be known. Before the war ended, Yamamoto was killed when a plane in which he was flying was shot down by a U.S. Army Air Corps P-38 Lightning, and historians have been left to study the diaries and recollections of his closest associates in their attempts to reconstruct his thinking. According to some of his contemporaries, the Aleutian part of the overall campaign was a "diversion." But if Yamamoto's purpose was to draw the U.S. carrier fleet into a battle at Midway, why he would want to divert any part of the U.S. fleet to another part of the ocean is hard to understand. Another suggested explanation is that Doolittle's raid had a profound impact on Yamamoto, who regarded the security of his homeland and the safety of his emperor with near-religious concern.

At any rate, Nagumo's carriers, Kondo's invasion troops, the Aleutian expedition, Yamamoto's own "main force" and the irrelevant submarine cordon now waiting for the carriers somewhere between Midway and Hawaii were the four elements of Yamamoto's great June 1942 flotilla. Of these, only the carriers would be of importance to the men who served on the *Yorktown* and her sisters, the *Enterprise* and the *Hornet*.

Scouting squadrons from the three carriers took turns throughout the day, June 3, searching unsuccessfully for the Japanese carriers.

As dark fell on June 3, Fletcher and Spruance moved closer to Midway.

On the two tiny islands, Navy, Marine Corps and Army Air Corps personnel braced for the assault they knew was coming.

At 2:45 A.M., flyers on the *Akagi*, the *Hiryu*, the *Kaga* and the *Soryu* were awakened. At 40 minutes before sunrise, they were ordered to assemble in a briefing room and a few minutes later were running to their planes, which waited for them on the carrier flight decks. Fuchida, recuperating from his appendectomy, got out of bed and dragged himself to the *Akagi* flight deck, unable to resist watching the attack begin, even though he would be unable to participate in it.

"Plane engines were started and livid white flames spurted from exhaust pipes," he recalled. "The flight deck was soon a hell of ear-shattering noise." Floodlights suddenly illuminated the deck.

"A Zero fighter, leading the flock of impatient war birds, revved up its engine, gathered speed along the flight deck and rose into the air to the accompaniment of a thunderous cheer from *Akagi*'s crew. Caps and hands waved wildly in the bright glare of the deck lights."

Within minutes, the four carriers had 108 planes in the air and on their way to Midway, now 240 miles to the southeast. Fifteen minutes later, the sun rose.

Fuchida summed up Nagumo's understanding—or misunderstanding—of his circumstances:

1. The enemy fleet will probably come out to engage when the Midway landing operations have begun.
2. Enemy air patrols from Midway will be heavier to westward and southward, less heavy to the north and northwest.
3. The radius of enemy air patrols is estimated to be approximately 500 miles.
4. The enemy is not yet aware of our plan, and he has not yet detected our task force.
5. There is no evidence of an enemy task force in our vicinity.
6. It is therefore possible for us to attack Midway, destroy land-based planes there, and support the landing operation. We can then turn around, meet an approaching enemy task force and destroy it.
7. Possible counterattacks by enemy land-based aircraft can surely be repulsed by our inteceptors and antiaircraft fire.

Even though he thought no enemy ships were in his vicinity, Nagumo sent search planes south, east and north of his strike force.

It is important to understand that Nagumo ordered a "single-phase" search. Each search plane was to fly 300 miles, dogleg left and fly 60 miles, then turn left again and return to the fleet. Had he chosen a "two-phase" search plan, a plane would have taken off before daylight and flown mostly in darkness, coming to the outer reaches of its assigned search sector as the sun came up. This provided search coverage at the outer limits of the admiral's area of concern as early as daylight was available—but left the interior part of the search zone uncovered because the scout was flying that area in darkness. Therefore, a second scout would be sent to search the inner area at sunrise. However, in choosing a single-phase search, Nagumo intended to send only one plane for each search sector. Therefore, he held the scouts back so that more of the internal part of each sector would be flown during daylight. The Japanese assumption that no U.S. carriers were in the region no doubt contributed to Nagumo's decision to employ the less rigorous search plan.

Luck struck her first blow in the *Yorktown*'s behalf when this phase of the Japanese carrier campaign was put into effect. In addition to scouts from his flagship, *Akagi*, and another carrier *Kaga*, Nagumo sent scouts from three cruisers, altogether seven planes to search seven sectors. The cruiser planes were seaplanes that were launched by catapult. The catapult on the cruiser, *Tone*, malfunctioned and by the time it could be repaired, two float planes from *Tone* were delayed.

From post-war reviews of records from the Navy and Marine defenders at Midway, the Japanese Imperial Navy and the U.S. fleet, historians have produced a minute-by-minute time line of the unfolding of events.

At 2:45 A.M., crews were awakened on the Japanese ships.

At 3 A.M., reveille on the *Yorktown* and her sisters.

At 4 A.M., scouts took off from Midway.

4:30: Nagumo began launching his attack force.

4:37: sunrise.

4:42: *Tone* launched its first reconnaissance plane.

5:00: *Tone* launched its second reconnaissance plane. Both *Tone* scouts were a half-hour late in launching.

5:34: Midway scout reported finding Nagumo's force.

5:45: Midway scout reported "Many planes heading Midway."

6:03: Midway scout reported "Two carriers and battleships

bearing 320 degrees, distant 180 miles (from Midway), course 135 degrees, speed 25." The scout was 40 miles off but now Fletcher and Spruance both knew the approximate location of their enemy.

6:15: B-17s and other attack planes took off from Midway to bomb Japanese carriers.

6:30: Japanese planes began bombing and strafing runways, hangars, power plants, a hospital and other facilities on the two islands.

7:05: The leader of the Japanese bombing force reported to Nagumo that a second attack on Midway will be necessary.

And with that succession of events, the conditions were put into place from which the Battle of Midway would move toward its devastating end. Too bad for Admiral Nagumo that he had never talked with the *Yorktown*'s Red Maag, for the winds of war were about to shift forever in the northern Pacific Ocean, and Nagumo had belayed his sheet.

Fletcher wanted to recover the search planes he had launched at 4:30 A.M., so at 6:07 A.M., only four minutes after receiving the scout's reported carrier sighting, he ordered Spruance to attack the Japanese carriers immediately. *Yorktown* planes would follow as soon as he had recovered his Dauntless scouts, he said. It was a crucial decision because by directing the two task forces toward separate activities, Fletcher caused them to become separated. The *Yorktown* was now alone.

At 7 A.M., the *Hornet* began launching attack planes. At 7:06, planes began taking off from the *Enterprise*.

On the *Yorktown*, dive-bomber and torpedo crews were told they were being held "in reserve."

Aviation Radioman 3c. Lloyd Childers had been flying in Devastators for only three months. Early in his training in Torpedo Three at Hawaii's Kaneohe Naval Air Station, he attended a special intelligence briefing at which he and other radiomen and pilots were told that whenever a 15-plane formation of Devastators attacked enemy carriers, the Navy expected only three of the planes to penetrate enemy defenses and deliver torpedoes.

"This bleak forecast unnerved me considerably," Childers said later. "However, as we walked out of the room, everyone seemed to be joking about it. I thought, 'Well, if the others can do it, I can too.'"

After reveille on June 4, Childers stood talking with his brother, Wayne. They shared a locker in the *Yorktown*'s compartment for Torpedo Three enlisted men. Lloyd Childers laid his wallet and his wristwatch on a shelf. "Wayne, if I don't come back from this flight, these are yours." Wayne nodded his head but said nothing. It was Lloyd Childers's 21st birthday.

At breakfast, aircraft crews found themselves being served steak and eggs.

"Last meal for the condemned," one man joked. The others laughed.

Childers would recall later that after the briefing at which *Yorktown* crews were told they would be held in reserve, another radioman-gunner declared sadly: "Someday, one of my grandkids will ask me, 'Grandpa, what did you do at the Battle of Midway?' I'll hang my head and say, 'I was held in reserve.'" But that man would never be a grandfather.

Nagumo was also holding reserves. After launching his first-wave attack on Midway, he held 93 planes on his four carriers in case he had to engage in a battle with enemy aircraft carriers—which he still had no reason to believe were anywhere nearby. These included "Val" divebombers, "Kate" torpedo planes and Zeroes. Of course, the "Kates" were armed with torpedoes, the best weapon yet invented for sinking aircraft carriers. But like the Devastators, "Kates" could deliver either torpedoes or bombs. Those used in the first-wave attack on Midway had carried bombs.

When word came back from Midway that a second attack on the islands would be necessary, Nagumo ordered the torpedo planes taken below to his hangar decks and the torpedoes replaced with bombs for a second Midway attack.

At around 7:15 A.M., high altitude Army Air Corps "Flying Fortresses" from Midway reached the Nagumo carrier force and began dropping bombs. None of the bombs ever hit a ship. Other U.S. planes, including dive-bombers, also attacked. However, with little training in dive-bombing, Marines from Midway chose to "glide" bomb the Japanese carriers, basically to fly over and drop bombs. Again, there were no hits and Zeroes in the Japanese combat air patrol shot down many of the low-flying dive-bombers, as well as their fighter escorts.

This action was underway when the message that would stop the clocks on Nagumo's flagship arrived. The second *Tone* scout, one of those delayed 30 minutes by the faulty catapult launcher, reported: "Ten ships, apparently enemy, sighted. Bearing 010 degrees, distant 240 miles from Midway. Course, 150 degrees. Speed, more than 20 knots. Time, 0728."

Had Nagumo ordered a two-phase search, this plane might have been in a position to sight these ships not at 7:28 but near sunrise, nearly three hours earlier. At a minimum, it might have been 30 minutes sooner with its sighting, but for the delay in launching it from the *Tone*.

It took a few minutes for the message to be relayed from the *Tone* to Nagumo on the *Akagi*.

Ten ships, apparently enemy? Fuchida said the information hit the *Akagi* bridge "like a bolt from the blue." Until that moment, no one in the Imperial Navy had thought that so many American ships were anywhere near the Midway Islands.

At 7:47 A.M., a message was flashed to the *Tone* scout to "ascertain ship types."

The scout had spotted the *Yorktown*'s Task Force 17 and was staying in clouds almost on the carrier's horizon, out of fear of running into fighters in the task force combat air patrol.

At 7:58 A.M., the pilot of the scout plane sent a message, saying only that the ships had changed course. Exasperated staff officers on the *Akagi* told him again to determine the composition of the enemy force.

"Enemy ships are five cruisers and five destroyers," the scout reported at 8:09, and some members of Nagumo's staff began to relax.

At 8:20, the scout added: "Enemy force accompanied by what appears to be an aircraft carrier, bringing up the rear."

By now, some of Nagumo's torpedo planes had been rearmed with bombs for the second Midway strike and were back on the flight deck. He had intended to launch them, along with dive-bombers and Zero escorts, in a second-wave attack on Midway, then start recovering his first wave, which was returning, low on fuel. Facing a likely imminent carrier battle, Nagumo could not send these torpedo planes to bomb Midway, so he ordered them back to the hangar decks and ordered weary hangar deck crews to switch them back to torpedoes.

While Nagumo was landing the first-wave planes returning from Midway, a U.S. submarine, the *Nautilus*, was watching the Japanese force, radioing reports of its speed and bearing to Midway. The commander of the submarine later reported that he was attacked by a cruiser and fired one torpedo that missed. Destroyers rushed toward the *Nautilus*. It descended to 50 feet. A few minutes after the *Nautilus* submerged, the Japanese force changed direction and the change went unreported. The destroyers started dropping depth charges over the *Nautilus*, which somehow survived and retreated from the battle area. The Japanese destroyer *Arashi* took up the chase and fell behind the Nagumo force. After the war ended, American historians and war crimes investigators would read of that bit of sidelight action with unusual interest.

On the *Yorktown*, Fletcher had ordered Spruance to launch a "full load" attack on the Japanese ships, meaning to use all available planes. However, the Midway scout had reported seeing only two carriers, and Nimitz's Op Plan 29-42 had said the enemy would bring four or five fleet carriers to the battle. Fletcher at first was unwilling to send the remainder of the planes available to either task force on an attack. What if the other two or three carriers were found later and all the torpedo planes and dive-bombers were gone? However, at 8:38, he had received no further reports of Japanese carriers, so he decided to stop holding his own forces in reserve and to launch an attack also.

Suddenly, the "held in reserve" status of Torpedo Three changed to, "Pilots and crews, man your planes."

"God, this is it," thought Childers.

Fletcher launched half of his dive-bombers, all his torpedo planes and six Wildcats to fly escorts.

Thach, Torpedo Three commander Lem Massey and bombing squadron commander Maxwell Leslie discussed whether Thach's Wildcats should accompany the high altitude bombers or the low-flying torpedo planes en route to the Japanese carriers.

Massey said he should stay with the bombers because at the Battle of the Coral Sea, Japanese Zeroes defending the *Shokuku* had concentrated on *Yorktown* bombers. Leslie said he should concentrate on defending the torpedo planes.

Thach was irked that the other two squadron commanders were playing what he later called an "Alphonse and Gaston" game with him—"After you. No, after you. No, after you."—he told them he would determine where his fighters flew and decided to stay with the torpedo planes. He had been told he would have eight Wildcats as escort planes. He was furious when he learned at the last minute that he would have only six. He felt he knew why the number was reduced, and that only made him angrier.

When the *Yorktown* was allowed to become separated from the *Enterprise* and the *Hornet*, Thach said, the possibility of mutual defensive support was lost. The two task forces would have to be defended separately, meaning more fighters would have to be held back to defend the *Yorktown.* Thach felt one of the oldest principles of warfare was being violated, and his life, the lives of his pilots and the lives of the men they were charged with defending would be jeopardized as a result. Thirty years later, he was still angry about it.

"I think one of the basic principles of warfare was violated, not intentionally, I presume," he said in his Naval Institute interview. He referred to the principle of concentration of force. By allowing the ships of Task Forces 16 and 17 to become scattered out over a distance of 50 miles or more, admirals had left all three carriers more vulnerable, Thach believed.

"It wasn't just an edict or Bible, because the basic principles of warfare weren't invented, they were discovered," he said. "They exist as a law of nature, the laws of strategy and tactics, and the people who violate any one of them are at a disadvantage."

Asked if he were bitter at any particular person about the way the ships became separated, he replied: "Well, yes, Admiral Nimitz, Rear Adm. Fletcher, Rear Adm. Spruance and Capt. Buckmaster. As I said, I was a young lieutenant commander then and since then, having grown up and gotten to be a captain with more experience in task group, task force and fleet operations and had command of two carriers, then rear admiral of a task group, and a vice admiral of a task force and finally a four-star admiral of forces in Europe, I haven't changed my mind one damned bit."

But at 8:30 Thursday morning, June 4, 1942, Lt. Cdr. Jimmy Thach couldn't argue strategy or principles of war with his superiors. He frantically appealed for two more fighters and was turned down. The *Yorktown* attack force took off.

17

When the *Tone* scout plane reported sighting the *Yorktown*, Rear Admiral Yamaguchi, the colorful commander of Carrier Division Two in the Nagumo force, flashed a message to Nagumo from his flagship, the carrier *Hiryu*: "Consider it advisable to launch attack force immediately."

But Nagumo hesitated and decided it wiser to complete the recovery of his planes from the first-wave attack on Midway and to rearm and refuel his Zeroes. Since all of the fighters either were escorting the attack planes or flying defensive formations above the carriers, to attack at that moment would have meant sending bombers and those torpedo planes that were still armed with torpedoes against the U.S. carrier without fighter escorts. While he recovered the Midway attack planes, an attack against the U.S. carrier was hastily organized. He decided to send 18 "Val" dive-bombers, 54 "Kate" torpedo planes and 12 Zeroes (three from each carrier) as escorts. At that point, some of the "Kates" were armed with bombs and some with torpedoes.

Before the attack plan could be carried out, destroyers and cruisers screening the Japanese carriers began reporting the approach of enemy carrier planes. Soon, the number of approaching planes made it clear to Nagumo that he was being attacked by more than one American carrier. Desperately, he ordered the preparations to launch his own attack force speeded up.

The first American planes to attack were Devastators from the *Hornet*, 15 of them flying low over the water. Zeroes fell furiously upon the *Hornet* squadron and sank all 15 planes. Not a single American torpedo hit a Japanese ship. Members of the crew of the *Akagi* cheered as the torpedo planes hit the water. Of 30 men, pilots and radiomen-gunners, there was one survivor, Ens. George H. Gay, who two hours earlier had taken off from an aircraft carrier with a torpedo-armed plane for the first time in his life. He crawled out of his downed plane, grabbed a flotation device and spent the next several hours hiding beneath it in the middle of the Japanese carrier force. He had seen the planes of his comrades bursting into flames all around him. Later, he would be awarded the Medal of Honor.

The commander of the fighter squadron escorting *Hornet* attack planes had chosen not to fly with the torpedo planes, but with the *Hornet*'s dive-bombers—which got lost and never found the Japanese ships.

Steaming about a mile behind Nagumo's flagship was the *Kaga*. Torpedo planes from the *Enterprise* went for it. Again, the Zeroes slaughtered them. Of 14 *Enterprise* Devastators, 10 were shot down immediately.

Nagumo was now within five minutes of launching his counterattack.

Five minutes.

At this point, the Japanese carriers were clearly winning the battle. They had been attacked by B-17s and "glide bombers" from Midway and torpedo planes from the *Enterprise* and the *Hornet* and not one ship was scratched.

The first Zero of the *Akagi* attack group lifted off the deck when a lookout screamed, "Hell-divers!"

Dive-bombers from the *Enterprise* also had trouble

locating the Japanese ships. When they arrived at the point where they expected to find Nagumo's carriers, they found empty ocean. This apparently happened as a result of the course change Nagumo had ordered minutes after the *Nautilus* was forced to submerge. For several minutes, Lt. Cdr. Wade McClusky Jr., the *Enterprise* air group commander, who was leading that ship's dive-bombing squadron, searched unsuccessfully for the Japanese fleet.

According to after-action reports, it was at this point that Capt. Miles Browning, Spruance's chief of staff, shouted to him over the radio from the *Enterprise*, "Attack! Attack!"

"Wilco [will comply], as soon as I find the bastards," McClusky replied.

Then he spotted a white wake and a ship he thought was a cruiser hurrying across the sea. Assuming the ship was headed for the Japanese fleet, he turned to the direction in which it was steaming and minutes later found the four carriers. Three of them were steaming in a "V" arrangement with the *Akagi* and the *Soryu* at the top ends of the "V" and the *Kaga* behind them, at the bottom point. The *Hiryu* was eight miles ahead of those three, alone.

Approaching the "V" from the left side, McClusky divided his bombers and attacked the *Akagi* and the *Kaga*.

Virtually unopposed by the Zeroes, which had been busy defending against the obsolete and helpless Devastators, the "slow but deadly" SBD Dauntless dive-bombers screamed down through desperate antiaircraft fire, toward Nagumo's decks. The *Akagi* had 40 planes on her flight deck, along with gasoline tanks being used to refuel them for an attack on the *Yorktown*. The first bomb crashed through the flight deck and exploded below on the hangar deck, where torpedoes and bombs had been stacked during the frantic switching back and forth earlier in the morning. Another exploded among the planes and fuel tanks on the flight deck. Within minutes Nagumo's flagship was engulfed in flames and the secondary explosions of his own bombs, torpedoes and gasoline tanks.

Fuchida had gone to his quarters, exhausted, and was lying down when the bombs began to hit the *Akagi*. He got up and climbed topside. There he met Genda.

"We goofed," Genda said, and the two went their separate ways.

In minutes, the *Kaga* also was on fire.

The Zeroes that destroyed the *Enterprise* and *Hornet* torpedo planes had attempted to regain altitude. Had they done so, they might have been able to stop at least some of McClusky's dive-bombers.

One reason they never reached altitude was the Thach Weave. The other reason was Torpedo Three from the *Yorktown*.

When he finished flight school at Pensacola, Chief Petty Officer W. G. Esders had never seen a Devastator torpedo plane, and when he arrived in San Diego in 1938, he decided it was the most beautiful plane he had ever seen. As an enlisted "Naval Aviation Pilot," he would fly his first combat mission in a Devastator at Midway, a member of Torpedo Three on the *Yorktown*. Then he would know what an unworthy plane he had.

The *Yorktown* attack force was 12 miles from the Japanese carriers, not far behind the *Hornet* and *Enterprise* torpedo squadrons, when Massey led it toward the carrier north of the "V," the *Hiryu*. The Zeroes promptly attacked. Esders looked around and estimated that 20 or 25 Zeroes were after the *Yorktown* Devastators. He could hear the bullets ripping through his fuselage. An exploding shell from one of the Zeroes' 20-millimeter cannons exploded against the armor plate on the back of his seat.

His radioman-gunner, Aircraft Radioman 2c. Mike Brazier, called him on the interphone and said he had been hit and was too badly wounded to defend the plane. Esders dropped his torpedo, passed just ahead of the *Hiryu*'s bow and began to concentrate on escaping. Thach had lectured

Torpedo Three pilots at one briefing and told them their best defense against Zeroes would be to fly low so that the attacking aircraft could not get under them, and to fly slow, something the Devastator did rather well. He said they should wait until the very last second when a Zero attacked them, then make a sharp turn. With four Zeroes on his tail, Esders tried the tactic, and evaded all of them.

"The four Zeroes chased me between 20 and 25 miles," he wrote years later, "but failed to hit me. The last fighter to make an attack flew alongside about ten feet off my wingtip. The pilot hesitated momentarily, raised his right hand, bending his arm at the elbow, apparently executing a half-salute. What he intended to indicate, I will never know. . . ."

Another enlisted pilot, Warrant Machinist Harry L. Corl, was at the controls of the plane in which Lloyd Childers was radioman-gunner. As they approached the Japanese ships, Corl shouted into the intercom, "Up ahead! Up ahead!" Facing to the rear, where his single .30-caliber machine gun was mounted, Childers strained to look around and saw what he believed were at least a dozen Zeroes, coming head on.

"Immediately, all hell broke loose," Childers recalled. "The Zeroes were all over us from several directions as we chugged more or less straight ahead. I was shooting every time I had a decent shot."

"Look at the skipper!" Corl screamed, and Childers glanced over in time to see Massey's flaming Devastator hit the water. Esders also saw it and said later that Massey was out of the cockpit, standing with one foot on the wing and another on the seat, apparently hoping to use his parachute. But the squadron was flying at only about 250 feet. A parachute would have been useless.

Flying above the torpedo planes, Thach and his five comrades from the fighter squadron began to engage the Zeroes, hoping to take some of the pressure off. Lt. (jg) Brainard T. Macomber, one of the holdover pilots from Fighting Forty-two, was flying even with Thach—but too close, because for

Thach's "weave" maneuver to work two cooperating fighters had to have at least a turning radius between them. Thach motioned for Macomber to move away and Macomber appeared bewildered. Thach tried to radio him to open up space, but Macomber's radio was dead. At that point, Thach realized that he had expected Lovelace to brief the Fighting Forty-two pilots on how the fly the weave maneuver, but Lovelace had been killed before he had a chance to conduct the briefing. The only briefing the Fighting Forty-two flyers had received was Thach's last-minute admonition, "Don't be a lone wolf."

Macomber had taken this advice to heart and was snuggling in as close to the skipper as he could.

"I had spent a year of effort developing what I thought was the only way to survive against the Zero and we couldn't seem to do it," Thach said. At about that time, Ens. Edgar Bassett of Philadelphia was shot down by a Zero and fell in flames.

Thach and other flyers from his VF-3 squadron began weaving among the Zeroes. It was the first time the maneuver had ever been used and the Zero pilots were obviously having trouble with it.

Several Zeroes went down, and Thach started keeping records on the pad he had strapped to his knee.

"Then I realized that this was sort of foolish," he recalled. "Why was I marking marks on my knee pad when the knee pad wasn't coming back? I was absolutely convinced that nobody could get out of there, that we weren't coming back and neither were the torpedo planes."

The weave seemed to work better and better. Thach teamed up with any of the three pilots from his VF-3 squadron, enlisted pilot Machinist Tom Cheek, Ens. Daniel Sheedy, or Ens. Robert A. M. "Ram" Dibb.

"Skipper, there's a Zero on my tail. Get him off!" Dibb yelled at one point. Thach banked straight toward Dibb and, as taught, Dibb banked back toward the squadron commander. The maneuver led the Zero in front of Thach's guns. The Japanese plane hit the ocean in flames.

Ram Dibb was flying fighter No. 23. Before taking off, he had scribbled his signature, attesting to the plane's ready condition, on the "yellow sheet" handed him by its plane captain, Petty Officer 3c. Joe Fazio.

The five surviving planes from Fighting Forty-two would be the only fighters from any of the three American carriers to take on Zeroes that day. The *Hornet* fighter escorts had gotten lost with that ship's dive-bombers, and the *Enterprise* fighters had chosen to stay with the dive-bombers, while their torpedo planes were attacked by Zeroes.

Finally, as Thach looked toward a Zero against which he was maneuvering, he saw a glint from the sun out of the corner of his eye. It was the *Yorktown* Dauntlesses starting their dives on the *Soryu*, eight miles away.

"It just looked like a beautiful, silver waterfall, those dive-bombers coming down," he recalled. A short time later, the Zeroes slacked off, and Thach looked around at the sea for the first time. Three carriers, the *Akagi*, *Kaga* and *Soryu* were in flames.

"One of them was burning with bright pink flames, and sometimes blue flames," he recalled. "I remember looking at the height of the flame from the ship and noticing that it was about the height that the ship was long, the length of the ship, just solid flame going up. And, of course, there was a lot of smoke on top of that."

The fourth Japanese carrier, the *Hiryu*, had not been scratched by Torpedo Three.

Thach and the remaining four members of his squadron returned to the *Yorktown*. Edgar Bassett, who once thought he might become a king among natives of New Guinea's jungle and who believed only a few months earlier that he had defeated his birthday jinx, would remain behind forever.

For all the trouble Thach and his four remaining squadron-mates had given the Zeroes, many were left to attack the *Yorktown* torpedo planes, and only two planes from the *Yorktown* squadron of twelve survived.

Corl jettisoned his torpedo and began zigging and zagging as best he could in the cumbersome Devastator. Childers could feel the slipstream from the side as the old plane skidded about. Then he felt two bullets hit his left thigh.

"At this point, I fully realized that war is not like a football game," he recalled later. "The bullets were hot but, strangely, I felt very little pain. I raised my leg and looked at the bleeding and continued talking to myself, 'Childers, you damned sissy, you're not really hurt.'"

He kept shooting at the Zeroes. Then he felt an intense pain in his right leg and realized that he was hit just above the ankle, and his leg was broken.

"It hurt like hell," he recalled of his second wound. "It was like being hit on the shin with a baseball bat." He kept shooting at the attacking fighters. He looked down and a Zero had moved under them and had slowed to fly at the Devastator's speed. The Zero was bobbing up and down and Childers decided the Japanese pilot was trying to cut the Devastator's tail off with his propeller, probably having shot up all of his ammunition.

"I jerked my seat up so I could shoot below our horizontal stabilizer," he said. "I could see the pilot's face as I fired pointblank at him. The Zero disappeared."

More planes came and Childers's gun jammed. He took his .45-caliber pistol and began firing at them with it. Then, almost suddenly, the Zeroes left. He and Corl headed back toward the *Yorktown*, oil streaming from their engine and pressure falling on the oil gauge in Corl's cockpit.

Soon they were joined by Esders and the badly wounded Mike Brazier. Esders was flying slowly in order to conserve fuel, but Corl had to fly as fast as possible in order to get back to the ship before losing all his oil and having his engine freeze.

Brazier had been hit at least seven times by 7.7-millimeter

slugs from Zero machine guns and twice by exploding shells from the 20-millimeter cannons. Yet he managed to change coils in his radio, a change necessary to use the instrument as a homing device. Esders ditched the plane near a destroyer, climbed out and inflated the rubber life raft.

"I removed Mike from the aircraft. I could see the large bones in each leg as I got him into the life raft," he said. Then Esders climbed into the raft to discover it had a bullet hole and was leaking. While he worked at patching the hole, he kept talking to Brazier.

"Of course, he bled to death," Esders said later. "Yet, this young man was still able to talk to me in the raft, expressing how badly he felt that he wasn't able to perform better or longer. This was the kind of men we had in Torpedo Three."

Three torpedo squadrons had been sent against Japanese carriers, 41 Devastators, 82 men. Not a single one would return to its own ship. Five, one from the *Hornet*, two from the *Enterprise* and two from the *Yorktown*, would land in the ocean. A handful of men, including the *Hornet*'s Ensign Gay, would survive. As far as can be determined, not a single American torpedo exploded against a Japanese ship.

Yet their role in the battle was critical. Only because the Zeroes were forced to attack the Devastators were the Dauntlesses able to bomb the *Akagi*, the *Kaga* and the *Soryu* and score not just a few hits but enough to destroy all three carriers. Whether they realized it or not, U.S. commanders had sent 82 men in the three torpedo squadrons on a virtual suicide mission.

For his part, Thach would remain convinced for the rest of his life that with two more Wildcats he could have saved many aviators from Torpedo Three.

It would take Corl and Childers nearly three hours to find their way back to the *Yorktown* task force. During that time, the fourth Japanese carrier, the undamaged *Hiryu*, would launch a counter-strike.

"All planes are taking off now for the purpose of destroying the enemy carriers," Yamaguchi messaged at 10:50 A.M. He sent "Val" dive-bombers, escorted by Zeroes, in his first attack.

But the Japanese scout from the cruiser *Tone* had not found enemy "carriers," but instead only one of them, the *Yorktown.* At Yamaguchi's request, the scout was ordered to remain near Task Force 17 and transmit a radio beacon the Japanese attack force could follow.

18

While the destroyer *Arashi* pursued the U.S. submarine *Nautilus*, the rest of the Nagumo force disappeared over the horizon. Yasumasa Watanabe, commander of the *Arashi*, finally gave up on finding the submarine. He turned and raced at flank speed toward his task force. His was the wake that had directed Lt. Cdr. Wade McClusky of the *Enterprise* dive-bomber squadron to the Japanese ships.

As the *Arashi* sped to rejoin the Nagumo carrier force, observers on the ship reported a strange sight, a man swimming in the ocean. Watanabe ordered the swimmer taken aboard.

The captive was Ens. Wesley Osmus of Torpedo Three. He seems to have attempted to reach the Midway Islands in his badly damaged Devastator but either was forced to ditch or crashed into the sea, his Devastator in flames. His radioman-gunner, Benjamin Dodson Jr. of Durham, North Carolina, apparently went down with the plane. Japanese sailors said Osmus was exhausted and badly burned when he was taken prisoner. He was fed and his burns treated, they would say later.

Much of what happened on *Arashi* that afternoon was

reconstructed by American military war crimes investigators after the war and by military historian Robert Barde of Connecticut.

Osmus was interrogated, while being threatened repeatedly with a sword. He answered many questions. During part of this interrogation, Watanabe had been ordered to bring the *Arashi* alongside the burning *Akagi* and assist in fighting the carrier's fires. That would mean Osmus was aware of the devastation visited upon the Japanese force and could see three carriers in flames. This factor may have affected his willingness to respond to questions. Dr. Barde points out that, for whatever reason, Osmus revealed critical facts. They included the following:

1. That three carriers were in the American force and that they were the *Yorktown*, *Enterprise* and *Hornet*. That there were also six cruisers and about 10 destroyers.
2. That the *Yorktown* was acting independently of the other two carriers and was accompanied by two cruisers and three destroyers.
3. That the *Yorktown* had arrived in the vicinity of Midway about June 1.
4. That there were no other capital ships at Pearl Harbor.

The key fact was that there were three carriers in the American force. Until then, Japanese commanders had only the report from the *Tone* search plane that the U.S. force consisted of "five cruisers, five destroyers and . . . what appears to be an aircraft carrier, bringing up the rear." That there were three carriers, not just one, in the American fleet was immediately transmitted to Yamamoto.

However, the significance of Osmus's disclosure doesn't seem all that clear.

After the *Tone* search plane had reported to Nagumo on the *Akagi* that the U.S. force consisted of "five cruisers, five destroyers and . . . what appears to be an aircraft carrier, bringing up the rear," Nagumo had ordered *Soryu* to send out a new high-speed reconnaissance plane to contact the enemy and confirm his strength.

According to Fuchida, the plane's radio malfunctioned, so the pilot flew back to the Japanese force to deliver his report personally. By then, the Americans had attacked Nagumo and finding the *Soryu*, the *Akagi* and the *Kaga* all in flames, the search plane pilot landed on the *Hiryu*. He reported to Admiral Tamon Yamaguchi that the American force included three aircraft carriers—and named them, the *Enterprise*, the *Hornet* and the *Yorktown*.

The conversation appears to have taken place at around noon, up to an hour before Osmus, who was a few miles away, also surrounded by burning Japanese aircraft carriers, revealed the same information.

After he was questioned, Osmus was taken to an officer's cabin and confined there while the damage-control efforts at the carrier continued. Late in the day, he was murdered. His captors took his wallet, a pen and a photograph of him and an attractive young woman, according to members of the *Arashi* crew.

Despite numerous interviews by war crimes investigators and by Dr. Barde, the exact method by which Ensign Osmus was killed is not known. According to one account, he was shot. Another had it that he was decapitated with a sword.

But the report Dr. Barde said was given most credence by war crimes investigators was that Osmus was killed with an axe. An *Arashi* telegraph operator, to whom war crimes investigators showed a copy of a photograph of Osmus and a young woman, said it was identical to one shown to him by crew member Ken Sato immediately after Osmus was killed.

Sato was interrogated by war crimes investigators in July 1948. He said that as leading petty officer on the ship, he was ordered by Watanabe to execute Osmus. He said he replied that he could not carry out such an order and was told to get someone else to do it. Therefore, he said, he passed the order on to a subordinate who told him 20 or 30 minutes later that the American flyer was dead. Sato said he related this to Watanabe.

The telegraph operator told investigators that Sato told him Osmus was taken to the stern of the destroyer and ordered to face aft. According to this account, Osmus was gazing at the ship's wake when he was hit in the back of the neck with a heavy fire axe. The blow failed to decapitate him and for a few minutes he clung to the rail chain in great pain, Japanese sailors said. Finally, he fell over into the sea. The disposition of the pen, wallet and photograph of Osmus and the attractive young woman is not known.

Despite over 30 interviews by investigators, no one was ever brought to trial for the murder of Ens. Wesley Osmus. Most of those believed to have participated in his murder, including Watanabe, were killed in action before the war ended. A Lt. Kiyosumi Tanikawa, the man who interrogated Osmus, told investigators he had been too busy rescuing survivors from the *Akagi* to pay any attention to what happened to the prisoner.

The Navy would not learn of events on the *Arashi* until after the war. On November 4, 1943, it launched a destroyer escort in Ens. Osmus's honor. According to stories in the *Bay City (Michigan) Times*, the ship slid easily from its ways at the Defoe Ship Building Co. shipyard and into the Saginaw River. During the commissioning ceremony, Capt. C. D. Swain reviewed Ens. Osmus's heroic record of naval service, noting that the Torpedo Three ensign had been awarded the American Defense Service Medal with Fleet Clasp and the Navy Cross and cited for extraordinary heroism for his action on June 4, 1942, according to the newspaper account. The new destroyer, the U.S.S. *Osmus*, was sponsored by Ens. Wesley Osmus's mother, Mrs. Louisa Osmus of Chicago.

Thach and his fighter pilots headed back to the *Yorktown*. The badly wounded Sheedy landed his crippled plane on the *Hornet*. He came down hard and the plane veered starboard. Sheedy's machine guns were jarred into action when he hit the flight deck, spraying the *Hornet* island structure with .50-caliber bullets. Four enlisted men and an officer, Lt. Royal Rodney Ingersoll, were killed. Ingersoll was the son of Adm. R. E. Ingersoll, Nimitz's counterpart in the Atlantic.

Every Dauntless dive-bomber from the *Yorktown* returned to the ship intact. However, pilots were waved off so that Thach and his three remaining pilots, all low on fuel, could land instead. By then, the ship's radar had detected the attacking dive-bombers from the *Hiryu*, 46 miles out and beginning to climb to diving altitudes. The *Yorktown* dive-bombers had to land on the *Enterprise* and the *Hornet.*

Thach and two other fighter pilots landed safely, but Machinist Cheek's plane crashed into the cable fence barrier, cartwheeled and flipped over on its back.

"Get me the hell out of here!" he reportedly yelled as members of the deck crew rushed to his plane. Not seriously hurt, he was pulled out and the plane was lifted onto a large dolly that had four free-swiveling wheels, making it easy for deck crews to quickly push it to an elevator, and it was "struck below" to the hangar deck. Several planes in the *Yorktown*'s combat air patrol had landed just ahead of Thach. Their fuel tanks were topped off and they were back in the air, heading for Yamaguchi's dive-bombers.

Thach hurried to the bridge to brief Fletcher on the destruction of the three Japanese ships. Joe Fazio signed in Dibb and fighter No. 23 at noon, Midway time. The plane and those of Thach and Macomber were pushed to the stern with a view to refueling them, reloading their guns and adding them to the ship's defensive patrol, but there wasn't enough time.

With the Japanese bombers minutes away, the *Yorktown*'s gasoline lines were flooded with carbon dioxide. Plane handlers folded back the F4F-4 wings and tied the three fighters to the flight deck, one line from each wing and one from the tail. Fazio walked around No. 23, counting the holes in it. He later said in an indignant letter to his younger sister back in Connecticut that the plane had been "riddled with bullets from enemy Zeroes." He said it was amazing that Dibb survived.

"One bullet went through the cockpit cover, narrowly missed him, and embedded itself in one of the instruments," he wrote. "Others went through the wings, fuselage and reserve fuel tank."

The dive-bombing attack began at 12:20 P.M.

In addition to the five-inch guns that were mounted at the four corners of the flight deck and the four batteries of 1.1-inch "pom-pom" guns, a row of .50-caliber machine guns and Swiss-made 20-millimeter guns lined the catwalk that ran along either side of the flight deck. Most of the .50-caliber guns were manned by Marines.

By the time the "Vals" started diving on the *Yorktown*, all of these guns were firing furiously. But those weren't all.

At some point in the *Yorktown*'s many voyages, members of the crew discovered that the .30-caliber machine guns used to defend Dauntless dive-bombers could be easily mounted along the catwalk that surrounded the flight deck. Metal posts that supported catwalk restraining lines were almost exactly the size of vertical rods on which the machine guns fit in the rear cockpits of the two aircraft.

Thach sat in the pilots' ready room and listened to the antiaircraft fire outside.

"You can hear the antiaircraft fire in the ready room," he recalled. "You're not supposed to be out on deck where bullets are flying around. That's not your job. We were in the ready room, which is at the flight-deck level on the *Yorktown*.

"You can hear the five-inch going off at a slower tempo than the smaller caliber, then the 20-millimeter and finally the little machine guns, so it begins with a roar and builds up to a crescendo of gunfire. When you hear the small caliber, you know that the enemy aircraft is pretty close, and I counted this sequence four times, and we felt a couple of thuds, but it seemed rather remote from the pilots' ready room.

"So, if only four got through, they were very accurate, because they got three hits on the *Yorktown.*"

David Pattison of Iowa was one of many crewmen who had taken spare machine guns and mounted them along the catwalk, hoping to add a few more rounds of opposition to any plane that might attack the ship. As the bombers descended on the ship and the antiaircraft gunners desperately tried to fight them off, Pattison twisted this way and that, popping away with his .30-caliber two-cents' worth, wherever he could.

The catwalk was about four feet lower than the flight deck, so that when a man stood on the catwalk, the deck was about waist- or chest-high.

Pattison glanced across the flight deck and saw a man he knew lying on his back. The sailor had been hit by strafing fire from one of the dive-bombers.

Pattison grabbed a first aid kit and ran to him. Blood was spurting from the sailor's groin. He already had put his hand between his legs and found nothing there.

"What happened?" Pattison asked as he got to the man.

"They shot off my balls!" the desperate sailor cried. "They shot off my balls!"

Moments later he observed sadly: "It blowed 'em right away."

Pattison and another sailor managed to get a tourniquet around the wounded man's upper leg and stop the relentless spurts of blood. The man's crotch was soaked with blood. Overhead, Japanese dive-bombers had just begun to "roll over" and plunge toward the *Yorktown.* A medical corpsman stopped, examined the tourniquet and told Pattison it should be loosened periodically. Every time he relaxed the pressure, however, the blood began spurting again. The corpsman returned with stretcher bearers and the wounded sailor was taken below to a first aid station. Pattison ran back to the catwalk and his .30-caliber volunteer machine gun.

As he had in the Battle of the Coral Sea, Buckmaster left the armored conning tower and stood outside on the navigation bridge, shouting his orders to the helmsman through the slits. When the dive-bombers that had survived attacks by the ship's Wildcat defensive air patrol began to roll over on him, Buckmaster increased the ship's speed to 30½ knots and made radical evasive turns.

Below, on the hangar deck, the Machinist Cheek's flipped Wildcat was still on its dolly, with the free-swiveling castor wheels. As Buckmaster maneuvered the ship, the free-rolling platform swung wildly about the hangar deck. Boatswain's Mate 2c. Joseph Lewis of Asheville, North Carolina, and men working under him frantically chased it, back and forth.

The first bomb to hit the ship was the one that destroyed the 1.1-inch battery at Mount Four, killing 14 men and wounding six, and either killing or wounding all but two at Mount Three.

At Mount Three, one of the two men who were not wounded was Ensign John D'Arc Lorenz, although he was temporarily knocked out. Mount Three was elevated from the deck about six feet, resting on top of a large steel box-like structure known as the "ready magazine." Over 60,000 rounds of 1.1-inch shells were stored in the ready magazine. The box was about 15 feet square, making the top of it large enough to support the gun mount. Inside the box two petty officers passed clips of the shells through an opening in the top to other gun-mount crew members, who passed them on to the loaders.

When the dazed Lorenz surveyed the devastation of his gun mount, he saw smoke coming out of the ready magazine. If the shells stored in the magazine were to start exploding, the result could be nearly as damaging as the bomb itself. He jumped down to the flight deck and opened a hatch into the ready magazine. Fragments of the bomb had torn through the steel walls and penetrated some shells, setting powder on fire. But by penetrating the sides of the shells, the bomb fragments provided an opening for heat from the burning powder. Therefore, instead of exploding, the shells were merely burning, spewing fire and smoke through the openings. Lorenz's mind summoned memories of boyhood firecrackers and "cat-and-dog fight," the tendency of a small firecracker to hiss and snap but not explode when it is broken in half and lit.

The two sailors in the box were both burned but were busy isolating the sizzling shells and trying to put out the fires. There was little room in there, and Lorenz realized he would be in the way. He climbed back to the gun mount on top of the ready magazine.

Gunner's Mate Edward Zimmerle was dying. Concerned that the one-point-one gun at Mount Three might fail to properly eject empty shells and jam—a continuing problem with the weapon—Zimmerle had been lying on his back under the gun with tools, ready to make repairs if it jammed. He had been a Golden Gloves boxing champion in Nashville, Tennessee.

"I saw Zimmerle," Lorenz recalled later. "His eyes were closed. He was pale. He opened his eyes and our glances met. He was trying to tell me something."

A doctor came by and Lorenz asked him to look at Zimmerle.

"He finally got around to him," Lorenz said. "I asked him if Zimmerle would make it, and he shook his head. When he moved on, I stayed with Zimmerle. He was in great pain and asked me to get him a drink of water. I made my way through the wounded and brought him a drink. I lifted his head. He didn't take much. He looked me full in the eyes and his thin, purple lips moved. It was difficult for him to speak.

"'Tell my folks this isn't the end,' he said. But the war had ended for him."

The bomb had killed the trainer, Seaman 1c. Rupert C.

Gibson. Members of the crew said later that only his lower torso and legs remained in his seat on the right side of the battery. But his counterpart on the left side of the battery, Seaman 2c. Harold Davies, was still in his pointer's seat, unscratched.

Davies was reared on a farm near Dillsboro, Indiana, one of twelve children. He and his older brother, James, joined the Navy in Cincinnati in August 1940. Before the war was over, another Davies brother, Howard, also would be in the Navy and two more, Francis and Delano, would be in the Army. Besides that, the husbands of three of their sisters were in the Army. Altogether, Harold Davies's mother had five sons and three sons-in-law in combat at the same time. All came back from the war alive, although Howard, who had suffered a head wound, died a few years later of a cerebral hemorrhage.

"Zimmerle was hit really bad," Harold Davies recalled. "I guess a big piece of bomb came up and hit him. The pointer was on the left and the trainer was on the right. The trainer was killed. I was just lucky. Johnson was leaning up against the rail next to Lorenz, I think, and he was killed too."

Davies continued to fire the one-point-one, even though the water jacket had been blown away, and there was no trainer to move the barrels from side to side. When the uncooled barrel became too hot to fire, he stopped. Later, he was awarded the Silver Star.

Killed instantly was Seaman 2c. Pearl Greison Prince of Bradenton, Florida. The quiet, twenty-four-year-old Prince's personal sadness, the deaths of his wife and baby in a car wreck a few months earlier, had inspired the sympathy of his shipmates.

Chief Gunner's Mate Albert S. Noland was wounded but not critically. He did his best to fix guns damaged by the explosion and began loading for Davies. Eighteen-year-old Seaman 2c. D. M. Smith, "painfully and severely wounded with bomb splinters in his back and both legs," helped

Nolan load the gun, according to an officer's recommendation that he be cited for gallantry.

The bomb blew a 12-foot hole in the flight deck. Fragments sprayed the hangar deck and several more men were killed there.

Harold Davies's brother James was a gunner's mate and his battle station was high on the island structure, where four .50-caliber machine guns were deployed.

The second bomb did not tumble. One sailor said it looked "like a big, black bowling ball" descending on the ship.

It penetrated the flight deck and a succession of decks below before crashing though the side of the huge stacks through which air was drawn down to the boiler fires. Exploding in the air uptakes, the bomb literally blew out the oil fires in five of the ship's six boilers. The steam that had been driving the *Yorktown*'s turbines stopped.

The blast also roared back up the air intakes and the ship's smokestack. It ripped soot and unburned oil out of the stack and sent an enormous cloud of smoke and fire rolling over the ship.

The Japanese pilots were holding their bombs and not releasing them until they were only 500 feet above the ship, according to Buckmaster's after-action report. For them, this strategy appeared to deliver the result it produced for the *Yorktown*'s Ens. John "Jo-Jo" Powers at the Battle of the Coral Sea: While it greatly improved their accuracy, it reduced their chances of survival to approximately zero. Buckmaster said he was convinced that none of the seven that made it past the Wildcat interceptors and antiaircraft fire from ships in the *Yorktown*'s screen survived.

A third bomb hit the forward elevator, penetrated to the third deck and exploded in a rag locker, setting fire to the rags. It also broke open crates of powdered soap stored above the rags and as the soap poured from the crates, it did much to smother the fires. They were doused with water and put out—almost. Just forward of the rag locker and below it was a tank containing thousands of gallons of aviation fuel and magazines containing ammunition for antiaircraft guns. The magazines were immediately flooded with water.

Little has been said about the fourth bomb. It near-missed and exploded close astern in the water. Fragments flew up onto the fantail, killed two men and started small fires.

While the battle was underway, Machinist Corl and his radioman-gunner, Lloyd Childers, finally reached the point where Corl's dead reckoning told him the *Yorktown* should have been. When he did not find it, he began to backtrack along the ship's intended course. Corl's oil pressure gauge had been reading zero for miles and Childers had lost so much blood from the wounds in both legs that whenever he lifted his head, he passed out.

"We can't land on that ship," Corl said into the intercom when he spotted the *Yorktown*, dead in the water.

"Why not?" Childers mumbled.

"Can't you see that hole in the deck?" Corl replied.

But Childers could not lift his head, so he could not see the hole or the hundreds of sailors who stood on the flight deck and watched him and Corl slowly pass the ship at low altitude. The silent group of seamen included Childers's brother, Wayne. Several other Torpedo Three enlisted men pointed out to Wayne that Lloyd was not moving in the rear seat and was probably dead.

The *Hornet* and the *Enterprise* were 40 miles away. Corl headed for them.

"Standby to hit the water," he said a few minutes later and crash-landed the Devastator near a destroyer, the *Monaghan*.

The life raft was stowed in the middle cockpit, and as soon as the plane was in the water, Corl hurried to get it out and inflate it. However, oil from his engine had blown back over the canopy, making it too slick to open.

Still in his rear cockpit, Childers saw the destroyer lowering a whaleboat to rescue them.

"We don't need it," Corl shouted, referring to the life raft. "Let's go." He jumped into the water and Childers slid over the side of his cockpit, wearing his inflated Mae West life jacket. Corl grabbed the life jacket and tried to tow Childers away from the plane as it sank. In a few minutes, the whaleboat arrived and a crew member shoved a boat hook at Corl. He shouted for them to take Childers on first. There was a doctor on the whaleboat. He laid Childers face-down on the floor of the boat and began pressing his back. Water squirted out of Childers's mouth. Later, aboard the *Monaghan*, the doctor told him that had he gone another 30 minutes without medical attention, he would have died.

19

Two hours after he sent the "Val" bombers to attack the *Yorktown*, Yamaguchi ordered a second-wave attack by 10 "Kate" torpedo bombers, escorted by six Zeroes.

Of course, "Kate" was the plane's American nickname. The Japanese knew it as the Nakajima B5N2, Type 97, carrier attack plane, and if the Devastator was slow and awkward, the "Kate" was anything but. It had a top speed of 235 miles per hour.

Lt. Joichi Tomonaga, the man who had sent the message from Midway telling Nagumo a second attack on the islands appeared to be necessary, insisted on leading the torpedo attack on the *Yorktown*. However, as planes were being readied for the second-wave attack, deck crews informed Tomonaga that one gas tank of his plane had been "holed" and there had not been time to repair it. He told them to fill the other tank and get his plane ready to take off. Although a single tank of gasoline likely would not be sufficient to get him to the U.S. carrier and back, Tomonaga brushed aside tearful pleas from other pilots to be allowed to exchange planes with him. The other nine torpedo planes and six escort Zeroes lined up behind Tomonaga and took off at about 1 o'clock in the afternoon. The deck was hushed because no man on the ship, including Yamaguchi, believed Tomonaga would be able to return.

With three fleet carriers in flames, Yamamoto set out to regroup. He ordered two small carriers that had covered the Aleutian invasion force—which had taken two nearly unpopulated islands without U.S. resistance—to move south and rendezvous with Yamaguchi's *Hiryu*. Admiral Kondo, who was holding back 600 miles south with the invasion troop transports, radioed Yamamoto that he was sending battleships, cruisers and destroyers north at 28 knots.

Yamamoto also was informed that the *Yorktown* had been bombed. Despite losing three carriers, he could still have the American force outgunned.

With the *Yorktown* dead in the water, Fletcher moved his flag to the *Astoria*, one of the carrier's cruisers. His executive officer, Capt. Lewis Spencer, several other members of his staff and some enlisted men, including Marine orderly Henry L. Boitnott and Yeoman Frank Boo, accompanied him. As they moved from one ship to the other on a whaleboat, they encountered hundreds of empty brass powder casings from the five-inch guns bobbing in the water. Thrown overboard, the brass casings had begun to fill with water. The open ends had sunk, causing the shells to turn to a vertical position and capturing air inside. They looked awfully like submarine periscopes, Boo recalled.

In fact, he would remember the half-hour whaleboat ride to the Astoria as the most tense event of the day. Everyone on the boat was concerned about submarines or being strafed overhead, Boo said.

Repair crews and medical corpsmen swarmed over the flight deck of the *Yorktown*. In about 30 minutes, carpenters had the bomb hole patched with beams and steel plates.

Ensign Lorenz continued to do what he could for members of his gun crew. Johnson, the tough, hard-boiled gun captain, was still alive. Lorenz dragged him to the edge of the ready magazine and, with the help of a sailor who happened by, eased him to the flight deck. Together they started carrying him to the dressing station, immediately below the flight deck. By the time they got there, he was dead.

"I went back to the flight deck," Lorenz wrote. "The ship had no way on her now. She was dead in the water as a result of a direct bomb hit on the intakes. It was now, for the first time, that I actually knew what had happened. I looked around me and in a few seconds saw the entire scene. Dead and wounded lay everywhere, and debris was scattered all around. We were in bad shape, stopped dead in the water and burning in numerous places.

"Suddenly, I heard cheers. I saw men waving their hats and shouting."

Lorenz looked up. Someone had taken down the small ensign that normally flew aft of the island structure and run up a larger Stars-and-Stripes, at least 10 feet wide and 15 feet long, he said.

He went back to his gun mount and found Seaman 2c. William Sullivan of Grand Rapids, Michigan, badly wounded but trying to stand. With help, Lorenz got Sullivan to the dressing station below and gave him a shot of morphine.

But the greatest emergency was five decks below. Smoke and fumes filled the engine room, and there was no immediate way of knowing how badly the boilers and fire rooms had been damaged by the bomb that detonated in the air uptakes. Only Boiler No. 1 remained in operation. The explosion had knocked loose many of its insulating firebricks and soon the outside of the firebox was starting to glow, red hot. The fires in Boilers 2, 3, 4, 5 and 6 were blown out.

In charge of Boiler No. 1 was Water Tender 1c. Charles Kleinsmith of Long Beach, California. Originally from Zionsville, Pennsylvania, Kleinsmith was 37. He had enlisted in 1922 and served on a battleship, the U.S.S. *Wyoming*. He moved to cruisers, the *Cincinnati*, the *Milwaukee*, the *Portland* and others, working his way up the rates as a water tender. He went on the *Saratoga* as a water tender first class in 1939 and, in November 1940, moved to the *Yorktown.* His wife, Mary, and their three-year-old son, Charles Jr., were at Long Beach.

Although an officer ordered crewmen to leave the boiler rooms, Kleinsmith threatened and cajoled his crew of six to remain. Boiler No. 1 was the only source of steam for the generators that would power blowers, pumps and other auxiliary equipment necessary to repair the ship—if it could be repaired. They closed the throttle and got the heat under control, enough to maintain 180 pounds of steam pressure and run the auxiliaries. The compartment was filled with smoke from fires, fumes from the bomb explosion and soot from the turmoil inside the air intakes and stacks. Somehow, Kleinsmith kept his crew together and Boiler No. 1 going while engineers inspected the bomb damage.

At 1:30 P.M., one hour and 10 minutes after the bomb had exploded in the air uptakes, the engine crews had Boilers 4, 5, and 6 repaired well enough to get them back on line. Kleinsmith's No. 1, which was leaking fumes into the air uptakes of the other three boilers, was then shut down. Even with only three boilers, the engine room reported to Buckmaster that it could deliver 20 knots, maybe a little more if need be.

Lorenz recalled that he was still on the flight deck when he "felt a little motion, like we were getting underway again. I looked up at the yardarm, and they were flying the speed flags. I watched as they went up. First it said 5, then 6, then 7 and so on, and pretty soon it was up to about 13 knots. That was pretty good after getting pounded like that."

Buckmaster had only six Wildcats flying combat air patrol over the carrier. They had refueled on one of the other carriers, temporarily relieved by a patrol from the *Hornet*, which was then about 40 miles away. Ten minutes after the ship was underway, repair crews reported to the bridge that fires were sufficiently under control to warrant refueling the fighters on deck. Within minutes, the Yamaguchi torpedo planes were detected on radar. The gas lines were again drained and flooded with carbon dioxide.

There were 10 flyable Wildcats on the ship, and eight had as much as 23 gallons of fuel. Joe Fazio's No. 23 was not one of them. Too badly holed to fly, it had been pushed to the starboard side of the flight deck. Fazio had it "doubled up"—with two lines from the stub of each folded wing and two from the tail to deck cleats. He still hung around the plane, counting the holes in it.

Thach and seven other pilots lined up at the aft end of the flight deck, preparing to take off, even with little fuel.

As he and other plane pushers lined up the fighters, Seaman 2c. Joe Wetherington happened to be standing on a spot where oil had spilled on the flight deck, between two planes. When the one in front accelerated to take off, the backwash of its propeller caused him to slip on the oil and slide backwards, under the revving propeller of the next plane. One of his Fighting Forty-two squadron mates, a husky sailor from Oklahoma named Bruce Blocker, rushed over and snatched him from beneath the second plane just before it too roared down the deck. Blocker claimed in his ancestry the "Sooner" settlers who came to the Oklahoma territory, as well as Cherokee and Choctaw Indians who already were there. He was a first cousin of actor Dan Blocker, who two decades later would become a household name as "Hoss Cartwright" on the popular television Western *Bonanza*.

One Wildcat refused to start.

The fighter occupied by Ens. John Paul Adams of Kansas was pushed to one side to allow the next plane to get off. When his squadron mates were in the air, Adams was still gunning the unwilling plane with shell after shell in its shotgun starter. Navy mechanics would learn a few months later that the tubes leading to the engines from the chambers where the shells were fired became clogged with residue and had to be periodically cleaned. That might have been the problem or, as Adams speculated years later, he might have flooded it.

From the *Enterprise*, Spruance had seen the huge cloud of smoke appear on the horizon and assumed the *Yorktown* had been bombed. When notified that the ship was dead in the water, he sent two cruisers, the *Pensacola* and the *Vincennes*, and two destroyers, the *Balch* and the *Benham*, to her assistance. They joined the two cruisers and four destroyers already circling the stricken carrier. When the *Yorktown* gradually got underway, the screen steamed with it.

Captain Frank L. Lowe, commander of the *Pensacola*, was about a mile to the carrier's port when the torpedo planes were visually sighted by scout planes, 18 miles to his own port side. Five-inch guns and eight-inch guns on the *Portland* opened up on the "Kates" when they got into range. They were already being attacked by *Wildcats* in the combat air patrol and two had been shot down. The others kept coming. Fighter pilots radioed back that the intruders were carrying torpedoes.

The Japanese planes disappeared in clouds and when they appeared again, they were about 10 miles out, Lowe said, and were flying in a formation that indicated that five of them would pass ahead of his ship and three astern, trying to get to the *Yorktown*. His five-inch guns opened fire but failed to stop any of the "Kates," which by then were rapidly decreasing their altitude in steep glides as they prepared to swoop low over the water and drop their "fish."

When they came into range of the *Pensacola*'s 1.1-inch guns, she opened up with those guns. Still, the Japanese carrier attack planes came.

Soon, the leading torpedo planes were between the *Yorktown* and the *Pensacola*, almost skimming the water as they maneuvered to drop their torpedoes. Firing into the water in front of them, the *Yorktown*'s five-inch guns created reverse torrents of sea water. One plane cartwheeled over a wall of water and fell into the ocean. The others flew through it.

With the torpedo planes between them, the *Yorktown* and the *Pensacola* were firing just about everything they had directly toward each other.

"Both ships accepted the danger in an effort to stop those planes," Captain Lowe said. Thach and the four other fighter pilots who had taken off with him had been racing to intercept the torpedo planes. They flew into the antiaircraft fire and shot down several planes.

One Japanese torpedo plane was nearing the point where the pilot would release his torpedo when Thach took up chase.

"I made a good side approach on him and got him on fire," Thach recalled. "The whole left wing was burning, and I could see the ribs showing through the flames, and that devil stayed in the air until he got close enough and dropped his torpedo and that one hit the *Yorktown*. So, he was a dedicated Japanese torpedo plane pilot. Even though he was shot down, he went ahead and dropped his torpedo. He fell in the water very close to the ship. . . ."

Later comparison of Japanese and U.S. records of the battle left historians all but certain that the plane Thach downed was flown by Tomonaga. Another Japanese pilot said he watched Tomonaga lead the attack on the *Yorktown* and "in the next instant" after he dropped his torpedo, his plane disintegrated.

Ensign Adams's plane finally kicked over and started. He sputtered down the flight deck, manualizing the fuel pump in order to keep his RPMs up. He could tell the five-inch guns were firing on the port side. The Wildcat's tendency to bank left was for once a valuable asset, and Adams turned as sharply as he could, simultaneously cranking up the landing gear.

Adams turned into the antiaircraft fire and saw two torpedo planes, closing in on the *Yorktown*.

"I don't think I ever got much higher than 1,000 feet," he recalled later, "because I saw them coming. They were still over to my left."

"The first one was going too fast; he was going faster than I was," Adams said. "I think he was doing 175 or so. It was apparent that I wasn't going to get him. He just zipped on by, but the other one was coming and I was able to get on his tail and hit him."

Adams banked around and looked for more planes but had to clear out when gunners on a destroyer, mistaking him for the enemy, began to fire at him. He wobbled his wings in a friendly signal, but that didn't seem to satisfy them.

One plane dropped its torpedo and banked close to the carrier. Dozens of men on the flight deck and hangar deck said they saw the rear-seater in the "Kate" shake his fist at them as the plane flew by. Later, there was speculation that this may not have been an angry gesture, as *Yorktown* crewmen had assumed for over half a century, but a Japanese radioman's joyous reaction to the realization that his plane was not going to crash into the side of the carrier.

In a letter to the author, former Japanese radioman Giichi Hamada said it was he who waved his fist when the plane passed the *Yorktown*.

"I confirm the story about waving my fist," he wrote. "When our airplane dropped the torpedo, our plane was in bad condition because of American antiaircraft fire and fighters. When I saw three Japanese ships burning because of the bombing, I was filled with the feeling, 'I'll pay you back for this.'"

He also wrote that as his plane returned to the *Hiryu*, he was shot in the leg "by a pursuing Grumman [Wildcat]."

"While these events were taking place, I keenly realized what war was!" Hamada said, a comment that was remarkably similar to the observation of his American radioman-gunner counterpart Lloyd Childers, who, after being shot in the leg by an enemy fighter, realized fully that "war is not a football game."

Hamada added, "I believe we will have no more tragedy

of war. Instead, there will be peace and good relationship with your country forever."

As he had before, Buckmaster attempted to escape from the torpedoes by taking the *Yorktown* into radical turns, and he wrote in his after-action report that he had evaded "at least two" of them.

But in the end, the old girl just wasn't up to another go. The waltzing Matilda of the Pacific Fleet was all danced out and, with a top speed of only 20 knots, Buckmaster could not get away from all of them.

Two torpedoes exploded into the carrier on the port side.

"As the smoke cleared, the big carrier lost way and finally came to a dead stop," wrote *New York Times* correspondent Foster Hailey in a dispatch Navy censors held up for three months.

Hailey said he and officers of an unnamed cruiser had watched from the bridge as the torpedoes exploded in the carrier's side.

"Where the torpedoes had hit, girders could be seen, twisted and broken like match sticks. Debris littered her deck. Slowly she began to turn on her side.

"'My God, she's going to capsize,' an officer said, almost in a whisper."

Jerry Lemberger was striking for a job as electrician on a crew that worked way below decks, setting switches according to a gunnery officer's direction to control the fire of five-inch guns.

Their instructions were communicated over the ship's system of voice-powered telephones. The force of the talker's voice on the microphone in each unit generated a weak electric current sufficient to carry the voice to the listener on the other end of the line.

Lemberger heard the announcement on the ship intercom.

"Torpedo attack. Port quarter. We're going to be hit."

He was two decks below the waterline, working in a compartment that was in the port quarter of the ship. He and his fellow electricians silently exchanged glances, waited.

David Pattison had been peppering away at the approaching torpedo planes with his jury-rigged .30-caliber machine gun on the port-side catwalk. Beside him was a friend named Ed Duckwall. Bill Surgi, Pattison's fellow ordnanceman in Fighting Forty-two, had taken cover in a storage compartment under the flight deck. When he saw that the torpedoes were going to hit the ship, Surgi started yelling to Pattison, "Duck! Duck!"

Pattison thought somebody was calling Duckwall and continued to look for targets.

One deck below, Joseph Lewis saw the torpedoes coming and, in obedience to a sailor's instinct, hit the deck, falling on his stomach with his arms outstretched.

Each torpedo detonated with a force greater than the combined energy of all four bombs that had hit the *Yorktown* in her two great sea battles. The first explosion shook the ship, but the second heaved it upward violently. For the only time in his life, Lewis was knocked to his feet.

The explosions were several compartments away from that containing the fire control switchboard. Lemberger and the other electricians heard them, felt them, survived them. The compartment suddenly went dark as all steam and electric power on the ship failed. Somebody turned on a flashlight and the crew watched in silent horror as the angle of the water surface in a drinking jar began to tilt—more. And more. And more.

The steadily increasing list of the ship finally stabilized at 26 degrees.

The second torpedo had sent a geyser sweeping up the side of the ship with such force that it ripped the catwalk where Pattison was standing loose from its weldings and pushed it back against the hull. He was pinned in a tangle of metal. A piece of angle iron was driven through his thigh and he could not move. Surgi crawled out of his refuge under the flight deck and had to crawl over Pattison to get onto the deck. He started yelling for a corpsman.

Some men who had been standing on the port side of the ship when the torpedoes exploded had chosen not to lie down, and had their ankles broken by the violent upheaving.

And others were killed.

They included the heroic Charles Kleinsmith, who less than two hours earlier had browbeaten his crew of young sailors into keeping Boiler No. 1 in operation. In the end, it was this action, perhaps more than any other, that made it possible to get other boilers back on line and the ship moving again.

Had Yamaguchi's torpedo planes found the *Yorktown* dead in the water, it would have been a helpless target for them. Had it not gotten up to 13 knots, it would have been unable to launch Thach and five other fighter pilots—and one more exploding torpedo might have sunk or capsized it. It could be said that most of the more than 2,500 members of the *Yorktown* crew owed their lives to Water Tender 1c. Charles Kleinsmith, who was posthumously awarded the Navy Cross and promoted to chief.

20

It took Buckmaster only about 15 minutes to decide to abandon the ship.

As Pete Montalvo lay wrapped in bandages in a battle dressing station, he could see sailors clawing their way onto the steep stairs at one end of the compartment. In addition to their normally steep angle, the stairs were leaning to the side because the *Yorktown* was listing heavily, making them even harder to climb. Big flashlights, called battle lanterns, the only light available in the darkened, powerless vessel, were swinging wildly from the hands of some of the men.

Montalvo said the medical corpsman's voice froze the scrambling sailors. "Hey, I need help getting these wounded men out of here," the corpsman shouted. Several immediately came back to help get Montalvo and other wounded men to the hangar deck.

Buckmaster's first order, immediately after the second torpedo exploded, was for gunners to prepare for another attack. Ammunition was replenished and the batteries made ready to fire again. The ship was now dead in the water and listing to port, the side hit by the two torpedoes. While the captain consulted with his damage control officer, Cdr. C. E.

Aldrich, and engineering officer, Lt. Cdr. J. F. Delaney, the list increased steadily. Delaney reported that seawater had flooded the engine room and put out boiler fires, and all power was lost. An auxiliary diesel generator was operative, but electrical switchboards had been destroyed and there was no way to use whatever power the generator could produce. Without power, Aldrich pointed out, pumps that would be necessary to empty flooded compartments could not be operated. No one really knew what shape the many hatches and bulkheads were in following the hurried Pearl Harbor repair effort or how much further the *Yorktown* could list without capsizing. The worst nightmare of all was that the ship would "turn turtle," roll over with her keel up and trap most of the crew inside.

Buckmaster told Delaney and Aldrich to "direct all personnel to lay up on deck and put on life preservers."

But a few seconds after he issued this preliminary order, the ship lunged to port is if to capsize, according to Lieutenant Edward Kearney, the junior medical officer. The list then seemed to stabilize at 26 degrees, but Buckmaster had seen enough. He ordered the *Yorktown* abandoned.

"In order to save as many of the ship's company as possible, the commanding officer ordered the ship to be abandoned," he wrote in his action report to Nimitz. "The ship was in total darkness below decks, and it was very difficult to move around because of the heavy list."

The abandon-ship order was passed through the voice-powered telephone system and word-of-mouth. Ropes were dropped over the side. The ship would be abandoned from the high side, away from the direction in which it threatened to capsize. Thousands of kapok-filled life jackets had been stowed in large canvas bags overhead on the hangar deck. When ropes attached to the bags were pulled they opened and life jackets came raining onto the deck.

Minutes after they were ordered to abandon the *Yorktown*, hundreds of enlisted men and officers were climbing down the ropes and dropping into the water. Destroyers moved in as close to the *Yorktown* as they could and got ready to pick up survivors. Destroyer captains also sent whaleboats to take on wounded men, who were being lowered on stretchers.

Montalvo said two sailors helped him up the crazily slanting stairs to the hangar deck.

"I remember, two fellows were helping me and my shoulder was hurting like hell," he recalled. When he finally got to the hangar deck, he picked up a life jacket and realized for the first time that with his left arm immobilized under bandages he could not climb down a rope. At that moment, Seaman 1c. John Pallay of Linden, New Jersey, happened by. The two had been to boot camp together.

"You okay, Pete?"

"I don't think I can get down one of those ropes with my shoulder like this," Montalvo replied.

"I'll get you down," Pallay said. "You can stand on my shoulders."

Pallay climbed a few feet down a rope and Montalvo eased over the side. With his one good hand and Pallay's two good shoulders, he made it to the water.

A sailor took off his shoes before grabbing a rope and left them on the edge of the deck. Another came along and put his shoes neatly beside those. Then another. Soon, hundreds of shoes lay in a row along the edge of hangar deck, as if the owners expected to return in a few minutes and put them back on.

James "Chick" Liner left his battle station for the first time that day. He had worried for two hours about Curtis Owens, his best friend from Buffalo, South Carolina. He had talked Owens into joining the Navy, then turned down a chance to go to cook and baker school so they could be together on the *Yorktown*. Owens had endured unmerciful kidding about his huge nose and other sailors had nicknamed him "Pelican."

Liner knew Owens's battle station had been at Mount

Four, the one where every man was either killed or wounded in the bombing attack. Although he could not leave his own battle station at the starboard forward five-inch gun, he had learned from deck talk that Owens's gunmount had been wiped out.

He headed for Mount Four, making his way across the sloping flight deck. A photograph shows a sailor Liner would later say was he, still wearing his metal battle helmet, walking beside the island structure.

"Did anybody get off the ship?" he asked a pharmacist's mate, who was still at the mount. He was told some wounded men were taken to the dressing station immediately below the flight deck. He climbed down the stairs to the dressing station, found a flashlight and looked around. There were several men still lying on tables. They appeared to be dead. He went from one to the other with the battle lantern. None of those whose faces he could see was Owens. One sailor had had his entire head wrapped in bandages.

"I held the light over him and I saw that nose, sticking out of the bandages," Liner recalled years later. "When I saw his big old long nose, I knew it was him. . . . He was shot all to pieces. They'd knocked him out with morphine."

Still not knowing whether Owens was alive or dead, Liner picked him up and put him over his shoulder like a sack of corn and climbed back to the flight deck, then down other stairs to the hangar deck. With help, he got Owens—who was alive—onto a stretcher and down to a waiting life raft. Then he climbed down behind him. He was told to get into the raft with the wounded sailor and did so.

The torpedoes had broken open fuel tanks on the port side and tons of fuel oil oozed out onto the surface. Soon the ship was surrounded by a huge oil slick. Sailors had to swim through it. Many gulped oil and became wretchedly ill in the water. Others were sickened by the fumes.

Seaman 1c. Louis Rulli of Astoria, New York, climbed down a fire hose from the hangar deck.

"I dropped off the end of the fire hose about 15 feet from the water and when I hit, I got a mouthful of oil and started choking," Rulli wrote decades later in the *Yorktown Crier*, a publication of the U.S.S. *Yorktown* Club. "I kept trying to get the oil out of my mouth when I spotted a shipmate, James Liner. I called out to him. He seemed to be sitting on top of the water. He grabbed my life jacket and asked, 'What's the matter?' He was sitting in a life raft! I held onto the raft while I cleaned out my mouth and eventually quit coughing. Thanks, Liner."

Owens and Liner were picked up by a destroyer and transferred later to the *Fulton*, a submarine tender that was sent out from Pearl Harbor to bring back survivors. Owens was placed in the *Fulton*'s sickbay and Liner remained with him. Even at night, he slept on the deck beside Owens's bunk until they got back to Pearl Harbor.

Not all the men who left the ship were choking on oil.

Petty Officer Harvey Wilder of Doerun, Georgia, said in an interview in the *Atlanta Journal* three months later that some sailors amused each other by waving hitchhike thumbs at passing debris and calling, "Taxi! Taxi!" Wilder, son of the pastor of Doerun Baptist Church, said officers and enlisted men in one life raft were singing "The Beer Barrel Polka."

The Navy would not acknowledge the carrier was lost until September 16, over three months later. The Associated Press called it a "well-kept naval secret." A *Chicago Tribune* Washington correspondent called it "an open capital secret."

In a San Francisco interview picked up by the Associated Press, Chief Water Tender George Vavreck of Portsmouth, Virginia, said he and his engine room crew were unaware of the abandon-ship order until they heard men scrambling up stairs.

A member of his engine gang opened a hatch and called up, "What's everybody doing?"

"Hell, we're abandoning ship!" someone called back down.

Ship's cook Thomas L. J. Saxon stowed his pet white rabbit in a gas mask bag and he and the rabbit survived.

Before leaving the ship, Lorenz decided to slip back to his room and retrieve the photograph of a freshman drama student he had met at a dance when he was still attending Portland University. He had decided he would marry her when he got out of the Navy. He slipped her picture into his cap and went back to the hangar deck, where Cdr. M. E. Arnold, the air officer, told him to get off the ship.

First, Lorenz climbed to the flight deck. Buckmaster was on the top deck, urging members of the crew to leave the ship.

"You know, I can't leave until you leave," some would remember him saying.

Lorenz said he wanted to make sure no living sailors were still in the dressing station.

"There were red lanterns in there, and I got this lantern and looked around at all the bodies. I put the red lantern over this one guy, Sullivan, and he blinked his eyes. I knew then he was alive and I had to get him up to the flight deck. But I couldn't get him back up those stairs, because he was a big husky kid. I was stranded there. Pretty soon this other officer came by. I told him there was a blanket down on the hangar deck at the after elevator pit. I'll stay here with him if you go get the blanket. So he went after it."

The two young officers wrapped Bill Sullivan of Grand Rapids, Michigan, in the blanket and somehow got him up to the flight deck. With a rope, they dragged him across the deck and got ready to lower him into the water. Because of the list, the deck was 60 feet from the surface, Lorenz estimated.

They tied their life jackets to Sullivan.

"I said, 'One of us has got to go in. We can't just throw him over the side here,'" Lorenz recalled. "He jumped in and I lowered Sullivan down on the line to him. Then I climbed down the line."

Almost as soon as Lorenz hit the water, a swell caught him in the face and washed away his cap, along with the picture he had gone below to retrieve. Sullivan was badly wounded and only intermittently conscious. Lorenz and the other officer hung on to a timber leftover from the flight deck repair work and tossed overboard after the torpedo attack. Lorenz kept urging Sullivan to hang on and telling him about the girl whose photograph had just disappeared into the sea. He told the sailor he intended to marry her.

"Bill, if you survive, I'll name my son after you when I have one."

Somehow, Bill Sullivan survived.

Bill Surgi crawled out of his refuge under the flight deck and was making his way to stairs leading down to the hangar deck and the ropes over the side. He passed Joe Fazio, still hanging around Wildcat fighter No. 23. By then, Fazio had the plane tripled-up, with three ropes on each wing stub and three on the tail.

"Hey, Joe, we're leaving," Surgi called. "Why don't you get in there and take the clock out of that thing? It'd make a great souvenir."

"Oh no, I could never do that," Surgi recalled Fazio replying. (Fazio recalled his reply was, "To hell with the clock.") A short time later, Fazio left his much-loved plane behind and climbed down into the water.

Surgi's elbow had been broken, but he was able to get off the ship. Contrary to an officer's orders, he kept a metal battle helmet he had been wearing as a souvenir of the *Yorktown*. He took it with him 56 years later when he accompanied undersea explorer Robert Ballard on the expedition that located the *Yorktown*.

Mess Attendant Thomas E. Allen had been sent "down to the hole," the sailors' term for the magazine where shells for the antiaircraft guns on the deck were stored. He and other black crew members loaded the 50-pound shells and their powder casings onto a conveyor belt, which carried them to an elevator and up to the deck. Growing up in Richmond, Virginia, Allen had been encouraged by his high school principal to consider military service and, following graduation, had attended a brief civilian military training camp at Ft. Meade, Maryland.

However, when he enlisted in 1939 and found himself on the *Yorktown* in January 1940, the Navy had decided he should be a mess attendant.

"It was strictly a racial decision," he recalled years later, and although he was trained as a loader on an antiaircraft gun, most of his time was spent either cleaning up the living quarters of officers, keeping track of Officers' Mess supplies or working "in the hole" with stored ammunition.

When the order came to abandon the ship, Allen recalled later, the crew scrambled out of the magazine and up the now-canted stairs along the emergency evacuation route they had been drilled to follow. However, not far from "the hole" they encountered disappointment of the worst kind. A hatch had been blown in the Battle of the Coral Sea and during the rush at Pearl Harbor, repair crews had apparently decided they did not have time to fix it and merely welded it shut. Allen would remember more than 50 years later the feeling of fear hardening into panic in his chest.

Then he remembered his grandmother and a lesson from childhood. As a little boy, whenever he would get too excited to talk, she would stop him and insist that he take a deep breath and turn around three times.

"I didn't let the other guys see me turning around," he recalled, "but I took a deep breath, and I turned around in my mind. Three times." With his nerves thus settled, Allen turned to another route through the dark, listing ship and within a few minutes they were out.

Judson Brodie had grown up on a farm near Aiken, South Carolina, hoping he could someday attend Clemson University. As his high school graduation approached, his regretful father told him there was no money for Clemson.

Jud joined the Navy, became an ordnanceman and went to the *Yorktown* with Fighting Forty-two.

After swimming for what seemed like a very long time, he and other men reached the *Balch* and climbed up a net that had been draped over the side of the destroyer.

"None of us rescued by the *Balch* will ever forget the men of that ship," Brodie wrote in a brief history of Fighting Forty-two. "They opened their lockers and gave us everything they had. A *Balch* sailor took one of his blankets and tore it, giving me half and the other half to another survivor.

"I went up into one of the forward five-inch ammunition handling rooms and sat with some of the ship company men at their general quarters station. They were eating canned strawberries. I ate some and was told by one of the men that during all of the excitement of the battle, they had raided the officers' pantry. They were good berries. One of the men told me that he would be on duty all night and that I could use his bunk, a kindness I shall never forget.

"I brought my half-blanket with me and kept it throughout the war. My wife bound it and all three of our children used it as infants. I still have it and wish I knew the name of the man on the Balch who gave it to me. . . ."

Far below decks in the *Yorktown*, Jerry Lemberger and other members of the fire control crew waited in darkness. The torpedo had hit only a compartment or so abaft the one in which they were working. From time to time, they would use a lantern to check the terrible angle of the water in a glass drinking jug. Lemberger kept shouting "Hello" into a voice-powered telephone. Although there was no response, he thought he could hear sounds, maybe voices, on the other end. So he kept shouting and finally somebody picked up the phone.

"Eventually, a guy up in the forward gun director on top of the ship heard me," Lemberger recalled. "He said, 'Jerry, we're abandoning ship. You guys are supposed to be dead, because that's where the torpedoes hit.'

"They'd been abandoning ship for about 15 minutes and we didn't know it. We didn't have power or anything. The sound-powered phones got us out of there," Lemberger said.

They shone a lantern through a glass porthole in the hatch at one end of the fire-control compartment and determined that the next compartment was not flooded. The adjacent compartment was known informally as "Central Station" because several other compartments adjoined it. From the central compartment an escape tube ran to the upper decks. It had a ladder in it, but water was flooding into it from a compartment above them. They checked a hatch at the other end of Central Station and found it was not flooded. They cranked open the deadbolt-like "dogs" that held the hatch shut and climbed the stairs to the next hatch. One by one, they undogged hatches and kept climbing through the darkened ship.

When they got to the mess deck, they shone their lights around at the devastation.

"The deck up there was peeled back like you open a can," Lemberger recalled. "The torpedo had exploded below that and had just bent it back. We didn't hang around there long. We got up to the hangar deck next and there wasn't anybody around. The skipper, the exec, the first lieutenant, I think, the gunnery officer, they were up there and that's all I remember recognizing. There was maybe only 15 or 20 people. A few officers and guys that had just come from below decks were up there. We looked around for life jackets and there weren't any.

"An officer told me to get off the ship. I said, 'I don't have a life jacket,' and he said, 'Get off anyway. It's going to capsize.'"

Chicken Underwood also had business below decks that couldn't wait—the poker winnings he had stashed in his locker. When he thought no one was looking, he slipped through a hatch and headed down to the Fighting Forty-two compartment. Soon he was back on the hangar deck with his winnings—but there were no more lifejackets. An officer happened by and got a pilot's inflatable life jacket and handed it to Underwood. There was a brown canvas pilot's helmet with it, so Underwood put on the helmet too.

Then he did something that wasn't very smart. Rather than climb down a rope into the water, Underwood walked to the port side of the hangar deck, which had sunk to the point that it was only a few feet above the surface. He stepped off into the water and started swimming away from the ship. But when he looked around there were no destroyers in sight. They were on the other side of the carrier, picking up survivors.

There was at least one occasion when destroyer crews thought they had spotted a submarine periscope and the ships went to general quarters and took off in pursuit of the suspected U-boat. It turned out to be a false alarm, but several survivors would recall years later the frustration of swimming for what seemed like hours to get to a destroyer and have it suddenly rush away. Underwood's reliable luck came through for him when one of the destroyers was returning from chasing a phantom submarine and a member of its crew spotted his brown "pilot's helmet" above the water.

If the ship had capsized, David Pattison and the men working to free him from the tangle of iron that kept him pinned on the flight deck catwalk on the port side likely would have been doomed. Pattison was conscious but could not move.

Although he had shrapnel wounds in his leg from the bombing attack, Warrant Officer Chester E. Briggs Jr. of Minneapolis led a party of several men onto the precariously hanging catwalk to try to rescue Pattison. They could not move the metal that had the Fighting Forty-two ordnanceman pinned and skewered. Briggs remained with Pattison while others went for an airplane jack.

Briggs had enlisted in the Navy as an apprentice seaman

in 1930. He had moved around a lot before coming to the *Yorktown* as a flight deck plane director, a job that was something like a traffic cop for carrier aircraft. He probably never knew that the man working beside him as they jacked the bent metal off Pattison was also from Minneapolis. He was Marine Corporal Peter Kikos, who had stayed on the ship "to the last, searching for and removing wounded men while the ship was believed to be in immediate danger of turning over," the ship's executive officer said in recommending Kikos for a medal and a promotion to sergeant.

The executive officer's memorandum also recommended Briggs for a medal, saying he "repeatedly exposed himself to danger during the bombing attack and was cool and courageous in repairing flight deck equipment while the attack was going on. He was wounded while conducting repair work and fighting fire on the flight deck without protection. After the torpedo attack, and while himself still wounded, he played a major part in freeing shipmates who had been caught and wounded by the curling up of the port catwalk which was caused by the torpedo explosions. This placed him in a precarious position on the low side of the ship without regard for his own personal safety."

They finally got the metal that had pinned David Pattison off of him and pulled the angle iron out of his leg. Pattison, conscious all this time, recalled feeling no pain and joking with Briggs that "one of these days they're going to get rid of all you old warrant officers."

A pilot happened by and used his white silk scarf to make a tourniquet for Pattison's leg. The next challenge was to get Pattison to the high side of the flight deck to be lowered down to a waiting life raft. Kikos said blood from the devastated Gun Mount Four had run down the flight deck toward the port side. This meant the deck was not only sloped, but slick. They tied a rope around Pattison and dragged him 88 feet up the incline to the starboard side.

Pattison recalled years later that he was recovering in the

sickbay of a destroyer from surgery on his leg when he saw in a nearby bunk the sailor who had been shot in the groin on the flight deck at the outset of the bombing attack.

"I'm sorry about your balls," Pattison said.

The sailor grinned.

"I'm going to be all right," he said. "I guess I was just so scared, I had sucked them up into my chest or something."

21

The Wildcat pilots who fought off most of the attacking torpedo planes had been forced to land elsewhere when the ship was hit. Thach flew to the *Enterprise.*

"All this time, I was mad all over again," he recalled. "I was angry because here were the *Enterprise* and the *Hornet* sitting about 50 miles away with combat air patrol, plenty of it, over them and too far away to help the *Yorktown.* There was something wrong with this, and I was unhappy about it. If we'd just had one or two more airplanes in the air to fight this attack, the *Yorktown* would never have been sunk. I'm sure of it."

As soon as Thach had landed on the *Enterprise*, he was told Rear Admiral Spruance wanted to see him on the flag bridge.

"Well, how do you think we're doing?" Spruance asked.

"Admiral, we're winning this battle," Thach replied in his Arkansas drawl. "We've already won it, because I saw with my own eyes three big carriers burning so furiously they'll never launch another airplane.

"Of course, that fourth one . . . An unfound carrier is a dangerous thing. We certainly ought to be able to get him. I think we ought to chase them, because we've got the advantage now."

Thach recalled that Spruance "kind of smiled" at this advice.

"Well, you know we don't have any battleships," he said. "All we have is cruisers, and if we start chasing them, it's going to get dark pretty soon. If we suddenly catch up with them, they may be able to chew us up before we get within gun range at night, and we don't have much of a night attack capability."

"I think they're on the run, and I think we ought to chase them," Thach said.

A short time later, Thach was sent to take over the *Hornet* fighter squadron, then flying combat air patrol over the two carriers. Apparently neither man realized during the conversation that the *Hiryu* had been located by a *Yorktown* scout.

Minutes before it was attacked by Yamaguchi's torpedo planes, the *Yorktown* sent Fletcher a visual signal on the *Astoria*, informing him that a scouting plane had found the *Hiryu*. Coordinates the scout had reported for the *Hiryu* were also signaled to Fletcher. The information was immediately relayed to the *Enterprise* and must have reached Spruance minutes after the brief conversation between him and Thach.

Now the question for Spruance was not whether to pursue the Japanese force with his ships, but whether to launch a bombing attack against the *Hiryu*. In 45 minutes, he had cobbled together a dive-bomber force made up of orphans from the *Yorktown* and the remaining planes in his own Bombing Six.

Following the bombing attack on the *Yorktown*, Yamaguchi was told by pilots of returning Zeroes that his bombs had left a carrier burning out of control. The conclusion was no doubt based on the huge black soot cloud that enfolded the *Yorktown* after a bomb went off in its air intakes.

Two hours later, torpedo plane pilots returned to the *Hiryu* and told the admiral they also had struck and sunk a carrier. In reality, his planes had attacked the *Yorktown* twice—and it was still afloat.

But thinking he had sunk two of three U.S. carriers, he made plans for a third attack in hopes of finishing off the U.S. fleet. He had six Zeroes that would still fly, along with five dive-bombers and four torpedo planes he had not used. He sent the fast reconnaissance plane to locate the target. The exhausted and famished crew was served a meal at 5 P.M.—sweet rice balls—and the men ate voraciously while still at their battle stations.

Most would not finish the meal, for while they were eating Spruance's bombers arrived. Within minutes four bombs had exploded on the *Hiryu* decks. As dusk closed in, enormous, fiery clouds of black smoke boiled into the sky.

At about the same time, a remarkable exchange of messages was taking place between Spruance and Fletcher.

"Task Force 16 air groups are now striking the carrier which your search plane reported," Spruance radioed. "Do you have instructions for me?" Fletcher had been under fire for months, mostly from Admiral Ernest King, the chief of naval operations in Washington. King thought Fletcher did not have the stomach for a fight and urged Nimitz to sack him and put someone else in command of the Midway operation. Nimitz had brushed aside King's advice and responded that he believed Fletcher to be "an excellent . . . fighting naval officer."

Fletcher received Spruance's message while on the *Astoria*. Although realistically he could not command a carrier sea battle from a cruiser, he still was the senior admiral and he could have told Spruance that he was transferring his flag to the *Hornet* and to carry on until the transfer was done. That way, he would have remained technically in command of what appeared likely to be a major victory, not a bad mark to lay on the record next to King's criticism.

But that also would have been a cumbersome, time-consuming, not to say dangerous, procedure. Spruance would have been in charge, yet not in charge, when crucial decisions had to be made. Without hesitation, Fletcher messaged back: "None. Will conform to your movements."

That's the way admirals talk to each other when one of them is transferring his command to the other. Raymond Spruance was now in command.

It had been a long day. Aboard his great battleship *Yamato*, Admiral Yamamoto would learn shortly that the decisive battle he had sought was over and he had lost it.

The *Soryu* sank about 7:15 P.M. and the *Kaga* a few minutes later.

Even though a cruiser was brought alongside to fight fires on the *Hiryu* into the night, it became clear sometime after midnight that the carrier could not be saved. Yamaguchi summoned the crew topside and commanded about 800 men who responded to abandon the ship and "to continue your loyal service to his Majesty, the Emperor." He chose to remain on the ship.

At around dawn, the *Hiryu* was scuttled with torpedoes, while Yamaguchi and Capt. Tameo Kaku, who determined to remain on the *Hiryu* also, waved goodbye.

A few minutes later, the *Akagi* was scuttled also.

Buckmaster remained on the *Yorktown* until he was sure all other survivors were off. According to his action report, he inspected the hangar and flight decks. He then went to the fantail, climbed down and swam to a waiting whaleboat.

His decision to abandon the ship would be criticized forever.

"I was in the carrier until she was abandoned," said M. B. Laing, a British Royal Navy captain aboard the *Yorktown* as an observer. "I watched both torpedoes etc. and had a nice swim until I was picked up by the *Morris*. . . .

"I suppose the best thing Buckmaster could have done

was to get rid of the useless mouths and keep the damage control parties, gun crews, engineers etc., to fight and if possible to save the ship."

By 5:30 P.M., all the survivors had been taken aboard destroyers in the *Yorktown*'s screen. Although no one would ever know how many drowned in the ocean, there were so many reports of sailors assisting each other and giving their life jackets to others, the number is likely very small. Five destroyers reported taking on a total of just over 2,100 men and officers. Fletcher's final report said "about twenty-three hundred" survivors were picked up by destroyers.

With no fighters to defend it, the remainder of Fletcher's task force was vulnerable, so he decided to move it to Task Force 16. He left the destroyer *Hughes* to guard the *Yorktown*.

Although the *Yorktown* was adrift and abandoned, two admirals continued to be interested in her fate. From Pearl Harbor, Nimitz ordered the *Vireo*, a converted minesweeper that occasionally saw duty as a harbor tugboat, to go to the carrier and attempt to take it in tow. The *Vireo* had been standing by a few hundred miles away. A fleet tug was to follow. The *Vireo* was commanded by Lieutenant James C. Legg, who was 52 years old and had been commissioned the previous month, after years as a Navy enlisted man. He hurried toward the *Yorktown* through the night of June 4.

At 7 A.M. on June 5, Nagumo received a report from a float plane scout that the *Yorktown* was abandoned and drifting. He sent the Japanese submarine *I-168* to get her. Lieutenant Commander Yahachi Tanabe, commander of the submarine, headed to the stricken carrier.

By midmorning, when the *Vireo* came into sight, the *Hughes* was still standing by. Two *Yorktown* sailors who had been left on the ship the previous day had been taken off by a *Hughes* rescue party.

The *Vireo* passed a towline to the *Yorktown* sometime in midafternoon and attempted to take her in tow. But against a rising sea and a trade wind, the *Vireo* could make only about one or two knots. A small salvage crew from the *Hughes*, the *Vireo* and a second destroyer, the *Gwin*, which Nimitz also had dispatched, went aboard the carrier that afternoon and began to jettison loose gear. At about the same time, 150 miles away, Buckmaster and Fletcher discussed saving the *Yorktown*. A salvage party of around 150 men and 20 officers was assembled from *Yorktown* crewmen who by then were scattered among several different destroyers.

The following morning, June 6, at around 6 o'clock the *Hammann* pulled alongside the *Yorktown* and Buckmaster took the salvage party back onto his ship.

A few minutes after the salvage team went aboard, Lieutenant Commander Tanabe spotted the *Yorktown* on the horizon from a distance of about 11 miles. With day breaking, he dived and began to maneuver into a position to attack.

While five destroyers, the *Balch*, *Benham*, *Monaghan*, *Hughes* and *Gwin*, circled about 2,000 yards away, Buckmaster and his crew worked for several hours to reduce the *Yorktown*'s port-side list and correct the trim that had the ship down at the bow a few degrees. The faithful *Hammann*, which had rescued the carrier's downed flyers at Guadalcanal and stayed with her through her two great battles, was alongside to starboard, providing power.

Seaman 2c. Donald A. Blessum of North Dakota was sent with several other men to try finally to bring the fire still smoldering in the rag locker under control. The locker was near aviation fuel storage tanks and a magazine containing powder canisters and exploding projectiles for the five-inch guns. The magazine had been flooded with water and carbon dioxide gas was pumped into the gasoline tanks. It was hot work, pulling smoldering rags out of the storage area and dousing those that remained with water pumped by the *Hammann*. There was no air circulation and the *Yorktown* was hot and stuffy below decks.

Bodies of 35 men who had been killed were brought to

hangar deck and buried at sea after Buckmaster conducted funeral services. Under the supervision of Lieutenant Edward A. Kearney, the ship's junior medical officer, all but 10 were identified, and all were fingerprinted. Identifying documents, fingerprint records and valuables were laid in a pile on the hangar deck.

Several planes that had been parked on the port side of the hangar deck were pushed over the side. One five-inch gun mount on the port side was cut loose and cast off and workers started to cut loose the second. The *Hammann* pumped water into empty fuel tanks on the starboard side to add ballast to that side of the carrier. Submersible pumps on the *Yorktown* pumped water overboard from flooded compartments on the port side. By about noon, the list had been reduced by two degrees.

At around 1:30 the fire in the rag locker was out. Blessum and other members of his crew came up to the "foc'sle deck," a short, raised deck at the bow, below the flight deck and higher than the hangar deck, for a fresh air break. While they stood there, lookouts on the *Balch* noticed a disturbance in the water about 2,500 yards starboard of the *Yorktown*. Within seconds, four torpedo wakes could be seen, headed toward the *Yorktown* and the *Hammann*.

Lt. Cdr. Arnold True, commanding officer of the *Hammann*, sounded general quarters and signaled his engine room to take the destroyer full speed astern in an attempt to break free of the *Yorktown* and get out of the path of the torpedoes. Gunners on both the carrier and the destroyer fired frantically at the torpedoes but failed to detonate them.

Blessum and other members of the rag locker crew watched in horror as a sailor on the *Hammann* raced to the destroyer's stern, where scores of depth charges were racked to be rolled into the sea during an attack against a submarine. Blessum said the sailor was frantically going from one depth charge to the other.

True later reported that he had ordered all the depth

charges placed on "safe" status before he had the *Hammann* tied onto the *Yorktown*. The sailor at the destroyer's stern apparently was Torpedoman Berlyn Kimbrel, who was believed to have been checking the settings to make sure the depth charges were on "safe."

"That man was a hero," Blessum said.

One of Lieutenant Commander Tanabe's torpedoes went wild.

A second hit the *Hammann* amidships and exploded, breaking her in two. She sank within four minutes.

The two remaining torpedoes exploded against the *Yorktown*.

As soon as he realized torpedoes were rushing toward the two ships, *Vireo* commander Legg had a member of his crew cut the steel tow line with an oxygen-acetylene torch. Even before the torpedoes hit, he had circled back and was on his way to pick up survivors.

After treating a large number of broken ankles the night before, Dr. Kearney, the ship's junior medical officer, had told sailors on the salvage party that if they ever were on a ship that was torpedoed, they should try to lie down first. He was on the hangar deck when word was passed that torpedoes were headed for the ship. He lay down.

The *Yorktown* heaved upward when the two torpedoes detonated, almost simultaneously. Several men working to cut loose the second five-inch gun were blown into the water.

One of them was Cdr. Ernie Davis, the *Yorktown*'s hard-driving gunnery officer, who had been supervising the work to get the five-inch gun off the ship.

Lt. Cdr. Clarence C. Ray, the *Yorktown* communication officer, recalled that after being blown into the water, Davis swam back to the ship and began climbing up a rope he found hanging over the side.

Ray, who had not fallen into the sea, remembered that someone had collected some mattresses from below and brought them to the flight deck. Thinking they would be useful swimming supports for *Hammann* crew members, he started for them.

Why the *Hammann*'s depth charges exploded is anyone's guess. If only one had been set to "ready" and exploded when it sank to its depth setting, that would have been enough to set off chain-reaction explosions among the others, even if they were on "safe." True later said he believed one of the *Hammann*'s own torpedoes exploded and set off the explosions among the depth charges. Another theory is that as soon as True sounded general quarters on the *Hammann*, Torpedoman Kimbrel had started resetting the charges from "safe" to "ready."

The terrible shock wave from the nearly simultaneous explosion of the depth charges, any one of which could tear apart a submarine, ripped through the sea. The explosion sent three huge columns of water towering above the *Yorktown*. The carrier lurched violently.

"As she [the *Hammann*] was sinking, something made me turn back," Ray recalled, "and I saw perhaps a hundred heads, floating on the water as she went under. Just then, the depth charges all exploded.

"All those heads that had been on the water just before the depth charges exploded suddenly disappeared, something like a windshield wiper erases the droplets from your windshield when it's raining. They were all gone."

Although Davis, the gunnery officer, had started climbing up the rope back onto the carrier when the depth charges went off, he was still in the water from his waist down. Ray said he thought maybe it was that North Carolina corn whiskey that kept Davis alive—despite the fact that the shock wave left him with "several hundred" tiny perforations of his intestines.

Of the 251 men and officers who had served on the *Hammann*, 81 were dead or missing in the water. They included Ens. Robert Enright who had been in charge of the whaleboat that rescued downed *Yorktown* flyers Adams and McCuskey from the beach at Guadalcanal a month earlier, and Torpedoman Kimbrel, who was awarded the Navy Cross posthumously. Another 26 would die later. Lieutenant Commander True was nearly unconscious and covered with oil when he was finally pulled from the water. He was carrying the lifeless bodies of two members of his crew.

Among the losses this time were the records, valuables and fingerprints of *Yorktown* crewmen who had been buried at sea. All the material slid overboard. It would mean there was no positive identification of the dead and several dozen would be listed only as "missing in action," to be officially declared dead a year later.

Lying on his back on the hangar deck, Dr. Kearney saw an airplane that had been stowed directly above him start to rip loose from the lines that held it. He knew it was going to crash on top of him. Years later, he would tell members of his family that it was one of those odd moments when unlikely thoughts present themselves. As he saw the plane start to fall, he thought of his education at Manhattan College and the Columbia University College of Physicians and Surgeons, his residencies at Thomas Jefferson Medical Center in Philadelphia, Queens General Hospital in New York and City Hospital in Boston.

"What a waste," he thought.

Then the fuselage of the plane crashed beside him, and he was unhurt.

The *Vireo* had circled around and was coming toward the *Yorktown* from astern as Kearney and several members of the salvage party gathered on the fantail. Buckmaster and other members of the crew were on the foc'sle deck, nearly three football fields away.

When the *Vireo* drew within about 100 yards of the carrier, members of its crew seemed to be frantically motioning and waving their arms, as if urging Kearney and the others to abandon the ship.

Finally, Kearney ordered the men with him to leave the ship and they did.

"I then turned to the warrant carpenter and told him it was his turn," Kearney recalled years later in a written account.

The list of names on the salvage party is attached to Buckmaster's final action report. It does not include anyone identified as a warrant carpenter. The party did include two chief carpenter's mates, one of whom was Thomas Coleman, the 62-year-old retired chief who had rejoined the ship in San Diego in January nearly 40 years after his initial enlistment. His name appears on the salvage party list as: "Coleman, Charles, Chief Carpenter's Mate, U.S. Navy (Retired)."

As likely as not, it was Coleman to whom Kearney turned and said, "Your turn." If so, the old chief knew his *Blue Jacket's Manual.*

"No, it is your turn, doctor," Kearney recalled the carpenter replying.

"What do you mean? I am the senior officer here."

"But I am the senior line officer."

A ship's doctor would not have been in the line of command but a chief petty officer carpenter would. Still unsure, Kearney got the carpenter to promise to jump as soon as he did. When the two men understood each other, Kearney jumped and the other man followed.

Buckmaster did not abandon the ship immediately. In fact, the second torpedo attack had further reduced the list by counterflooding starboard compartments, but the ship was now lying deeper in the water. He had men go below as far as they could and close those water-tight hatches they could reach. At one point, someone reported hearing an incessant pounding noise somewhere in the ship. It turned out to be the sea, flooding into empty compartments.

Among those members of his crew Buckmaster would cite for service beyond the call of duty was a black mess attendant identified only as "Wilson, A., Mess Attendant 1c."

"The conduct of this man was of the highest order in that during the period following a submarine torpedo attack on June 6 and while the ship was in a precarious position, he volunteered to go below decks and to conduct a search for missing shipmates. He further produced from below decks some six mattresses which were used to transport injured and would have been very valuable as life-saving equipment if the injured had been compelled to swim. He displayed exceptional courage and initiative when the condition of the ship indicated that abandonment would be necessary in a very short time," the captain's report stated.

When Tanabe and the jubilant men on his crew felt the shock that they knew was the explosion of their torpedoes, the commander of *I-168* took the submarine down to 200 feet. Despite a furious attack by American destroyers, the sub escaped. Tanabe survived the war.

It soon was obvious that the *Yorktown* could not be saved. For the rest of June 6, she continued to settle deeper into the water and to turn slowly to port. The *Vireo* joined the five destroyers, *Monaghan*, *Gwin*, *Hughes*, *Balch* and *Behnam,* in an all-night vigil around her. At dawn on June 7, she was within minutes of sinking.

Torpedo Three radioman-gunner Lloyd Childers, who had nearly bled to death with bullet wounds in one leg and a compound fracture of the other following the attack on the Japanese carriers, was still on the *Monaghan*.

"The corpsmen came into my room and asked me would I like to watch my ship go down," he recalled. "They made a sling of their arms to hold me up so the three of us could watch the *Yorktown* slowly sink below the surface."

A few minutes before 5 A.M. the *Vireo* and the five destroyers half-masted their colors. On signal, all hands on the six ships came to attention and removed their hats and helmets. *Yorktown* crew members aboard the destroyers, including Buckmaster, wept and saluted.

At 4:58 A.M., six months almost to the hour after the bombing of Pearl Harbor sent her to war, the *Yorktown* rolled onto her port side and sank. Her battle flags were still flying, as was the new, oversized Stars-and-Strips that her eager and buoyant young crew had cheered in the midst of battle.

"It was an awesome sight," said Childers.

AFTERWORD

"Aren't you Lynn Forshee?"

Forshee did not recognize the emaciated American who confronted him in Japan.

After the *Yorktown* sank, Forshee had been sent back to the States for electronics training and flight school. Then he returned to the Pacific, serving in Guam, the New Hebrides and New Caledonia as a chief petty officer.

During leave he married his hometown sweetheart, Jennie, in Britt, Iowa. As this is written, they have been married 55 years.

Hostilities between the United States and Japan had ended, although the U.S.S. *Missouri* was waiting in Tokyo Bay for the signing of the formal surrender documents when Forshee arrived at Yokohama in a transport ship loaded with equipment to be used in setting up a support base for U.S. aircraft.

With a day to spare, Forshee had taken a short tour of the devastated Japanese countryside.

"Aren't you Lynn Forshee?"

"Yes, but I don't think I recognize you."

"I'm Ace Dalzell."

A few days earlier, Japanese guards had vanished from the prison camp near Lake Biwa and American, British and Australian prisoners of war had wrecked the camp.

"I took off for the hills there with some Marines, further up into the mountains," Dalzell said, "to get away from all of it. We didn't know what was coming off. We didn't know if the war was over or what. Somewhere along the line, some of our guys ran into a guy who said he was a war correspondent and he said, 'Don't go down into the Hiroshima area.'"

When guards abandoned the prison camp there was no food, so Dalzell and the Marines built a bonfire on a railroad track and when the engineer stopped to put out the fire, they slipped aboard and rode to Osaka. There they found food and a charcoal-powered truck, which they drove back to Lake Biwa.

Before long, the U.S. Army came in, emptied the camp and brought the former American prisoners of war to Yokohama where, Dalzell said, "we were debriefed and deloused." For the first time since shortly after they were captured near Jaluit in the Marshall Islands three years earlier, all six flyers from the two *Yorktown* Devastators were together again.

Dalzell would remain in the Navy for 30 years, retiring in 1967, and having a second career as a civil defense official in Florida. When he arrived home from Japan, he stayed briefly at an Army hospital in Georgia. His mother visited him and brought with her a young woman with whom she worked. A few months later, Dalzell and the young woman got married and 55 years later they were still married.

Chuck Fosha came out of the prison camp to learn that the commission informally promised to him by a Navy recruiter had been approved shortly before he was taken prisoner. Promotions that he presumably would have earned had he not spent three years as a prisoner of war were quickly approved, and he remained in the Navy for the next 38 years, retiring as a commander.

As this book is being written, he is 87 years old and he and Edna have been married 61 years. Fosha had to break off an interview at their home in Pensacola in order to get to his class in computer science at the University of West Florida.

In 1997, divers Matthew and Lucy Harris, working under contract with the U.S. National Park Service, were guided to a spot where native oyster fishermen in the Marshall Islands said they had seen a submerged aircraft. It turned out to be the Douglas TBD Devastator left there 55 years earlier by Lt. Harlan Johnson and his crew, Chuck Fosha and James Dalzell. Matthew Harris said the plane was lying on the ocean floor, "like a model aircraft discarded by a disinterested child."

By the end of the war, Joe Wetherington, who began his *Yorktown* service as a plane pusher, had become a chief petty officer working at an aircraft service facility in San Diego. He left the Navy at the end of the war.

In 1951, having lived through the Depression and World War II, he found himself face-to-face with another American trauma, polio. He fought his way through that one also and became a Hillsborough County deputy sheriff in Tampa. He and Etta had been married 57 years in 1999 and had reared two daughters.

Wetherington's close friend and Fighting Forty-two squadron mate, Judson Brodie of South Carolina, made the Navy a career, retiring as a lieutenant commander and later becoming tax commissioner of Aiken County, South Carolina. After more than 55 years together, he and Kari were dividing their time between their home in Columbia and a summer cabin near Wetherington's in the North Carolina mountains.

Among the records that slipped over the side of the *Yorktown* when torpedoes interrupted the salvage effort were those of Musician 1c. Gordon Leroy Roop, who had played flute and piccolo in the ship's band. When Mrs.

David J. Roop of 514 Normandy Avenue in Baltimore received the official notification that her son was "missing in action," she clutched for hope where there was no hope. She wrote to administrators of every hospital in Hawaii and on the U.S. West Coast, asking each if her son was a patient there. She enclosed a photograph of him, smiling in his dress blues and white hat. When other members of the band heard about her futile letter-writing campaign, they visited her in Baltimore and told her he was dead.

George "Judge" Barnes, the leading chief and surrogate father figure for many members of the young crew of Fighting Forty-two, retired from the Navy in August 1943, and returned to live near his family's farm in Albion, Maine. He never married. He died on October 21, 1968. After his death, members of his family found a locked seaman's trunk among his possessions but did not find the key. At this writing, the trunk remains closed.

Awarded the silver star and credited with keeping several dozen critically wounded men alive until they reached Pearl Harbor, Dr. Edward Kearney returned to New York and practiced general surgery in the town of Newburgh. He died in 1985.

An hour after the *Akagi* was scuttled, Admiral Yamamoto relieved Vice Admiral Nagumo of his command.

"I was once captain of *Akagi*," Yamamoto had told his staff just prior to ordering the great carrier scuttled. He then went into seclusion for several days.

When he emerged, he asked, "Is Genda all right?"

To the surprise of practically no one who ever knew him, John Smith "Jimmy" Thach reached the highest rank of anyone who served on the *Yorktown* at Midway. As a four-star admiral, Thach was commander in chief of all U.S. Navy forces in Europe.

He retired in 1967 and died in 1981. His older brother's name had become so much a part of him that some obituary writers formalized it and identified him as Adm. "James"

Thach. A guided missile frigate was commissioned in honor of him. The "Thach weave," which made the rugged but slow Wildcat fighter a viable foe of the Zero, retained its validity in a jet age and continued to be taught, along with its many variations, wherever fighter pilots were trained.

Carl "Red" Maag remained in the Navy after the war ended and, in his own words, "finally made chief" and retired.

John "Chicken" Underwood came back to Pearl Harbor after the Battle of Midway and found himself practically under 24-hour guard. A rumor had reached a Honolulu newspaper that a 15-year-old boy had been at both the Battle of Coral Sea and at Midway. Navy officials were determined to keep that story from getting out.

Despite his age, Underwood had served during two major sea battles and drumming him out of the Navy seemed as unthinkable as sending him back into combat. He was kept in the Navy—as a driver for admirals based at Pearl Harbor.

After the war he settled in California, where he became a fireman and dabbled successfully in real estate development, before retiring to a small cattle ranch near the town of Williston in north-central Florida. He hung onto the brown pilot's helmet he was wearing when a lookout on a destroyer found him treading water on the wrong side of the *Yorktown* in 1942. He kept it displayed, along with the trophies he won playing tournament poker in Nevada.

In his action report on the Battle of Midway, Captain Buckmaster pleaded for another carrier.

"During all these actions and the many weeks at sea in preparation for them, the fighting spirit of *Yorktown* was peerless," he wrote. "That fighting spirit remains alive even though the ship herself has perished gloriously in battle. The wish closest to the hearts of all of us who were privileged to serve in that gallant ship is that she might be preserved not only in memory but by the crew's being kept together to man, commission and return against the enemy in a new aircraft carrier, preferably another *Yorktown*."

Buckmaster would be promoted to rear admiral but he would not get the second carrier he hoped to command.

At Newport News Shipbuilding, the ship that had been provisionally named *Bon Homme Richard* was renamed *Yorktown* by Navy Secretary Frank Knox in September 1942. First Lady Eleanor Roosevelt was invited to sponsor the new carrier, as she had the ship that lay at the bottom of the Pacific Ocean near Midway. At first she was unsure, given the "sad fate" of the earlier carrier, but Knox urged her to "banish any fears you may have" and sponsor the ship.

She agreed and was there to smash the champagne bottle against the hull of the U.S.S. *Yorktown* (CV-10) as it slid down its ways and into the James River. Its first commanding officer was Capt. Joseph J. "Jocko" Clark, Buckmaster's bombastic executive officer who once thrilled young *Yorktown* sailors with his flight-deck exhortation, "Let's go to Tokyo."

The new *Yorktown* served during World War II, the Korean War and the Vietnam War and was retired to Charleston, South Carolina, where it became a floating museum, memorializing its service and that of its older sister.

John D'Arc Lorenz went back to Portland, Oregon, after the war. He found Delight McHale, the former freshman drama student whose picture was stolen from him by an ocean swell, and talked her into marrying him. Keeping his part of a bargain sealed on June 4, 1942, in the oily water of the northern Pacific Ocean, they named their second son after William Sullivan of Flynt, Michigan.

Ray Machalinski made a career of Navy communications, retiring as a chief petty officer in 1959. After that, he continued to work in electronics, most often as an employee of Navy or Air Force contractors.

When Machalinski was growing up in a Catholic orphanage in Erie, Pennsylvania, he never saw his mother, who lived not far away in a state hospital, her mental health permanently shattered by grief at his father's death. Once, on leave from the Navy, he took his new wife, Mable, to see her.

"Mother, I'm Raymond," he told her.

She smiled patiently. "No," she said, "Raymond's just a little boy."

When they were brought back to Pearl Harbor, Yorktown survivors were told to say nothing in their letters home about the loss of the ship. Mail was being censored and Bill Kowalczewski assumed that censors would delete from his mail home any reference to the death of his brother Victor at the Battle of the Coral Sea. His parents learned of Victor's death from a War Department telegram. Before the war was over, three more Kowalczewski brothers would join the military, one in the Navy and two in the Army.

In the tradition of the times, their proud mother, a first-generation American, displayed five stars in the front window of the house in Milwaukee, four blue and one gold.

Yeoman Frank Boo made a career of the Navy, then had a second career as a stenographer. In 1972, while visiting friends in Virginia, he decided he'd like to see his old boss, Admiral Frank Jack Fletcher, who had retired in La Plata, a town in southern Maryland. Boo had Fletcher's phone number, so he called to say he would like to stop by.

A woman who answered the phone listened politely while he explained that he had been the admiral's yeoman during the Battle of Midway and later at the Battle of Guadalcanal.

"I'm sorry," she said, "but you are six hours late. The admiral was buried this afternoon at Arlington National Cemetery."

As soon as leave had been approved following the Battle of Midway, Ensign John Paul Adams, whose F4F-4 Wildcat was the last plane ever to take off from the *Yorktown*, went to North Carolina to visit Dixie Palmer, the sister of his flight-school friend, Gus Palmer. Adams did not have a change of clothing and because the sinking of the ship was still being kept secret, he was not allowed to tell his host family why.

Later, Gus Palmer would come home from his assignment on the U.S.S. *Wasp* without a change of clothing and his family would know why.

Adams remained in the Navy and retired as a captain. At this writing, he and the former Dixie Palmer have been married 57 years.

Two months after the Battle of Midway, Navy publicists fed newspapers a story about the success of an initiative to incorporate Negroes into ranks and noted that they made excellent fighting men.

But Thomas E. Allen of Richmond, Virginia, who had learned he could turn around three times in his mind and find his way out of a stricken aircraft carrier, could not find a way out of his job as a mess attendant after the *Yorktown* sank.

"The messmen's branch was the only part of the Navy you could not get out of," he said. He tried for the rest of his enlistment to get into the "regular Navy" but failed.

After the war, he went to Howard University in Washington, D.C., on the GI Bill and became a pharmacist. He returned to Richmond, ran a pharmacy and served as chairman of the Virginia State Pharmacy Board and as a member of both the State Board of Health Professions and the State Board of Health.

Pete Montalvo left the Navy because of the wounds he received at Midway. Later, when he and Betty were picking a date to get married, he suggested April 4, the day the *Yorktown* was commissioned. "That way, I'll always remember our anniversary," he assured her.

Montalvo converted one room of their home in Saratoga Springs, New York, into a small *Yorktown* museum.

So far, he has remembered the wedding anniversary more than 50 times.

In fact, the large number of lengthy marriages among surviving *Yorktown* crew members seems to touch, if not define, a character trait of the young men and women of

1930s and 1940s. Only a very small fraction of the men who served on the ship have been interviewed for this account. Yet, even in this small sample, if the years of marriage among those who have passed "golden" wedding anniversaries could somehow be linked together, they would cover a span of time that would reach back to ancient days.

Former Aircraft Radioman 3c. Lloyd Childers suggested that the Depression may have had something to do with that. Those hard times defined and taught a disciplined code that affected everyone who lived through them, he said.

Childers said that did not mean that the men of the *Yorktown* and the women they married came from a superior or "greatest" generation—but possibly from a more disciplined one. He would command young Marines at Vietnam and swell with pride at the bravery with which they performed under fire.

Childers recovered from the wounds he sustained during the ill-fated torpedo attack on Japanese carriers at Midway and reported for flight training in December 1942. He was subsequently commissioned as a second lieutenant in the Marines. He later fought in Korea and in 1962 was promoted to lieutenant colonel, despite not having a college degree.

He later earned the degree while still on active duty. Following his retirement from the Marine Corps in 1968, he earned his Ph.D. and became a college administrator.

He was administrative dean of Chapman College in Orange County, California, when he retired from his second career.

Childers's pilot, Harry Corl, was shot down and killed at Guadalcanal a few months after the Battle of Midway.

Boatswain Chester Briggs, who led a team onto the *Yorktown* catwalk to rescue Fighting Forty-two ordnanceman David Pattison, served in Korea and Vietnam and retired from the Navy as a captain.

James Liner's best friend, Curtis Owens, also known on the ship as "Pelican," returned to Buffalo, South Carolina, after the Battle of Midway, discharged from the Navy because of the wounds he received at Midway. He died a few years before this book was written.

Liner remained in the Navy until the war ended. He too went home to Buffalo and became a home builder.

Chief Carpenter's Mate Thomas Coleman served one more enlistment in the Navy after the Battle of Midway, then retired permanently. When he died in 1972, he was 92 years old.

Joe Fazio moved to the *Enterprise* after the Battle of Midway. Like many of his former *Yorktown* shipmates, he would hear more bombs explode and again feel a carrier lunge helplessly when hit by torpedoes. He made a career of military service.

When he retired in 1963, he was a chief petty officer in the United States Navy.

ACKNOWLEDGMENTS

In my childhood, I had no idea that men like Rear Adm. Frank Jack Fletcher and Capt. Elliott Buckmaster commanded the U.S.S. *Yorktown.* I always thought that great ship answered to a man named Joseph L. Wetherington, whom I now know to have been a seaman second class "plane pusher," only a few months out of boot camp, on the day of the *Yorktown*'s last great battle. My confusion was not the result of any deception on his part. Rather, it grew more or less inevitably out of the fact that Joe Wetherington is my mother's baby brother, and in the heroic accounts she related to me, the *Yorktown* was always described as "Uncle Joe's ship." I grew up sort of thinking of it as our family aircraft carrier, even though I can't recall ever not knowing that it had been sunk and lost forever or that its sinking had something to do with a dark and terrible thing called war. So the first debt I owe in writing this book is to my Uncle Joe, for having been there. I am also indebted to him for helping me contact other members of the ship's crew. A familiar pattern developed during the scores of telephone calls I have made to *Yorktown* crewmen, requesting their help in assembling the story of the eager, idealistic young men who sailed on the ship at the outset of World War II.

After I introduced myself and said I was a newspaper reporter in Washington, D.C., and was writing a book about the *Yorktown*, there was usually a silent moment while the man I was calling waited, no doubt wondering what this call was all about. Then, when I said that my uncle had been a member of the ship's crew, I could almost feel the telephone warming in my hand, as if I had become a member of the family. Almost invariably, this information led to a question at the other end of the line—the same question every time: "Did he get off?" Of course, the official record contains the names of more than 160 men who did not get off because they died on the ship or were lost at sea in the fighters, bombers and torpedo planes that flew from her deck during the first six months of the war.

I am indebted to the men who talked with me on the phone and received me in their homes. Several went out of their way to guide me through this project. They include Joe Fazio, Pete Montalvo, Ray Machalinski, Lynn Forshee, Jud Brodie, Bill Surgi and the unforgettable Carl "Red" Maag. I thank the U.S. Naval Institute at Annapolis, Maryland, for allowing me access to its oral history interview of Adm. John S. Thach.

I have benefited from previously published work and would refer the reader who wishes to learn more about the *Yorktown* and the Battle of Midway to any of the following books: *Miracle at Midway* by Gordon W. Prange, McGraw Hill, 1982/Penguin Books, 1983; *History of United States Naval Operations in World War II, Volume IV* by Samuel Eliot Morison, Atlantic-Little Brown, 1949; *Incredible Victory* by Walter Lord, Harper & Row, 1967; *Combined Fleet Decoded* by John Prados, Random House, 1995; *Eagles of Mitsubishi: The Story of the Zero Fighter* by Jiro Horikoshi, English trans. by the University of Washington Press, 1980; *The First Team: Pacific Naval Air Combat from Pearl Harbor to Midway* by John B. Lundstrom, U.S. Naval Institute, 1984; *Midway: The Battle That Doomed Japan* by Mitsuo Fuchida, English trans. by Ballantine

Books, 1993; *That Gallant Ship* by Robert J. Cressman, Pictorial Histories Publishing Co., 1985.

I am grateful to my daughter, Susannah A. Nesmith, a gifted journalist and merciless editor, for reading this work, chapter by chapter, from her home in Bosnia and E-mailing her consistently helpful comments.

Finally, I am very indebted to a longtime friend and former assistant executive editor of the *Atlanta Journal-Constitution*, Lt. Cdr. Jim Rankin, USNR (Ret), who was my first night city editor and who agreed to edit this book. He is uniquely qualified for the task, having spent years slogging through my copy. But in addition to that, he knows the subject. He flew torpedo bombers from the U.S.S. *Kula Gulf* in World War II and antisubmarine planes from the U.S.S. *Viaroko* during the Korean War.

INDEX

C

M

N

O

P

U

V

W–X

Y

Z